PENGUIN BOOKS

A GAIJIN SARARIMAN

Asif Chowdhury is currently working as part of the executive management team at a global semiconductor company where he also serves as the head of their Japan business. During his thirty plus years in the semiconductor field, Asif has travelled extensively to many parts of the world, especially in Asia, giving him an opportunity to work with people from different cultures and various backgrounds. His career path has moved him and his family from Texas to Arizona to South Korea, to Japan to Massachusetts and more recently to Singapore. Asif worked as an expatriate in Seoul, Korea for three years and later in Tokyo, Japan for four years. His business development role in Japan took him all over the country and enabled him to work and interact with the Japanese people from all walks of life, but especially with the *sarariman* from many top Japanese companies.

He has written for various trade publications and magazines and is a regular contributor to the *Living in Singapore* magazine published by the American Association of Singapore.

Asif holds several degrees including a BS in Mechanical Engineering from University of Texas in Arlington, an MS in Mechanical Engineering from Southern Methodist University (Dallas, Texas), an MS in Finance and an MBA from Northeastern University (Boston, Massachusetts).

Asif currently resides in Singapore with his wife and teenage son, while his daughter is working as an aerospace engineer in Texas.

A Gaijin Sarariman

Asif R. Chowdhury

PENGUIN BOOKS

An imprint of Penguin Random House

PENGUIN BOOKS

USA | Canada | UK | Ireland | Australia
New Zealand | India | South Africa | China | Southeast Asia

Penguin Books is part of the Penguin Random House group of companies
whose addresses can be found at global.penguinrandomhouse.com

Published by Penguin Random House SEA Pvt. Ltd
9, Changi South Street 3, Level 08-01,
Singapore 486361

First published in Penguin Books by Penguin Random House SEA 2022
Copyright © Asif R. Chowdhury 2022

ISBN 9789815017809

Typeset in Garamond by MAP Systems, Bangalore, India

www.penguin.sg

While the stories in this book are all based on the author's real life experiences, some of the names have been changed to protect the individuals' identity and privacy.

For my loving parents,
M Nural A. Chowdhury and Ismat Chowdhury,
both of whom immensely enjoyed their Japan visits with us

Contents

Introduction:
Who Are These *Sarariman*?

Japanese sarariman are an enigma to the West and the rest of the world. There have been many movies, studies, documentaries, articles, and books about them. One can see thousands of sarariman in busy Tokyo streets, crowded railway stations, jampacked commuter trains and subways, on any weekday morning. Everyone dresses in suits and ties, carrying their office bags, quietly commuting to their respective workplaces. Some read newspapers, some read manga (Japanese comic/graphic books) and some sleep deeply on the trains and in subways—many doing so while standing. It's a sight to behold—in fact, a visit to Tokyo Station on a busy weekday morning to view these sarariman in action is often a part of Tokyo tourists' sightseeing itineraries. So, who are they?

There are many English words that have made their way into Japanese vocabulary. These are known as *wasei-eigo*, or words borrowed from English language. Words such as 'table', 'chair', 'Google' or 'door' are parts of the wasei-eigo and are used in everyday Japanese, with the pronunciations Japanized. In a nutshell, sarariman are millions of white-collar employees who work for traditional, large Japanese firms and draw monthly salaries. Just as the other wasei-eigo, sarariman comes from the English words 'salary man'. Since there is no letter 'L' in the

Japanese alphabet system, it is often pronounced as the letter 'R'. Salaried workers from large foreign companies based in Japan are also included in this category. But interestingly, it does not include all employees working for monthly salaries. Professionals such as lawyers, doctors, or freelance workers, are not part of the sarariman, even though they may also work for monthly salaries.

Sarariman may sound like a simple salaried worker to the non-Japanese, but the term holds a very special meaning in Japanese society. Japanese men dream of becoming sarariman, which would immediately elevate them to a higher social standing, regardless of their backgrounds. It is enough for a proud parent or an in-law to state that their son or son-in-law is a sarariman, to immediately conjure respect from the listeners—regardless of what the actual job may be—no further explanation necessary.

While sarariman gained prominence after the Second World War, the designation was first devised in the early part of twentieth century, around the 1930s, when Japanese companies were slowly becoming large conglomerates. These big companies, like Mitsubishi or Matsushita, would hire graduates fresh out of college or even high school, for a lifetime of guaranteed employment. In return, the employees were expected to show deep commitment and uncompromising loyalty to the companies they work for, often over their own families. The designation of sarariman is also synonymous with post-war prosperity. They are considered the foot soldiers who, through their hard work and dedication, enabled the meteoric transformation of Japan into a global economic powerhouse from amidst the ruins of the Second World War.

Like the famous *bushido* or the 'way of the warrior' of the old samurai clan, these sarariman are a breed of their own, with distinctive work ethics and social practices. Always in their uniform of suit and tie—even though the trend is going tie-less now—they essentially dedicate their working lives to their respective companies. They are known for working long hours, and then going out drinking, singing karaoke, or partying with their colleagues and customers well into the night, before returning home tired and drunk. The next day, as in the film *Groundhog Day*, it starts all over again. The philosophy is that your work is your extended family, and one must spend as much time with this extended family as possible. It is not unusual for a sarariman to work up to eighty hours a week.

There are so many incidents and stories of sarariman dying from working hard and long hours, that there is a term for this in Japanese known as *karoshi* or death by over-work. As a result of spending long hours with this extended family, many end up neglecting their wives and kids, their real families. Often, sarariman are transferred to faraway locations without their families for years on end, with only weekly or monthly visits to their wives and children on weekends. Going on for many decades, such a practice is widely accepted by society, much to the surprise of Westerners.

To really understand this concept, one must try to understand the role of gender, which has been accepted in Japanese society for centuries, going back to the feudal era. Men were the breadwinners, rulers and fighters, while women tended to family matters, including managing the home economics. There was clear and distinct division of labour. The philosophy was that such division of labour produced the best outcome for the family, society, one's own turf or fiefdom, and ultimately, the country. If men had to tend to family matters, that might weaken their ability to earn, rule and fight. To a large extent, the same fundamental thought process continues today.

Dr Brigitte Steger, an expert in Asian and Middle Eastern studies from Cambridge University, stated it perfectly, 'Japan's economic success in the post-war era has been built on a clear gendered division of labour: the reproductive housewife and the hard-working man.' One can argue that such discipline in maintaining the division of labour was a key factor as to why Japan had always been able to successfully defend its freedom from foreign entities. And perhaps this cultural norm played a key role that led to their successful expansion and occupation of Asian countries during the Second World War, even though Japan is a relatively small nation. Despite the complaint often rallied in the Western media against Japanese men neglecting their wives and children, it worked well for Japan Inc. to bring the country out of the ashes of the Second World War to reach the height of economic prosperity in a couple of decades.

While the fundamental work ethos of sarariman remains the same today, the Japanese government has been trying to push for a 'softer' image and focus more on work-life balance. New terms such as 'cool biz' have emerged, allowing sarariman to go without ties, especially during the hot and humid days. A more recent phenomena is the term *ikumen,* which implies sarariman spending less time at work and more time with their families, and participating in raising their children. A research graduate from Cambridge University, Hannah Vassallo, recently embedded herself with five such ikumen fathers and their families. She discovered that while the fathers enjoyed more time with their families, they disliked the association with the term ikumen, due to suffering significant abuse from their colleagues and bosses for having such a role.

Change in Japan doesn't come easily, especially when it comes to things associated with their heritage, history and culture. So, the battle continues to this day, with the sarariman marching on.

Preface

When I started to talk to people about writing this book, many would ask me if the book would be a memoir, or a 'self-help' kind of book for foreigners who are working or want to work in Japan. Indeed, my original plan was to write a book about the culture, customs and the background of the Japanese sarariman. The primary objective was to share this with people who are engaged in doing business with Japanese entities or plan to work for Japanese companies. To be successful in foreign lands, a solid understanding of their history, culture and customs is very important, perhaps even more so than the issue of the language difference. I hoped that armed with some fundamental knowledge, appreciation and understanding of the sarariman and the local culture, the probability of success in people's Japanese endeavours would increase.

Most people would emphasize language as a key issue when dealing with people from different countries. Language can be a barrier, but the lack of fundamental understanding of culture and customs of the land and the people can be a larger issue in successfully navigating and engaging with foreign entities. Yet, language differences invariably appear as an obstacle at the front and centre when dealing with foreign entities, while the cultural barrier remains invisible. One can easily find interpreters to do the required translations. But without a basic understanding of culture, one can easily get blindsided and thus behave inappropriately. This can jeopardize success.

As I started to write the book, I realized that the best way to meet my objective of conveying the Japanese culture and sarariman customs was through storytelling: recounting my first-hand experiences working for an American semiconductor company and encountering everyday Japanese folks and sarariman during my four-year expatriate assignment in Japan. This book is part-memoir for Japan enthusiasts and part 'business self-help' for people engaged with Japanese entities.

* * *

The Japanese politeness towards foreign tourists is world-renowned. But most foreigners who come to Japan to work and stay may face a different reality. It is very rare that the Japanese will easily allow foreign expatriates and workers to become a part of their working family and become a true sarariman. Japan has always been a relatively closed society and more inward-looking, compared to other countries. There has always been a fundamental mistrust of foreigners, which continues today to a large extent. Many foreigners who have been living and working in Japan for years are essentially treated as outsiders by the local employees, sometimes to their frustration.

The mistrust is rooted in history as for centuries, the Land of the Rising Sun had remained a distant and forbidden place for much of the world, especially during its self-proclaimed isolation for over 200 years (1639–1853) during the reign of Tokugawa Shogunate. Japan is the only country in the world to impose such a long self-isolation.

Especially for new immigrants, foreign workers, or expatriates, being accepted by their Japanese colleagues is an uphill battle. Accepting the Japanese way of doing things is critical for gaining such acceptance. Most often there is a hidden initiation process in which the local team teaches, trains, and observes to see how much the newcomers would conform to the Japanese way of doing business. On the other hand, most of the new foreign workers, especially from the West, find adhering to the Japanese work culture and social norms difficult and, in many cases, not so meaningful. This Catch-22 makes it even harder for foreign workers to integrate with the local team, often ending up with both sides being frustrated. However, to be truly considered as part of any Japanese team, group or company, following the local customs is a must.

Due to the nature of my assignment, I was able to immerse myself as a *gaijin* sarariman (foreign salaryman) for most of my four years in Japan, providing me a front row seat to some of the most interesting and unique aspects of Japanese culture, social norms and practices. I was sent to the Japan office of an American semiconductor company as a Director of Japan Business Development—so I wasn't employed by a Japanese company but was working at a local sales office of an American company there. But like many new foreigners, I too faced an uphill battle. However, the slope was less steep for me compared to what it would have been if I was working for a Japanese firm. My acceptance was accelerated, once my colleagues realized that I could be more of an asset than an impediment for them to advance their causes.

I realize now, in hindsight, that there are three key factors that led to this acceptance and immersion. A lot of it has to do with the nature of my assignment and my attitude towards the Japanese customs.

First, as mentioned above, it has to do with the fact that I was in a local sales office of an American company, as opposed to working for a Japanese firm. Other than being a relatively closed society, Japanese firms may not allow gaijin foreign employees access to many of their inner workings because the firm does not feel comfortable divulging such information to foreigners. In a Japanese firm, the local employees will always have the upper hand. However, if one is sent to work for their local Japanese branch, the situation is different, and if the expatriate plays his or her cards right, he or she may end up having the upper hand, albeit a slight one. By the time I was transferred to Japan, I had been working at the head office in Chandler, Arizona, for ten years. I knew the company well and had established relationships at all levels, including the top management of the company. So, it wasn't easy for my Japanese colleagues to isolate me, even though they tried to do so during the initial months. They soon realized that it was better for them to make an ally out of me and include me as a gaijin sarariman, than to cast me aside.

Second, most expatriates are usually sent as heads of local branches. Even if they are not sent for the top job, expatriates usually work at higher positions. In these top roles, the expatriates are the bosses. Due to the very hierarchical nature of Japanese society, the boss's word is the law (almost) and most of the time, they will not be required to truly integrate with the local sarariman to get things done. However, on rare occasions, such as mine, if one is sent as an expatriate at mid-management level, it becomes necessary to integrate with the local team to do one's job. On the plus side, not being the top boss made it relatively easy for me to make friends and integrate myself into Japanese society.

Third, and most important, as I mentioned above, one's attitude plays a significant role in being accepted by and integrated into the local team. Most Westerners will find many of the Japanese ways and norms to be unproductive, in some cases unnecessary, and many times, downright weird. The key to success is to not overanalyse them but to accept them for what they are—simply a set of rules to abide by while there. A sense of humour always helps, too. While the nature and position of my expatriate assignment was helpful, those by themselves could not have allowed me the access that I had, if it wasn't for my relatively positive attitude towards the Japanese ways.

Most of the time, I found the local customs and cultures comical and found myself more intrigued and amused by them than disturbed or annoyed. Besides, I had had a fascination for Japan ever since my childhood days, when my dad had visited the country. Upon his return, he shared so many interesting and amazing stories about the country and the people—the bullet trains that run precisely on time, the Japanese obsession with cleanliness, the old *samurai* castles, the traditional temples, parks where friendly deer roam around freely and so on.

I have been a student of Japanese traditions for many years. The assignment gave me a first-hand opportunity to learn more about the country I had loved since my childhood. So, my numerous questions and enquiries to my Japanese colleagues about their culture came from a place of curiosity and amusement, than complaint and ridicule. In fact, my Japanese colleagues found my interest in their culture and my keenness to become a part of it so intriguing that they gave me the title of '*henna* gaijin' or 'strange foreigner'.

Perhaps it was also relatively easier for me to do so because of my Asian heritage, which provided me with a fundamental understanding of Asian culture. Also, I was with my family in Tokyo, so when I came home from work, I was able to revert to our rules and customs. This allowed for a nice cultural balance where I didn't have to worry about the Japanese culture when I was home if I didn't want to.

However, I still had to go through quite a rough initiation process at first and it did take a few painful months to overcome all the hurdles that the local team kept throwing in my direction. But once I was accepted by most of my colleagues and coworkers, I found that I had access to the sarariman of other Japanese companies as well. Being in the semiconductor industry, I was exposed to almost all the big conglomerates such as Matsushita/ Panasonic, Sony, Toshiba, Renesas, Rohm, Fujitsu, Fuji and Sharp. Many of these companies are over a hundred years old and were instrumental in building modern Japan. Others started recently and helped rebuild post-war Japan. Companies such as Mitsubishi and Matsushita are steeped in Japanese culture and tradition, and hold conservative views, while others like Sony and Rohm are relatively modern, open-minded, and forward-looking by Japanese standards. Dealing with both management and the engineering communities from these companies allowed me to gain special insight into the Japanese sarariman culture.

This book is an account of my experience working in Japan as a gaijin sarariman for four years. These experiences are at times weird, amusing, entertaining, confusing, painful, funny, and often, all of them at the same time. Through recounting these experiences, the book will hopefully provide insights into the Japanese culture, the customs, and ways; particularly those of the sarariman. Additionally, *A Gaijin Sarariman* provides the background and historical context of some of these customs and cultures, where applicable. It also discusses why most of them work well for Japanese society, however odd they may seem to Western eyes. Hopefully, the readers will find some of my experiences and knowledge insightful. Perhaps it will help some readers appreciate the importance of understanding the culture of distant lands when dealing with their people. At a minimum, if the readers find the book entertaining and have a few chuckles, I will consider this endeavour a success.

Asif R. Chowdhury

Chapter 1

The Tokyo Assignment

As I looked down at the Pacific Ocean through the windows of the Northwest Boeing-747-400, I could almost make out the Japan coastline in the distance. The jumbo jet, rightfully referred to as 'heavy' by air traffic controllers, was preparing to land at the New Tokyo International Airport, more popularly known as Narita Airport. The flight attendants of my favourite business class cabin—located at the front of the lower deck—were busy getting the cabin ready for our arrival in Tokyo.

I was all too familiar with the process, so I got into my own landing auto-pilot mode, putting away my constant travel companion, a pair of Bose noise-cancellation headphones; my laptop, and some office papers back into my Tumi briefcase, storing the bag inside the overhead compartment. Our flight would soon cross over into the Pacific coastline, to the flat plain of Chiba Prefecture, well north of Tokyo city, as it prepared for its final approach, lining up with runway 34L. I could recount almost every moment of this phase of the landing from memory, as I had taken the same flight probably a hundred times before. A few times, the final destination was Tokyo for meetings in Japan. But most of the time, it was to catch connecting flights to Seoul, Manila, Hong Kong, Shanghai or other Asian destinations for my various business trips. But this time, the flight had a very different significance. This time, I was coming to Tokyo to stay, for at least two years, on an expatriate assignment to help grow our company's business in Japan. Tokyo would become our new home for the next few years. My wife and eighteen-month-old daughter would soon follow me. I was still in a state of disbelief, wondering how in the world I'd got to be so lucky.

'How the hell did you manage to get this expatriate assignment in our Tokyo office?' is a question I have been asked repeatedly, often in an unmistakable tone of jealousy, by many of my colleagues and co-workers, during and after my four-year stint in Japan. Some even hinted that I had done some major ass-kissing to have landed such a role. The question does have some merit. After all, the original opening was for a Vice President of Business Development; I was merely a Senior Manager at that time.

Expatriate assignments are few, rare and very difficult to come by. These assignments come with many perks. The company takes care of most expenses, allowing one to save money, while living a life of relative luxury. For example, most expatriate assignments pay for all basic family needs such as housing, cars, utilities and tuition for kids' international school. Most companies also allow a month-long annual home leave—paying for business class tickets for the entire family to visit wherever 'home' is, stateside. In our case, it additionally included an automatic 25 per cent increase in base salary, known as a hardship allowance. The idea being that the company was making up for the hardship of having to deal with a new foreign land, away from one's larger family.

I have also often wondered how I had managed to land such a coveted position. The simple answer is that like many opportunities in life, I just happened to be at the right place at the right time. Likely, it was also due to a mix of my exposure to all levels of management at the company and my experience of working for three years in Korea. I never even asked for the assignment; the opportunity literally fell into my lap. My contribution was to seize the moment.

Before this new Tokyo assignment, I was planning to return home with my wife to Arizona, after another three-year expatriate assignment in Seoul, South Korea. At that time, I was working for a semiconductor company, based in Chandler, about twenty miles southeast of Phoenix, Arizona. I was newly married when we moved to South Korea to work in the company's Global Research and Development Centre. My wife and I had immensely enjoyed our expatriate life there, making many new friends and travelling all over South Korea. We had our baby daughter during this period.

However, expatriates are invariably expensive as the company covers a lot of the living cost on top of the regular salary, and after three years, I was summoned back to our Arizona headquarters. I wasn't pleased with this abrupt end to our expatriate Korean life. I was also wondering about my new role stateside. So, before our permanent move back home, I decided to take a business trip back to Arizona to understand more about what my new role would entail. Once back, I couldn't help but express my displeasure with this imminent transfer to my friends and colleagues in Arizona. Soon and unbeknownst to me, the word regarding my unhappiness reached the management team.

The vice president of our product group was a gentleman named Tom McCann. Tom is one of those fatherly figures type— even though he didn't have any kids of his own—always ready to dispense good wisdom and advice when necessary, and help us when needed. He is a great guy and many of us looked up to him. One day, as I was leaving the office late in the evening, I noticed that Tom's office light was still on. So, I decided to stop by to bid him goodbye since I was going to be returning to Seoul within the next couple of days. Tom was in a talkative mood, and we chatted about various things, including my new assignment and my transfer back to Chandler. Much to my surprise and discomfort, Tom suddenly mentioned that he was well-aware about my reluctance and unhappiness regarding the move back from Korea.

I was completely taken aback by this and was at a loss for words. I didn't know how to respond. *Should I deny it? Should I just tell him the truth about how disappointed I was with the transfer?* I was certainly disappointed to know that my complaints to my friends had reached his ears. I knew that moving me back to the US had been Tom's idea. If I told the truth, would there be some sort of repercussions? Despite it being quite cool in the room with the air conditioning blowing at full blast, I found myself sweating a bit. I nervously but somewhat cautiously replied that we did indeed want to stay in Korea for one more year, if at all possible. Then I waited for some angry comments from him. But to my greater surprise, he replied that indeed if I preferred to be in Asia, there was a business development position open in the company's Tokyo sales office. Perhaps I might be interested in taking that job?

I was once again stunned at this sudden proposition, especially since I was expecting to get a heated lecture from him. I knew about the opening in our Tokyo office; it was for a Vice President role in charge of Japan Business Development. I would have to be promoted three ranks higher to be eligible for the position as per the official job posting. I said that I would be very interested but reminded Tom of the seniority requirement for the opening. He told me not to worry about that. He did want me to confirm that I would move to Japan if offered the job. Of course, I would, I assured him as we said our goodbyes for the evening; Tom told me to leave the matter to him and that he would get back to me soon.

Frankly, I didn't take our discussion about the position in Japan seriously. Why on earth would the company send me to

Japan to fill a position that clearly seemed to be for a more senior person? Despite the fact that we didn't want to move back, since the move back to Arizona had been finalized, we had just bought our first home that very week and were somewhat reluctantly looking forward to resuming our life back home. Besides, how bad could it be to be back in good old USA, closer to my parents and sisters, who lived in Texas? Indeed, I loved Japan and would have been delighted to take the job, but the offer from Tom just seemed too good to be true. I didn't give it a second thought and even forgot to mention it to my wife, Sharmeen.

The next day was my last full day at the Arizona office before I headed back to Seoul to pack our bags. The day was busy, filled with various meetings regarding my new role. I met with my new boss and the team members. I felt relieved that I had worked with all of them in the past, so I knew them relatively well. I felt that the transition back would not be very difficult. The day went by fast in all these meetings and interactions, and after the meetings, I was surprised to see that Tom had left several messages for me just asking me to call him back. He didn't say what it was about. 'There must be something urgent he wanted to discuss with me', I thought, but frankly, I had no clue what it could be.

I figured perhaps he wanted me to do something when I was back in Korea, or perhaps he wanted to me to carry something back for him. I tried to call Tom back, but he was unavailable for the rest of the afternoon. No matter. There was a farewell party at Tom's house that evening, which I planned to attend. One of the senior executives was retiring and Tom had arranged a small shindig in his honour. I figured I could catch up with him at the party. Interestingly, it didn't even occur to me once that he might be calling me about the position in Japan.

In the evening, I showed up at Tom's house for the farewell party. When he saw me, he immediately pulled me aside and mentioned that he had some good news.

'It's a done deal, Asif', Tom said with a broad smile, adding, 'congratulations!'

I had no clue what he was talking about. I was caught by surprise and felt a little reluctant to ask him about it as I felt I should be aware of it.

'That's great, Tom. But may I ask what is a done deal?' I asked sheepishly.

'Your transfer to Japan, of course. It's all approved.' Tom replied, sounding a little annoyed.

Tom went on to explain that he had discussed the Japan assignment with Robert Green, our Executive Vice President of Global Sales, and our CEO, Steve Sullivan. Both had agreed that I would be a good choice for the Tokyo assignment.

Yet again, I was completely taken aback. I found myself somewhat shocked and in a state of total disbelief. Did I hear him right? Did Tom just offer me the Japan assignment? I guess my looks and demeanour gave away my feelings, and now it was Tom's turn to be confused and worried.

'I asked you yesterday and you said you want the job. You are not going to back out on me, are ya? I really pushed for you with Robert and Steve', Tom said, his concern clear in his voice and tone.

Of course I didn't need any convincing to move to Japan on the assignment. But I was having a hard time believing that I had got the job that easily. Besides, I had just had a day full of meetings about my new role in Arizona. Everything seemed to be happening too fast.

'Of course, I want the job in Japan. But what about my role here, which we have been discussing for the past week?' I asked.

'Don't worry about it. I will talk to them. We would rather you be in Japan for now. Besides, you wanted to be in Asia for longer. It's a win-win', Tom replied.

I found myself in a mixed state of elation, confusion and worry, struggling to digest what Tom had just told me. How was it that my new role was approved in a matter of a day?

What I wasn't aware of at the time was that the company had been looking for almost a year to fill that position. Our management was concerned that our revenue from Japan was very low and had been stagnant for years. This, despite the fact that many Japanese companies were key players in the semiconductor industry. Management felt that they needed someone who had a clear understanding of how our factories operated, how the company worked, and knew key people in senior management. They also believed, rightly so, that the person had to be familiar enough with Asian culture in order to work closely with our Japanese employees and customers. They were worried that if the person was not suitable or a good fit for the job, the effort could backfire.

There were more qualified candidates, but they had kids in school and weren't necessarily keen on uprooting their family and moving to Japan. A few people had apparently shown interest in the position, but the management was sceptical about how they would fit into the role. So there I was, an Asian American, with a newborn baby, who had been with the company for ten years, knew all the key players, had worked three years in our largest factory in Korea, which is located close to Japan. Apparently, the management felt that my background made me a good fit for the role and was very pleased that I was interested in the position.

Many people at the party seemed to be aware of this—clearly, I seemed to be one of the last to know about my new assignment. I spent the rest of the evening in a daze, even though I managed to thank everyone and mingle with the other folks in the party.

On my way back to the hotel, it occurred to me that I had not mentioned anything about this Japan assignment to my wife,

Sharmeen. I wondered how she would react to the news of a 180-degree turn from our current plan to move back to the US. As much as we loved our life in Seoul and wanted to extend our stay there, Sharmeen had been slowly warming up to the idea of moving back. Having bought our first home, she even seemed a little excited about returning to the States. What if she just simply didn't agree to move to Japan? I started to proactively think of ways to try to convince her, just in case. But what if she didn't agree with it at all? How would Tom react if I had to turn down his great offer? Would he just fire me? Surely, he won't be happy. Slowly, my elation started to evaporate and instead a sense of uneasiness and fear started to creep in.

By the time I got back to the hotel late in the evening, it was morning in Seoul. So, I called Sharmeen and after a few minutes, summoned up the courage to tell her about the Tokyo assignment, unsure if I should show excitement or disappointment. To my great relief, she not only didn't reject it but seemed very open to the idea. It was just us with our eighteen-month-old daughter, Farhana. So, things like schooling were not a concern for us at all.

Sharmeen and I had taken a trip to Tokyo while living in Seoul and we had enjoyed it thoroughly. She had been quite taken in by Tokyo and liked the city very much. My concern now seemed completely unwarranted, and I felt a sense of relief as the feeling of joy and elation quickly returned. As we were discussing how nice life would be in Japan, Sharmeen suddenly stopped talking. I thought our line got disconnected. Just as I was about to confirm if indeed the line had been lost, Sharmeen said, 'But what about my USMLE preparation classes?' in a very concerned voice.

In my excitement, I had completely forgotten all about that. Sharmeen is a doctor and was preparing for the various steps of the United States Medical Licence Exam (USMLE) exams. I had registered her for the preparatory classes in the Phoenix area.

Could she take such classes in Tokyo? She made it clear that if not, then it would not be a good idea to move to Japan. Once again, my excitement evaporated. I told her that I will confirm this immediately and get back to her. I felt completely exhausted after having been on an emotional rollercoaster all that evening and decided to just go to sleep. As soon as I went to bed, I was completely out.

The next day, I looked into it and much to my relief, was able to confirm that there were indeed USMLE prep classes available in Tokyo. I felt an ultimate sense of relief and finally and happily started to wrap my head around my new role and the move to Japan.

Chapter 2

Why Are You Coming to Japan?

Before leaving Arizona, I had enquired of Tom about the new position and asked for a detailed job description. Tom simply said the job was to increase our business and revenue in Japan and didn't say anything beyond that. He did say that it was a new role, and I may have to define it as I go along. I wasn't totally surprised to hear this as our company was fundamentally not a very bureaucratic organization, which had enabled us to grow significantly in the last few years. Still, I found it both strange and interesting that the company didn't have a job description for such an important expatriate position. Obviously, the goals and expectations for the role must be defined by and aligned with management. But I wasn't too worried about it since by nature, I am a risk-taker. I figured I would just take Tom's word and define the role after I arrive in Japan. I also worried that if I pressed him too hard about it, management might change their mind about sending me to Japan. At this point of time, I was just glad to have got the role and was looking forward to starting the new assignment as soon as possible.

However, I soon learnt that it was going to take two to four months to get all the required documentation completed, such as visas and the work permit. It was a little disappointing as I was still in a state of disbelief and paranoid that someone might sabotage my coveted Japan assignment during this period. I had little choice but to wait. It was mid-summer and since we had not yet moved back to Arizona, I decided to work out of our facility in Seoul for the rest of the summer and move directly to Tokyo from there.

* * *

The head of our Japan office was a gentleman named Kento Satoh. I had met him a few times in the past but didn't know him well. He was in his late forties and had white hair, which gave him a distinguished look. I had heard that he spoke English quite well, which was a very positive thing for me since I didn't speak any Japanese. Tom had shared that Satoh San was aware of my new role. While I would be reporting to my boss in the US, I understood the importance of aligning with the head of our Japan office to ensure a smooth transition. I figured that it was important to have brief discussion with him, to introduce myself and discuss what his needs in order to grow the business were, and how I could be of help.

As I was contemplating having a phone call with him, I learnt that Satoh San was coming to visit our Seoul facility with some Japanese clients. I was quite excited to get this opportunity to meet him face-to-face and reintroduce myself. I had already reviewed various financial data from our Japan operation. Seeing the numbers for myself, it was obvious why our management had been so eager to send someone to Japan to drive the business growth. I figured Satoh San and I could take this opportunity to strategize on how to go about increasing local sales.

Since Satoh San was visiting the Seoul factory with one of our Japanese customers, I would have had a higher chance of catching him in our customer service department. The customer service office, located on the fifth floor of the old building, had a completely different decor from the rest of the factory. The factory looked old and drab; the fifth floor had a very new and posh look and feel, with wooden walls and marble floors to make it appear more welcoming to customers. My favourite were the bathrooms, which were much nicer than those in the rest of the factory. Most importantly, all the toilet seats were of Western style, something very near and dear to my heart and my rear. Other bathrooms in the factory—in fact, many older buildings in Seoul—still had Asian-style toilets, which are basically holes on the floor and not easy to navigate under any circumstances, but particularly difficult when one is wearing a suit.

I walked up to the fifth floor to see if I could locate Satoh San and make an appointment for a meeting. As I was about to ask the receptionist where I could find him, I saw Satoh San, with his unmistakable full head of white hair, coming out of one of the meeting rooms. The receptionist motioned me towards him. I was hoping to set up a meeting and wasn't expecting to run into him like this, all of a sudden. So, a little nervous, I walked up to him and introduced myself, hand outstretched, smiling broadly. He didn't smile back.

He quickly shook my hand and dryly told me that he had heard about my assignment. *That's a good start*, I thought. I asked politely if he had some time to perhaps discuss my new role. Satoh San replied that he was quite busy during this trip with his customers and, unfortunately, did not have any time for me. He sounded a little annoyed. That was strange. I figured that he would be very keen to discuss the new role. After all, it was to improve the Japan business and assigned by the head office itself. I didn't know what to make of his tone and reluctance to have a discussion with me. I asked him if he might have some time for a quick coffee or even dinner, perhaps.

'Do you speak any Japanese?' Satoh San asked instead, in a condescending manner.

I was somewhat taken aback at his directness. It was not at all what I had expected from a Japanese person. I replied that I didn't speak or understand any Japanese but was planning on taking some lessons before moving to Tokyo.

'Well, in that case, I am not sure why you are coming to Japan.'

Like a balloon losing air, his response completely sucked out my enthusiasm and wiped off my smile. For a few seconds, I didn't know how to respond. Frankly, I didn't know what to make of his apparent rude and unfriendly attitude. But I decided not to back down and pressed on.

'I understand the importance of the language, Satoh San, but perhaps we can discuss the assignment. I would like to hear your opinion about how I can help to grow our business and revenue, even though I don't speak any Japanese.'

'Frankly, I don't know what there is to discuss Asif San. Also, I am visiting with a customer and really don't have any time. Very sorry.'

With that, he turned around and went back into the meeting room, perhaps forgetting why he had come out in the first place. I stood there in the lobby for the next few minutes, shocked and confused.

The first thing that came to my mind was that our management had made the decision regarding my assignment without discussing or consulting with Satoh San. Or perhaps, they had discussed it with him and he did not approve, but they had decided to pursue the move anyway. If I was the head of the Japan office, I would also be upset if that was the case. Indeed, that might explain Satoh San's lack of enthusiasm regarding my assignment. Still, I was trying my best to justify his rude behaviour. What shocked me the most was to experience this kind of unprofessional behaviour and rather rude attitude from a Japanese person. My experience with the Japanese had been the complete opposite, and I had come to regard them as very polite. After all, the Japanese are known for their politeness worldwide. Also, they rarely communicate so directly. Was Satoh San an anomaly? I am sure there are a few outliers in every culture and society. Why would Japan be any different?

Little did I know then—though I was about to find out— that the Japanese can be 'not so polite' in certain environments, especially when a foreigner comes into their 'space', potentially upsetting the delicate Japanese *wa*. The concept of wa is an integral part of Japanese society. While it translates into English as 'harmony', it has a much broader meaning. It suggests a peaceful conformity within the broader society, a working group or among family members. The fundamental concept is to maintain social harmony by respecting and putting the need of the community above individual needs and aspirations. As strange as it may sound to foreigners, the concept of wa works like the invisible hand of a maestro that conducts most of the daily social interactions in all Japanese social settings, including workplaces.

As I would also find out later, Satoh San was indeed a little bit of an anomaly. Over time, I found Satoh San's frankness refreshing in a country where hardly anyone ever speaks their mind. In fact, Satoh San and I would go on to become friends in the coming years. But these are stories for later chapters. At that moment, I was more worried that he might put an end to my dream opportunity of working and living in Japan.

Bewildered and worried, I called Tom back in the US that night, and narrated my encounter with Satoh San in its entirety. He listened to me and simply advised me not to worry about it, reiterating that I was really needed in the Tokyo office. He promised that he would discuss my assignment with our Japan office, particularly with Satoh San, in more detail. I was relieved to hear Tom confirming that the transfer was still on. Indeed, he called me back in a couple of weeks to inform me that he had had a heart-to-heart with Satoh San and that all was settled, and

I should not have anything to worry about, going forward. I felt relieved after my conversation with Tom and tried not to give this matter any further thought. I also decided not to discuss the role with Satoh San, or anyone, for that matter, till I moved to our office in Tokyo. Still, the whole encounter left me worried and shaken about my assignment. My euphoria was now turning into a fear of the unknown, unsure of what else I might encounter once I started my new role in Tokyo.

Chapter 3

The Move and the Uphill Battle

Summer was coming to an end, but our paperwork still wasn't ready. I started to get a little impatient and bothered our legal team on a weekly basis, asking them the status of our work permit. Finally, in mid-October, it was approved along with the dependent visas for Sharmeen and Farhana. In early November, with all our required paperwork completed, we were ready to move to Tokyo. We decided that it would be best for me to go by myself at first and try to find my bearings in the new city. There was no point in both of us struggling in the new surroundings, especially since we had a two-year-old. Sharmeen would fly back to the US with our baby daughter to spend some time with my parents and sisters. Then they would join me in a month or so.

As my plane landed at the Tokyo Narita Airport on a Sunday afternoon, I was both excited and anxious. I couldn't believe that Japan was going to be my new home for the next few years. The company had put me up at the Hyatt Hotel in Shinjuku, a lively district in the heart of Tokyo. By the time I arrived at the hotel, it was already past eight o'clock in the evening. As soon as checked in, I left my luggage in the room and went outside the hotel to explore my new home. The concierge desk encouraged me to walk about ten minutes to the Shinjuku station, as there were all kinds of restaurants and eateries around it. I found a small ramen shop and gulped down some hot ramen noodles. The hot ramen hit just the spot on that cold Tokyo evening. After my light dinner, I walked around Shinjuku for hours, taking in the Tokyo scenery, just in awe of all the bright signs and stores and the sheer number of people, despite it being so late at night. Finally, around 1 in the morning, I decided to go back to the hotel to get some rest as I had to be in the office the next day. I found it difficult to fall asleep as I was still too excited, but ultimately, managed to get some shut-eye.

The next day, on a beautiful, sunny, cold and crisp winter morning, I showed up in our Ebisu office. Ebisu is considered one of the high-end areas of Tokyo—though most areas in Tokyo looked high-end to me then. Our office suite was located in a modern building with a lot of technology and automation, way ahead of its time. The elevators had no buttons, for example. Instead of up and down buttons, there was a small digital tablet where the tenants were supposed to punch in what floor they wanted to go to. The elevator would show up and take them to their designated floor while talking to them, providing vital information such as the top news of the day and daily weather. All lightings were automatic, and the brightness of each floor and office space were automatically adjusted according to the ambient light. On a cloudy day, the office lights would shine brighter. Everything looked clean and shiny, as if someone had just polished it. Everyone was dressed in suits. Having worked in a drab factory for the past three years, this definitely felt like a major upgrade. As I stepped into the elevator, I tried to hide the broad and satisfied smile on my face, in case people around me thought that I was crazy.

I was met by Erika Toda, the head of the Human Resource (HR) department. It was our first meeting, and she welcomed me to the office. Toda San asked me to follow her and showed me my office space. My laptop was already on the desk, along with my new mobile phone, chargers, etc. Typical Japanese efficiency, I thought—everything done on time and ready to go. While it wasn't an office with a door as I was used to at our Arizona headquarters, it was quite a spacious cubicle. She offered to show me where the pantry was, which I welcomed. I was ready for my much-needed morning coffee. Just as I was about to get settled at my desk, having finished a cup of freshly brewed coffee, Toda San appeared again and asked me to follow her to the HR area, where I was to fill out some necessary paperwork. As the forms were in Japanese, Toda San helped me fill them out in English. She came across as a no-nonsense, very task-oriented kind of person, cordial but with a hint of coldness in her attitude. In my usual manner, I tried to make a few light remarks but soon stopped, as I was not getting much of a response from her. A plump, single woman in her forties, Toda San reminded me more of the strict schoolteacher every student is scared of, as opposed to a typical friendly and warm HR person. But I felt pleased with her ability to communicate in English—the language issue had been on my mind since my brief encounter with Satoh San. With no Japanese language skills, it was imperative that some of the key folks in the company spoke some level of English. Toda San seemed quite fluent in it.

After the formalities, she offered to take me around to introduce me to the other members of the office. Our Japan office was relatively small, with about twenty or so employees. I had met some of them during my past business trips, but that was a few years back. After my unfriendly encounter with Satoh San, I was a little worried as to how the others in the office would react to the arrival of a new gaijin sarariman in their midst. Much to my relief, most of them were quite pleasant and welcoming. At the end, Toda San brought me to Satoh San's office. My anxiety level jumped up as I saw him again. While he wasn't friendly, he did welcome me to the office. As I was about to leave his office after our very brief encounter, he mentioned that I could come to him in case I needed anything. *Well, that was very nice*, I thought. This time around, he was much more pleasant—very different compared to our first encounter in Korea. Either he had accepted my new role or decided that there was no point fighting it. At any rate, I felt at ease with the overall initial reception and was ready to get to work.

The first few weeks were uneventful. I got settled into my new office, but not into my new role. No one spoke to me, other than chiming in with the usual *ohayou gozaimasu* (good morning) each morning and *otsukaresama deshita* (a common phrase used when leaving the office, which translates to 'you must be tired') in the evening. I would show up in the morning, do my e-mails and review our Japan business report—the same report I had been reviewing for the past few months. I wanted to approach Satoh San a few times but decided against it, based on my Seoul encounter with him. I figured that it would be best to see if he would approach me, this time around.

Toda San had kindly pointed out a few convenient places for lunch in the office's vicinity. I was hoping that people would invite me to go to lunch with them to discuss my role or even perhaps to welcome me to the office. But I didn't receive any such invitations. Every day, I would contemplate inviting someone to lunch but then invariably end up just walking around and exploring the area by myself and trying out different restaurants. I guess I was eager to avoid any further negative interaction at this very early stage of my assignment.

* * *

During my fourth week, I got a call from Tom. He wanted to see how I was doing and if I needed anything. I mentioned that everything was fine except that no one in the office seemed to know why I was there.

'What do you mean?' Tom asked, surprised.

'Well . . . I have been in the office for over three weeks now, and no one has approached me or spoken to me about my role.'

'What? Really? Satoh San was supposed to talk to you', Tom said, sounding incredulous. 'Have you tried to talk to him?'

I sighed, choosing my words carefully and doing my best to keep my frustration at bay. I didn't want Tom to think that I had no control over what was going on.

'You know what happened the last time I tried to have a discussion about my role with Satoh San, Tom. I truly don't want a repetition of the same thing again. I would rather not start my new job on any further negative notes', I replied, still sounding a little frustrated.

Tom told me to take the bull by the horns and start strategizing with Satoh San on how to increase our business in Japan, even if I had to do it forcefully. Clearly, Tom wasn't well-versed in the Japanese way of doing business. You can't force yourself into a role in most of the places in the world, least of all in Japan. As I would find out later, here, a team or a group is like a family—one must be invited in. To try to fit in forcefully will invariably cause pain and frustration to both sides. Luckily, I had the common sense not to force anything on anyone in the office. But I agreed with Tom to cut our conversation short.

'These Japanese guys! I will have another talk with Satoh San', Tom promised, sounding frustrated before hanging up.

After the phone conversation with Tom, I wondered if this might make Satoh San even more upset and less willing to cooperate with me. But I decided that there was no choice but for Tom to push him; in the end, Satoh San would have to listen to Tom as he was one of the big bosses at the head office.

I wasn't surprised when Satoh San invited me to lunch the next day. I was sure that Tom had spoken to him. But I wondered how he was going to react. I tried to figure out by carefully judging his demeanour and his body language and tone during the brief encounter when he invited me, but I sensed neither any hostility nor a friendlier attitude. Both of us were quiet as we walked to a restaurant close to the office. But as we sat down for lunch, Satoh San asked me how things were and how I was liking Japan. To my very pleasant surprise, we had a great lunch, discussing the country, the culture, language, etc. Of course, I was very eager to learn about Japan and had many questions, and Satoh San seemed pleased to be taking up the role of a *senpai*, an experienced mentor. While I was quite pleased with our lunch meeting, it occurred to me later that Satoh San had not mentioned anything about my work or our Japan business. I decided to let it pass. Perhaps it was better to ease into the new role than to force my way into it, I thought.

In the meantime, Sharmeen had joined me in Tokyo with our baby, Farhana. Tom was kind enough to allow us to upgrade to a suite at the Hyatt, so we were quite comfortable. I was very pleased to have them around after almost a month and a half, especially Farhana, as I didn't want to miss any part of her growing up. It also allowed me to get my mind off work. After coming back from the office, we would go out to eat and explore the Shinjuku area. Some evenings, we would venture out to other parts of the city. It definitely helped to ease my stress levels.

After we had our lunch, I waited a week to see if things would start to move. But when there was no progress, I decided to invite Satoh San to lunch, which he readily accepted. Once again, we had a great discussion, and he seemed genuinely interested in quenching my thirst to learn about everything Japanese. But this time, towards the end of our meal, I cautiously brought up the subject of my role. He told me that the team is arranging an introductory meeting with me to give me a detailed status of the Japan business. He added that after the introductory meeting, he would like to discuss my new role in detail. Needless to say, I was quite happy, even though I felt that this meeting should have taken place weeks earlier. Tom's intervention seemed to have paid off.

I was excited and looking forward to the said introductory meeting. Finally, things seemed to be progressing. I spent a few days working hard to create a presentation with my thoughts on how we could all work together to improve our business. I had all sorts of financial data to show how we had been doing and had also done some market analysis to show the areas where I thought we could improve. At the end of the week, I asked Satoh San about the meeting, and he politely said that everyone had been busy but he would schedule it soon. He didn't define what 'soon' meant and I also forgot to ask him. But I figured it would take place in the next few days. However, another week went by and there was still no such meeting scheduled. Disappointed once again, I went to see Satoh San in his office. This time, he seemed even nicer. He apologized for the delay, adding that the team had been busy and promised to have the meeting the following week. I wondered if he was giving me the run-around. I had heard that it is not uncommon for the Japanese to say 'yes' or 'maybe' when the answer is really a 'no'. The idea is that you keep saying 'yes' to appease the enquirer with no intention of ever really taking up or accomplishing the task. Eventually, the enquirer would get the message and stop asking, and things would just remain *sono mama* or the same. The precious *wa* would be maintained. I couldn't help but wonder if this was my first initiation into such Japanese practices.

It turned out not to be the case. The following week, the much-anticipated introductory meeting appointment showed up on my calendar. Much to my surprise, it was a three-hour meeting, which included a detailed review of our Japan business by sales account and by customer.

On the designated day, the meeting started right on the dot and Satoh San began by introducing me to the team, first in English and then in Japanese. He emphasized that I was here to help grow the business and that people should feel free to seek my help as needed. I presented my slides in English, not sure if most of the people were able to grasp what I was trying to say about working together to grow our revenue. At the end, there were no questions—which didn't surprise me—perhaps the language, my assignment and the new charter to grow were too much for them to digest. Then each of them presented business details about their respective customers and clients. Of course, I had many questions, which they tried their best to answer. It was a very productive first meeting. In fact, after waiting all those weeks, I felt like things were finally moving in the right direction.

However, another two weeks passed after the meeting, and no one came to me for any kind of business discussion. Everyone was very polite and friendly, but it was back to square one—the meeting didn't seem to have any implications whatsoever with respect to my work.

While I was having not-so-meaningful, pleasant encounters with Satoh San and the rest of the team members, there was another issue brewing on the HR front. Toda San's demeanour invariably always came across as cold, giving me a distinct feeling that I was a burden to her and distracting her from more important duties. Getting any help from HR required her approval and it felt like pulling teeth. Toda San's first answer was always a 'no' to everything I would ask for, even though she would be indirect about it. For example, she would pretend to go into a deep meditation whenever I asked for something. Then she would come back with a response like, 'Wow, that is very difficult, Asif San. Frankly, we may not be able to help even if we try.' If I pressed on, she would find a way to deflect it, letting me know that either it wasn't HR's job, or that they were simply not equipped to help me with such requests. It was quite painful and frustrating as HR's help was indispensable, especially in order to get my family settled in Tokyo.

For example, being new in Japan and not being able to communicate in the language, we needed help with almost every basic thing, like finding a home, opening a bank account, leasing a car, finding a daycare centre for our daughter, getting our cable set up and so on. All these institutions (like the banks, cable companies etc.) preferred to deal with local entities and people as opposed to a new foreign arrival. Besides, all the contracts were in Japanese. So without help from the local office, things would be very difficult. Toda San's continual refusal to help us with some of these things was becoming very frustrating. But I wasn't going to give up so easily either, and politely kept asking her for help, deliberately ignoring her excuses. Finally, Toda San did come through and did a wonderful thing. Since our HR department apparently wasn't equipped to deal with a new expatriate, she hooked us up with an external company that would help us with all our needs to get settled in Tokyo. But I still wonder if she had to make life so difficult for me in the process. Regardless, I was quite happy with this very positive development and glad to think that I wouldn't have to ask Toda San for any more 'favours'.

But much to my dismay, it turned out that my feud with Toda San wasn't quite over yet. As part of my expatriate contract, the company was supposed to pay for all the major local expenses, including our monthly rent and our car lease payment. While the payments were not the issue, the mechanism of payment became a problem. Typically, the local office would make these payments directly to the local entities on behalf of the expatriates. Then they would bill back the relevant expenses to the head office. Toda San insisted that the Japan office did not have any precedence and procedures to take care of such things for me. It was going to be a major issue if Toda San refused to take care of these expenses. I felt very tired at this point and had no energy to pursue the matter with her any longer. I decided to take it up with our finance team at our Arizona office.

When I discussed the matter with our finance team at the head office, they seemed quite baffled. The Japan office was regularly billing several items to our head office, which routinely got paid back by the corporate finance team. So they didn't understand what the issue was for Toda San to pay for these critical high-cost items on my behalf. As I discussed this in depth with the finance team, it became quite apparent that she simply didn't want to do this for me. Her boss was Satoh San, who had already decided that my assignment was a waste of time, since I could not speak any Japanese, despite his recent, nicer and more polite demeanour. I felt that talking to him wasn't going to be of much help either. I almost felt like calling Tom and telling him that this was not going to work out and perhaps it was best for me to return to Arizona.

Just around this time, when my frustration was about to reach its boiling point, to my great surprise, I met another American expatriate from our head office at our Ebisu office. One morning, as I was sitting at my desk, minding my own business as usual, this American gentleman stopped by and introduced himself as Brad Saler. Apparently, he had also been sent to Japan from our head office as an expatriate. This whole time, I had been under the impression that I was the only expat there. I was shocked and surprised to learn that there was another expat here who was just like me. How come no one had ever mentioned Brad's existence? And how come I had not seen him all this time? I found this quite annoying and mysterious. However, I was very pleased to meet Brad, eager to pick his brain on how to best deal with the folks in the office. Surely, Brad had gone through similar experiences and if so, perhaps he could shed some light on my current predicament and guide me on how to navigate all these barriers.

I immediately invited him to lunch, hoping that he would be available, so that we could talk outside the office environment. He said he was available and at 12 p.m. on the dot, the two of us dashed out of the office. Brad took me to a small burger place and we talked for almost a couple of hours. I found out that Brad had been working for the company for three years and had been at the Tokyo office for two. He worked in the corporate procurement group and had been sent to Japan to manage our Japanese suppliers. His wife was Japanese, and he had lived in Japan before, so this was not his first assignment in the country. He seemed quite well-versed in the Japanese ways.

I shared with Brad what I was going through, describing all my troubles with Satoh San, including his reluctance to accept me in the office and Toda San's resistance to providing any help at all. He just smiled and said that he wasn't surprised at all. Apparently, he had also faced a similar fate when he had first moved to Tokyo. He had found many people in the office to be quite unhelpful. In fact, Toda San had also refused to take care of his local expenses, just as she had refused to take care of mine. But Brad had decided that he would not put up with 'such crap'. After working at the office for a few months, he had apparently stopped coming to office altogether. He worked out with his boss that he would be working from home. He took care of all his local expenses like rent and childcare by himself, and just applied for reimbursement directly to our Arizona office. He mentioned that he showed up in the office only when it was absolutely necessary, such as to file his expense reports or to attend meetings with suppliers, or if there was a specific reason for him to be there. He encouraged me to strike a similar arrangement with Tom.

Unfortunately, this was just not an option for me. Since Brad's role was to manage and deal with the local suppliers, his job had nothing to do with sales. Our Japan office was a sales office, and my function had everything to do with sales and the local office staff. There was no way for me to do my job being away from the office: I *had* to work with the local team. So while I was happy for Brad, the discussion proved not to be of much help in my current predicament. However, I couldn't help but feel a sense of relief to learn that I wasn't the only one suffering from these unwarranted pushbacks from HR and the unwillingness of the local team to engage with me. While it didn't solve my problems, it felt good for some reason nevertheless.

Looking back, and having been exposed to Japan for a long time now, I have a better understanding as to why I faced such an uphill battle to gain acceptance from my Japanese colleagues and team members. In fact, it is common for foreign employees to encounter some level of resistance and challenges from the local folks when they first start to work for a Japanese company. Japanese workplace rules are typically rigid with very little to no room for flexibility. Most local employees follow these rules religiously and rarely question or challenge them, even though they may find many of them quite unnecessary and sometimes devoid of logic. On the contrary, most employees often come across as being thankful and grateful for the benefits and opportunities the company provides them with, whatever they may be. Questioning the employer, or any authority for that matter, is not a very common practice in Japan and such behaviour is frowned upon by the broader society, at least in public. The idea is that when everyone follows rules, it helps to maintain order and prevents chaos in the workplace. Again, the all-important wa is maintained.

From the viewpoint of the Western work ethics and culture, some of the local company rules, regulations and customs will likely not make much sense. For many of us who are indoctrinated in the Western ways, we tend to think that rules have to make some sense for us to follow them. It is not unorthodox or uncommon to question them in the US or Europe when they don't make sense, and such behaviour, while it may not be very popular with employers, is generally accepted. As a result, the Japanese believe that foreign employees tend to be less willing to conform to all the local rules and regulations and are more demanding. So most of the time, the local team tends to go a little overboard, being unduly strict during the orientation process of the new foreign employee to ensure that he or she 'fits in' with the Japanese way. The new employee invariably finds this uphill battle a little challenging.

For example, when we moved to Japan, we wanted to decide where to live, what kind of house or apartment we wanted to live in and what kind of car we should lease. In Japan, the company providing housing quarters and transportation typically does not enquire into the employees' preferences. The company decides what is appropriate for the employee, most often based on his or her rank or position. So right off the bat, my requirements and demands were not in sync with the Japanese way of doing things. From our perspective, there was no way we would let Toda San decide on our accommodation. Also, when Toda San refused to pay our rent out of the Japan office, a Japanese employee would rarely challenge her. They would simply accept it, however inconvenient it may be. However, I kept pushing her, insisting that she take care of our needs. Just as her behaviour didn't make any sense to me, what I had failed to comprehend at the time was that my behaviour didn't make much sense to her either. In fact, she probably thought I was being rude and arrogant, typical of foreign employees. These kinds of gaps in understanding and expectations, arising from differences in work culture and ethics, can become a source of frustration for both sides. If not managed properly, that frustration can fester into bigger issues, resulting in the failure of an otherwise important assignment.

In my case, I did have a slight upper hand as I wasn't working for a Japanese company but the Japanese branch of a US firm. Furthermore, I had been sent there by our top management from our head office in the US. Despite this, I still had to face quite an uphill battle to establish my place in the local organization. A foreign employee in a Japanese firm would have no choice but to follow the local policy and practices. In hindsight, one right decision that I made was not to rush into things and continue to be polite and respectful towards everyone in the office, including Toda San, despite the pushback and however frustrated I felt. Also, instead of just getting mad, I desperately tried to understand why they were acting the way they were, simply due to my intense and sincere interest in Japanese culture. In the end, it was my patience and attitude, along with my deep knowledge of our company culture, which would help me to win over my Japanese colleagues.

Chapter 4

These Houses Are Not for You, Asif San

While I was facing the challenges at work with the local team, my wife and I were facing another challenge on the home front. Our first order of business was to get settled in Tokyo with our daughter. While we were enjoying our life at the nice, posh and comfortable mini-suite at the Shinjuku Hyatt, it had almost been a couple of months, and we were eager to move into our own home and start our life in Japan.

Settling down in any foreign country with a family is not easy. We discovered that when there is a language barrier, it can compound the task. Relatively simple things such as opening a bank account, getting a local mobile phone subscription, signing up for a cable TV service, finding the right school for the kids, buying or leasing a car, acquiring a local driver's licence or finding the right medical facilities can prove to be daunting tasks, unless there is someone local assisting the new family. There are obviously communication issues due to the language barrier, plus all the paperwork and contracts are written in Japanese. So it is vital to have someone local assisting in these endeavours, especially one who is knowledgeable about the needs of both sides and can translate and communicate with us in English.

One great thing we had going for us was that my aunt, Anowara Ahmed, was also living in Tokyo at the time. She is my father's younger sister and we are very close, as our families used to live together when I was a child. Her husband, Dr Monzoor Ahmed, was serving as the head of UNICEF in Japan. We called my aunt Fupu and her husband Fupa. They had moved to Tokyo from New York on a three-year assignment. By the time we arrived, they had already been living there for about two years. Both Sharmeen and I are very close to them, and it was wonderful to have some family in this foreign land. I was regularly consulting with Fupa about various things, and he reiterated several times that without help from the local office, it would be difficult for us to get settled in Tokyo. I had shared all the stories with him about Toda San and my frustration with our local office, but he said that I should keep pushing my office to provide guidance and help. I was doing exactly that but wasn't getting anywhere until Toda San hooked us up with the external agency. I do believe that if I hadn't respectfully and politely pushed back on Toda San, she might not have provided us with this much-needed service. The agency she hooked us up with turned out to be the HR group of a large American company in Japan that specialized in handling the needs of expatriate families. At one point, the company had many expatriates working in Japan and their local HR department had a small, dedicated group to take care of that community. Over the years, they became so good at it that they had started to offer this service externally.

The challenge of getting us settled fell to a woman named Miku Watanabe. She was middle-aged, with a very pleasant demeanour, extremely polite, thoughtful and ready to help, with great attention to detail, quite consistent with her Japanese heritage. Most importantly, she spoke fluent English, having spent some time in the US. During our first meeting in the lobby of the Hyatt, she explained to us all the things that she would help us with to get settled in Tokyo. So under the supervision and guidance of Miku San, one of the first thing we did was embark on our journey to find a suitable place for us to live.

I was quite unfamiliar with Tokyo, even though I had visited the city a few times in the past for business meetings. My familiarity with the city was limited to Ebisu, where our office was located, and the touristy districts such as Shinjuku, Roppongi or Shibuya. Tokyo was a big city with twenty-three wards or municipalities. So we were at the mercy of Miku San to find us the right place in the right neighbourhood.

She would show up exactly on time in the lobby of the Shinjuku Hyatt for our house-hunting trips. She would have already made the necessary appointments beforehand. She would pick us up and ferry us around in her car to each of the appointments for the day. During each of these trips, Miku San would take us out to see two to three homes and we made three to four such trips every week. Every detail of this process was planned, from which house we would visit first to where we would park for each of the appointments. She would print the detailed itinerary with descriptions and photos of each of the houses we were supposed to visit in triplicate—one for me, one for my wife and one for herself. After making a few trips with her, both my wife and I felt that we were in good hands. Every house-hunting trip went smoothly and as planned. Everything, except finding the right home. The houses or condominiums we liked were either at the right locations but too expensive, or within our price range but at the wrong locations.

For decades, Tokyo has been ranked top of the list of the most expensive cities in the world. Here, a melon, perfectly rounded and beautifully packaged, can cost up to $80. A single banana, once again perfect with almost no spots, immaculately wrapped in clear plastic, can cost over $3. I remember my first dinner experience many years ago, when I was a young engineer visiting Tokyo for a one-day business meeting. During dinner, having been forewarned by my colleagues about how expensive the city could be, I cautiously ordered just a small bowl of soup and a plate of pasta, no wine or any other drinks, except for water. While I can't recall the exact location, it was a small restaurant by a station, nothing fancy whatsoever. The bill for the dinner came to over $90. Our company's policy allowed about $30 for dinner for one. The next day, on my flight back home, I spent most of my time worrying that my boss wouldn't approve my expensive dinner, in which case I wouldn't be reimbursed for it, and might even get reprimanded for such an extravagance.

I had been worried for nothing as my expense report was promptly approved without any questions. I had almost forgotten about this incident if not for the current nightmare of a situation with very steep monthly rents.

Even though we moved from Seoul, which is also not a cheap place to live, my wife and I still could not comprehend the outrageous rents in Tokyo. For example, the rent for a small two-bedroom apartment in central Tokyo can be over $10,000 a month. On top of that, the tenant may have to fork up an additional $1,000 a month if he or she requires a parking spot. As one radially moves away from central Tokyo, rents drop. This, of course, is a common phenomenon in any big city such as New York or Boston, except that the base rent in and around Tokyo is so much higher. There are places outside Tokyo that are reasonable—most consisting of one room with a small kitchenette, a tiny bathroom and a shower.

For the past three years in Seoul, we had been living on the ninth floor of a nice four-bedroom condo, perfectly located on top of a hill, with a full glass wall providing a breathtaking view of the Han River, some of Seoul's high-rises and beautiful mountain ranges in the distance. We didn't feel comfortable moving into a tiny one-room condo from all that luxury; downgrading is invariably tough. Also, we had a daughter to raise, so while we could live without the likes of the luxury of our apartment in Seoul, we wanted some space. Additionally, we were expecting to have family and friends visit us. So we decided that a very tiny place simply won't do. The rents posed quite a conundrum in our quest to find our home. In the meantime, we were getting tired of hotel living, despite the relative luxury. Plus, I was getting worried that my company would soon throw us out of the hotel—a mini-suite at the Hyatt Regency in Tokyo is not cheap by any means.

To ensure success in our quest to find our ideal home, we had provided Miku San with certain criteria. At the top of the list was a budget. Our daughter was nearing two years of age, so schooling was not a concern, which provided us with more flexibility with respect to location. Still, we told her that it should not be more than thirty minutes' ride by car or by train (or subway) from my office, and it had to have three to four bedrooms. Another key criterion for us was that the house or the apartment should be no more than ten minutes' walk to a train or subway station. This is because we would only have one company car. We figured a ten-minute walk with a two-year-old in tow would not be unreasonable.

At first, Miku San appeared unfazed by any of our criteria. However, she mentioned that while she was confident about finding us a home with relative ease, our budget could be an impediment. This was a very legitimate concern. She kept asking us to try to increase our budget, especially if we wanted to live closer to a station. Alternatively, we could find something cheaper, i.e. within our budget, if we were okay with living outside Tokyo. This could make my commute well over an hour long. Miku San explained that many people lived outside the city and an hour's commute to work was not at all uncommon. She added that some people's commute took two hours each way, and about four to six million people commuted to the city daily from their homes outside Tokyo. However, the prospect of such a long commute didn't appeal to me.

We found ourselves in quite a conundrum. Clearly, what we were looking for was available, but our budget was on the lower side for these places. Sharmeen and I discussed and decided that we will not settle and will go for what we want. Of course, this meant that I had to do some renegotiation with our head office, i.e. with Tom. I wondered how he would react. Things weren't going so smoothly on the work front. Tom was aware of this. Now if I ask for a higher budget for our home, would he just ask me to come back to Arizona? After giving the matter some thought, I decided to go for renegotiating our housing allowance, regardless of the outcome. If they want me to pack up and move back, so be it. But instead of just asking him for a higher budget, I decided that there might be a higher chance of convincing people back home if I could show them how expensive Tokyo is, compared to Phoenix and Seoul. So I collected all sorts of data and even made a small PowerPoint presentation for Tom. I put together a comparison of some basic living costs such as grocery items, a movie night for two with some popcorn and drinks, school fees, parking fees, road tolls and of course, rents for equivalent places. The data clearly showed that Tokyo was about 1.2 to 2 times more expensive. I summoned up the courage and presented this data to Tom, and explained to him our trouble with finding a suitable home. It turned out that my company needed me in Japan more than I had realized. Tom approved my request right during the call, much to my surprise. In fact, he sympathized with us, saying that he was aware of the high cost of Tokyo living. Armed with the higher budget, Miku San promised that our house-hunting battle with all our requirements would soon be won with relative ease. On weekdays, we would make two to three house tours, much to the annoyance of my Japanese colleagues, who didn't seem to understand my involvement in this family matter, especially since I had to take time off from work.

Sarariman in Japan rarely take time off for family issues; taking time off on a regular basis is almost unheard of. The company is the family. How can a sarariman abandon this work family on a regular basis? Such was the attitude of my colleagues towards my weekday house-hunting trips, even though no one in the office seemed to make any effort to utilize me on the work front.

Frankly, I was enjoying the time away from my colleagues, out of the office with my wife and daughter, looking at homes to rent. I felt I was being more productive this way. To ensure that this didn't become a big issue with the folks in our office, I cleared this with Tom in the US, reiterating the importance of spending the initial months getting the family settled, so that I could focus on work. He not only agreed with me but also didn't quite understand what the issue was, clearly unaware of the strict work culture of the sarariman.

During one of our house-hunting excursions, we came across a place we really liked. It was in a very nice and quiet neighbourhood known as Himoniya in the Meguro-Ku ward of Tokyo. It was on the top floor of a three-storey, cozy apartment building, what we would call a condominium back in the US. In Japan, they call it a *maanshon* or mansion, another wasei-eigo that has made its way into the Japanese vocabulary but is pronounced with a Japanese twist. While it was nothing like a mansion in the US, it was a very spacious two-bedroom condo with a large living room, adjacent to an equally large patio that had a beautiful Japanese garden. Most of the rooms had floor-to-ceiling glass windows. Both Sharmeen and I immediately fell in love with it. The closest station was about fifteen minutes away, a little longer than what we had wanted, but Miku San assured us that the walk to the station was pleasant, through a nice and quiet Tokyo neighbourhood. We decided to take the walk and see for ourselves how long it would actually take while pushing a stroller with our little Farhana in it.

Indeed, the walk took us through a very quiet and pristine neighbourhood—the kind quite common in an otherwise busy and bustling Tokyo. Small houses were lined up on both sides of the narrow street. Each house had a small gate and very limited parking space, which in many cases seemed to be smaller and narrower than the cars themselves. I always wondered how they managed to get out of their vehicle even if they somehow managed to park in such a narrow space. All the houses were neatly decorated with colourful seasonal flowers. It looked as if every house had been painted and cleaned that morning. The whole neighbourhood was indeed nice and neat, just as Miku San had promised it would be.

As we were walking through this tranquil neighbourhood, I noticed a few homes had signboards. They were in Japanese, but they seemed like they were rental signs for rentals. I was curious. I asked Miku San what they said, and she confirmed that they were indeed rental signs for the houses. From outside, the houses looked very nice, not very different from what we would have liked. I wondered why Miku San hadn't shown us these properties. After all, they were closer to the station. Was the rent for these places much higher than our budget? They didn't look very different from what we had seen in other areas, which were all within our new, higher budget. Curious, I again asked Miku San if these houses were really available for rent.

'Yes, of course, Asif San. As I mentioned, you can see the signs', Miku San replied.

'I guess the rent must be much higher', I said.

'I don't think the rent is much higher in this neighbourhood.'

'Really?' I was surprised and a little irritated. 'How come you didn't show us these homes, Miku San? They are obviously closer to the station.'

'*So ne* (a common Japanese expression) Asif San, very sorry but these houses are not for you. But you will like that maanshon. It is very nice and quiet. Also, there are two other expatriate families living there, so you will have nice neighbours—' Miku San continued.

'What do you mean, "not for us"?' I interrupted her mid-sentence.

'Oh. Very sorry. Yes, these houses are for rent but for *Nihonjin* (Japanese people) only. They are not available for gaijin. Very sorry, Asif San', she said.

I could not believe what I had just heard. Did Miku San just say that we were not eligible to rent these homes because we were not Japanese? I was so shocked that I just stood there, unable to speak for a moment. To me, it sounded like discrimination in broad daylight. How was it possible in a developed nation such as Japan, especially in this day and age? What I found even harder to believe was how nonchalant Miku San was about the matter. I felt somewhat outraged. But I managed to calm down and pointed out to Miku San that this practice seemed a little discriminatory, while simultaneously trying not to offend her.

'Very sorry, Asif San, but I think you misunderstand. Of course, this is not discrimination', Miku San said. 'Many Japanese feel comfortable only with renting the house to other Japanese people because we understand each other well. Also, many of these people can't speak English and find it difficult to communicate. So they prefer Japanese tenants. No discrimination, Asif San. Please don't say such things.'

As in many other countries, subtle discrimination is not uncommon in Japanese society. The question I continue to struggle with is whether this kind of Japanese practice is truly discriminatory in the real sense of the word. There are Japanese establishments today that will entertain only Japanese clients and won't allow entrance to foreigners. For example, there are signs in front of some bathhouses that read 'Japanese only' much to the dismay of foreign visitors. While they don't allow foreign guests, most of them will be willing to let foreigners in if they are accompanied by a Japanese person. More often, these establishments simply find it difficult to deal with foreigners, mostly due to language barriers. Also, most Japanese establishments tend to follow and enforce certain practices, customs and rules, with no room for flexibility, similar to what one encounters in Japanese workplaces. To most Westerners, some of these customs and practices may seem unnecessary, and they may decide not to follow them—a very un-Japanese thing to do. Westerners tend to be more argumentative about the local practices if they feel that the rules don't make sense or somehow do not apply to them. Perhaps, such practices are not so much discriminatory as they are meant to simply avoid any unpleasant encounters with foreign guests.

At any rate, we found Miku San's comment about Japanese landlords' preference for having Japanese tenants both amusing and shocking. A part of me couldn't help but wonder if perhaps, she did have a point. Is it truly discrimination to try to avoid any unnecessary altercations with foreign tenants who had little to no understanding of Japanese customs? I certainly didn't feel any sense of discrimination in her tone whatsoever when she responded to me. If indeed Miku San thought that this practice was discriminatory in nature, wouldn't she be a little hesitant to bring it up so openly? While I wasn't fully convinced, I decided not to argue with her further. We had already found a place we liked. Better not to disturb the 'wa of the moment', I thought.

At any rate, the walk to the station from the maanshon was just a little over ten minutes, and Sharmeen and I figured that this was definitely something we could live with. We finally ended up renting the place in Himoniya. After living for two months in the luxury of our spacious mini-suite at the Shinjuku Hyatt Regency, we were very glad to move out into reality, into our new home. Thank God the landlord of the maanshon was willing to rent it to a gaijin.

Chapter 5

My First Sarariman Adventure—The Weird Meeting in Hon-Atsugi

While things were moving along nicely in the home front with us moving into our maanshon, things in the office seemed stagnant. I was yet to have any meaningful discussion with Satoh San or others as to how I could contribute. I kept minding my own business, trying to avoid getting in anyone's way. Finally, one fine day, Satoh San showed up in my office with a woman from the customer service group. There was an urgent enquiry from Toshiba, one of our big potential customers, and they didn't quite know to whom at the USA branch or Korea branch they should be directing that enquiry. Clearly, they were in a bind, otherwise they wouldn't have come to me. The enquiry was about the manufacturing capacity of a product in our Korea factory. Having worked in our Korean factory, I knew most of the key people there. While they were standing in my office, I called one of my friends at the Korea site and got the answer for them in less than five minutes. It was obvious that Satoh San and the customer service lady were not only relieved but also quite impressed with the fact that I was able to provide them with the answer so fast.

The next day, Hiroshi Hasegawa San, one of the sales guys, showed up in my office with enquiries. Hasegawa San, a skinny and extremely polite gentleman, was one of our account managers. His primary account was Sony and he also had a few other key accounts such as Panasonic. His English was okay, but not quite as good as that of Satoh San's. He mentioned that he was struggling to answer some questions from another one of our top semiconductor customers, Panasonic. Panasonic engineering had asked him to provide some details on a technical specification. Hasegawa San had reached out to the right person in the US, but despite several reminders, he wasn't getting any response. I assured him that I would get him the answer the next day. That evening, I called up Barry Miles, the head of that division in the US, and asked him to provide the answer to Hasegawa San. I'd known Barry for a long time, and he was a friend. Hasegawa San got his response the next day, along with an apology for the delay. He came to my office and wouldn't stop bowing and thanking me; I started getting worried that he might hurt his back.

Soon, the word got around that I could help people get answers to their enquiries quickly. Our salespeople sought out my assistance and advice regarding various matters. In most cases, I could answer the questions immediately, or advise them well on who to go to for those answers. I was also able to follow up separately to ensure that they got their answers on time.

Not everyone was coming to me for help even if they needed it. Obviously, there were other barriers that I would have to overcome to gain acceptance as a real team member, but I was still pleased to have these meaningful interactions with some of the sales folks. I felt like I was making progress and adding value.

During my fourth month in Japan, Satoh San stopped by my office to discuss a potential business opportunity with Sony. Apparently, Sony was coming up with a new PlayStation model and there might be an opportunity for our company to manufacture one of the key components for this model. Using his business connections, Satoh San had been able to set up a meeting with some of the top guys at Sony's semiconductor packaging research and development group.

I understood that it's not easy to get an audience with Sony for new suppliers. So the fact that Satoh San was able to set up a meeting with their key people was an accomplishment in and of itself. 'This could be our opportunity to get our first business from Sony, and we must make a good impression', Satoh San added. I thought he was going to ask me for help to prepare for this meeting, but to my astonishment, he invited me to join the meeting with Sony. Needless to say, I was very excited about this opportunity. This would be my first sarariman adventure in Japan. Besides, if we could indeed get business from Sony, I could show it off to my boss in Arizona as one of my first accomplishments.

The meeting was going to be in one of Sony's research and development centres in a town called Hon-Atsugi, forty-five kilometres southwest of Tokyo. Hasegawa San was also going to join us. It was scheduled for the afternoon. The plan was for me to meet up with them at Hon-Atsugi station around lunchtime. Two days before the meeting, Satoh San gave me very detailed instructions on how to get to the venue.

First, I would take the Yamanote Line train from Ebisu Station to Shinjuku Station; our Tokyo office was a ten-minute walk from the Ebisu Station. There, I would change trains and take the Odakyu Line, which would take me to Hon-Atsugi. Satoh San probably spent fifteen minutes explaining to me how I could get to the Odakyu Line platform once I had arrived at Shinjuku station. Plus, he kept emphasizing that I board one of the first six train compartments of the Odakyu Line. Apparently, at some station along the way, the first six compartments of the Odakyu Line separate from the rest of the train and go towards Hon-Atsugi, while the remaining compartments go towards some other station. Satoh San kept on saying that the Tokyo train system was not so easy to navigate, especially for foreigners, and there was a high possibility that I would get lost. While I appreciated his concern regarding my lack of navigation skills around Tokyo, as indeed I was new, I felt that it really was a little overbearing and unnecessary. It was as if he was giving directions to a child, assuming only Japanese people had the necessary skillset to navigate their rail system.

The next day, once I arrived at Shinjuku Station, it became clear why Satoh San had given me such explicit instructions on how to navigate my way to the Odakyu Line. The sheer vastness and complexity of the place, along with the sea of morning commuters as far as I could see, was simply overwhelming. I had some idea as to how busy many of the train stations could get in Tokyo, especially some stations such as Shinjuku Station or Tokyo Station. But I was not aware that Shinjuku Station is registered in the *Guinness World Records* as the busiest station in the world. About 3.5 million people go through Shinjuku Station *every day*. The station has over 200 exits. A few times, I had accidentally taken the wrong exit to come out of Shinjuku Station, only to find myself thirty minutes away from my desired destination. I felt like a child lost on his first day at elementary school.

It is worth spending a paragraph on the Tokyo commuter rail system for the reader to appreciate its complexity and how punctually it operates. The Tokyo train and subway system together form the best-connected commuter system in the world. Japan's railway system ranks among the world's best in many categories. For example, out of the top fifty-one busiest train stations in the world, forty-five are in Japan. Tokyo city alone has over 880 railway stations, with 285 of them being part of a complex subway system. It is estimated that the Tokyo railway and subway carry an average of 40 million passengers daily. It is also among the most complicated systems due to the sheer number of trains and subway lines within Tokyo and connecting various stations all over Japan. Even more amazing is how such a complex system is run with absolute precision, day in and day out. Trains arrive and depart exactly on time. A mere five-minute delay on a busy line makes it to the news. For someone new in the city, the system can be downright intimidating. I got my first glimpse of this vast network of the train system that morning.

At any rate, I was very happy and grateful that Satoh San had provided such detailed instructions on how to navigate the chasms of the Shinjuku Station. Plus, I felt a little guilty for being annoyed with him the day before for the same and made a mental note to thank him later.

After about an hour and a half into my train ride, stressing over the fact that I might be in the wrong train compartment and could end up in some other town, I was glad to hear the conductor announcing something in Japanese that contained the words 'Hon-Atsugi'. I didn't speak or understand any Japanese at the time, but it was clear that we would arrive at Hon-Atsugi station soon. Once the train stopped at Hon-Atsugi station, I darted for the door to ensure that I was indeed at the right station. Even though Hon-Atsugi station is much smaller compared to Shinjuku, but it was still a challenge to navigate its few labyrinthine exits. After some confusion and fumbling around, I thankfully managed to exit through the right gate and land right into the arms of a visibly relieved and delighted Satoh San and Hasegawa San. Truth be told, part of me had been stressing out that I would get lost and would have to ask either one of them to come and rescue me, which would have made us late for our very first and very important meeting with Sony (and would not have boded well at all for my new gaijin sarariman ego either). As it turned out, they had been worrying over the same thing, too.

It took us another ten minutes by taxi to get to the Sony facility from the station. We signed in at the front desk inside the visitor's centre and waited in the lobby for our meeting, admiring the amazing display of various electronic gadgets and products that Sony had produced from the past to the present. It was like a museum. I noticed a number of receptionists in the lobby area, all women, immaculately dressed in Sony uniforms. I found it interesting that all of them not only were young and pretty, but also had remarkably similar physiques, tall and slim. It was as if Sony had a mould that each of these receptionists had to fit into before they could be hired for the job. Hiring receptionists because of their appearance is not an acceptable practice in most developed countries today. However, in Japan, it doesn't seem to be a very big deal. In fact, there is one semiconductor company in Japan that only hires former *All Nippon Airways* flight attendants. Additionally, they publish their annual calendar with pictures of these receptionists scantily clothed. This remains a common practice in Japan, even though a light wind of the #MeToo movement has started to blow in the country.

One of the receptionists came to greet us and take us to our designated meeting room. She took a deep bow, almost at a ninety-degree angle. We followed her into the meeting room, where she asked us our beverage preferences. As she left the room, promising that our beverages would arrive soon, she bowed once again. Soon enough, the beverages arrived as promised, this time bought by two different lady attendants, immaculately dressed as well. They were wearing gloves to add to the neatness of their appearances. They bowed deeply when they came into the room, bowed a little after serving each of us our drinks and then bowed deeply again before leaving the room. No other place in the world can promise this level of attention and politeness to their guests. I have found this characteristic of the Japanese to be soothing. This kind of courtesy and politeness are the crown jewels of Japanese culture and are on full display when one visits any place—from trains to offices to shopping centres to a Japanese home.

As soon as I put down my office bag on one of the chairs, Satoh San summoned me to the other side of the table. He wanted me to sit between Hasegawa San and himself. Here, I got my first lesson in Japanese sarariman meeting etiquette. In a business meeting, there are customs related to the seating arrangements for the customers and the suppliers, Satoh San explained. Typically, the customer would sit facing the door or the window, and the supplier would sit on the opposite side. I would find out later that the highest-ranking person sits in the middle.

In the US or Europe, no one cares as to who sits where. The Japanese way has some inherent benefits. When a third person enters the room, it is easy to understand who the customers and suppliers are. In addition, one can assess who the top guys or the decision-makers are from the seating arrangement. I figured that it was better to do as the Japanese do when in Japan, and I squeezed in between Satoh San and Hasegawa San as per his instruction. As expected from the punctual Japanese, three gentlemen from Sony showed up exactly on time. All three of them were wearing Sony jackets: it is common for Japanese companies to have their own jacket, kind of like a uniform. People at all levels are expected to wear these jackets during working hours. The first gentleman to enter the room portrayed a sense of confidence. The other two persons following him seemed to have a relatively submissive demeanour. *Perhaps the first person is the boss*, I thought. All three of them were tall and wore similar types of glasses. Wearing the same company jacket, for a moment, they all looked alike to me, and I started to worry that I might not be able to tell them apart during the meeting. Satoh San quickly nudged me and asked me to exchange business cards with the Sony folks.

Business cards, or *meishi*, as they are known in Japanese, are an integral part of not just Japanese business life, but the Japanese society in general. It is very common for a Japanese person to give you his or her meishi when you meet them for the first time, even in a non-business setting. The first time I went to our local neighbourhood hair salon to get my hair cut, much to my surprise, the lady who was going to cut my hair introduced herself by giving me her business card. Of course, coming from the US, I wasn't in the habit of carrying my business cards around and could not reciprocate in that situation.

There is also a proper way to exchange meishi. The meishi exchange etiquette involves holding your business card with both hands and holding it out with your name facing upwards for the benefit of the receiver. The idea is for them to be able to see your name and more importantly, your title, while taking the card from you. The title dictates how deep one bows to the other. The higher the title, the deeper the bow.

Once all the meishis were exchanged and we all sat down, the meeting started. Turns out, the person with an aura of confidence was indeed the boss. He introduced himself as Kento Yamazaki, the head of Sony's semiconductor packaging R&D. The other two gentlemen were Masato Sakai San and Masaki Suda San. Satoh San very politely thanked the Sony folks for their time and introduced me again, even though I had already exchanged visiting cards with them. The meeting was conducted in Japanese, as I had expected. It didn't bother me at all. Why should they switch to my language and stress over conducting the meeting in English when we were in Japan, and I was outnumbered five to one? The objective was not to have the meeting in English but to get the Sony business. I didn't care about the language, as long as it helped us advance towards our objective. Besides, Satoh San would lean towards me and translate what was being said, every so often. This was extremely helpful, of course, and even made me wonder if he was finally accepting me as a part of the team.

Satoh San started by introducing our company to the Sony team using our corporate presentation. Turned out that the Sony folks didn't know much about our company and had a lot of questions, politely interrupting Satoh San now and again during his presentation. Whenever the Sony guys would ask Satoh San a question in Japanese, he would invariably turn and ask me the question in English if he didn't know the answer. Luckily, having worked in various roles for the company for a long time, I knew the answers to almost all their questions and was glad that I could provide them with those right on the spot. I could sense that Satoh San was quite pleased with my instant contributions.

Recognizing that I was able to answer their inquiries in real-time, the head of the Sony R&D, Yamazaki San, started to ask me the questions directly, even though he was asking them in Japanese. Again, Satoh San would translate and I would answer in English, directly to Yamazaki San. It seemed that the gentlemen from Sony understood my answers in English most of the time. I find it common for many Japanese sarariman to have a fair ability to understand spoken English if it is spoken slowly, using simple vocabulary. Their capability to write English is also strong. It is merely their English-speaking ability that is lacking.

About an hour and a half into the meeting, I noticed that the discussion was getting quite intense. Then suddenly, the meeting room went quiet. Was the meeting over? After a few minutes, I leaned over to Satoh San and asked if we were done with the meeting. Satoh San whispered back that they were at an impasse. He explained that indeed there was an opportunity for us to do business with Sony. Apparently, there was one key component that we could manufacture for them in high volume. This, of course, was music to my ears. However, the technical requirement for that component was more stringent than the industry standard, and the solution was not readily available. It certainly was not available in our company. It would take time to develop the solution, time that Sony didn't have, based on their product introduction schedule. Everyone was wondering how to proceed.

Despite the fact that we had all agreed that no one in the industry had a solution for their quality requirement, Yamazaki San kept insisting that our assembled part must meet their stringent requirement if we wanted to participate in the Sony PlayStation business. We could develop the solution, but it would likely take about six months to a year. Yamazaki San shook his head and once again pointed out that such a long schedule could not work for them. I looked at Satoh San, surprised—I thought we all agreed that no one had the solution ready. I asked Satoh San to translate this. Before Satoh San got a chance, Yamazaki San said in broken English that he fully agreed with my assessment. I was even more confused now.

Yamazaki San had already told us that his job was to find an external partner who would manufacture this particular component for PlayStation cost-effectively in high volume. But if he already knew that no other external parties had the solution or could come up with a solution within the required timeframe, what was he going to do? This discussion went on for another thirty minutes in Japanese while I sat there. I didn't understand the point of the discussion when there seemed to be no solution at hand. I whispered to Satoh San that there was no way Sony could come up with the solution that fast and that perhaps they should be realistic and look at the possibility of delaying their product launch schedule. 'But Yamazaki San said that Sony already has the solution', Satoh San whispered back to me.

At first, I thought I heard it wrong. They already had the solution? Then why had we been discussing how to proceed for the last hour? Somewhat incredulous and a little annoyed, I came up with the perfect solution to proceed. I told Satoh San to ask the Sony team if they could provide us with the solution under a non-disclosure agreement (NDA). If they were to provide this to us, we would, in turn, provide them with a very cost-effective and high-volume manufacturing solution for their product within the provided timeframe. Seemed like a reasonable solution to me. But Satoh San seemed a little uncomfortable hearing my suggestion to ask Sony about it. At first, he ignored it altogether.

After I repeated it, he whispered, 'We cannot ask Sony for such a thing, Asif San. This is Japan!'

I didn't quite understand why not. To my non-Japanese mind, I thought it was a simple and elegant solution. Besides, what does Japan have to do with it? His last sentence was even more baffling.

I insisted that Satoh San at least ask the Sony team about the possibility of providing us with the solution. As we were talking, the Sony team were looking at us, especially at Satoh San, and expecting him to translate it to Japanese for them. I could sense that Satoh San was feeling awkward, perhaps stuck between some Japanese custom, clear from his 'this is Japan' comment, and his new gaijin colleague's insistence on asking such a direct question.

After a long pause, he told me to ask the Sony folks for the solution directly. 'You can ask in English, Asif San. I will translate to them in Japanese, if necessary', Satoh San said when I reminded him that I didn't speak any Japanese. By then, we had been well over four hours into this meeting, and I was getting impatient. I didn't see what any of us had to lose at that point by asking Sony for the solution. I looked straight at Yamazaki San and asked as politely as I could if Sony would be open to providing us with their solution. I promised that, in turn, we would provide Sony with a very cost-competitive, high-volume manufacturing solution within Sony's product launch schedule. At first, Yamazaki San didn't seem to understand what I was asking and looked at Satoh San with a blank face. Again, I sensed a distinct discomfort around the room as Satoh San reluctantly translated my enquiry for the Sony team.

I will never forget what happened next. It was quite interesting and provided an important glimpse into the indirect method of communication that Japan is well-known for. Once Satoh San translated my question into Japanese, everyone went completely quiet for a minute or so. Then, Yamazaki San made this weird sucking sound, sucking air in through his teeth, while making a face. As he kept making this sound, he took turns looking at the other two gentlemen from Sony who also appeared to be in distress. It seemed as if I had asked for something precious, and they had no clue how to provide it to me. Soon, the other two gentlemen also started to make the same sound by sucking air through their teeth. Now all three of them were making the sucking sound in unison. It sounded like a not-so-pleasant acapella by the three of them. This went on for what felt like a very long time. I was taken aback by this turn of events and didn't know quite what to do. I kept looking around, at the Sony team first and then at Satoh San, to see if I missed something.

Then an even stranger thing happened. After everyone stopped the sucking sound and making faces, the discussion resumed where it had left off before I had asked my stupid question. I leaned over to Satoh San to ask what was going on, trying to assess the situation. I realized that Satoh San was ignoring me at this point, so I stopped asking him and decided to go with the flow. Within fifteen minutes, the meeting was over. Hasegawa San, who had been quiet during the entire meeting, finally opened his mouth to summarize the meeting and action items. There was not one word mentioned about my enquiry, as if I had never even asked my question. I'd had enough experience in Japan to know not to belabour the point. However, I couldn't wait to get out of the Sony offices and ask Satoh San what had just transpired.

On our way back from Hon-Atsugi, Satoh San explained to me what had happened, and taught me another key lesson about Japanese sarariman business culture and customs. Satoh San explained that such a direct method of communication, like asking for a design, is not an acceptable practice in Japan and it's typically avoided in business meetings. He emphasized that it's especially rude for a low-level foreign supplier to ask such a direct question of a Japanese giant like Sony. In Japan, one must wait for the customer to make such an offer instead of asking like I had. If indeed we wanted the solution, the ideal way would have been to call one of the junior Sony guys the day after the meeting, and then politely allude to the possibility of us getting the technical solution from them. Then the engineer would subtly take the proposal to his bosses, essentially to the team we had just met at Hon-Atsugi. The engineer would then let Satoh San know of Sony's collective decision. If the answer was 'no', the engineer would politely inform Satoh San while apologizing profusely. The end.

Japanese communication is inherently indirect. Often, what is not said is more important than what is actually communicated. When I asked Yamazaki San for the solution, he was not able to say 'yes'. In an American company, they would just inform us one way or the other, or offer to get back to us with the information. That's not how it's done in Japan. Yamazaki San was likely taken aback by the directness of my enquiry. Secondly, he probably preferred not to say 'no' directly—although that would have been so much easier—so we could move on. But that's not the Japanese way, Satoh San explained.

What was with the sucking sound that the gentlemen from Sony were making? Apparently, that's a very Japanese thing to do when one doesn't have an answer or especially if the answer is a 'no'. The sucking sound implies that the person is in deep thought on how to answer the question, as the answer is probably negative. The listener is supposed to understand this and quickly rescue the person from his or her ostensible anguish by either withdrawing the question or offering some other solution. In our case, all the Sony folks were making the sucking sound as they didn't know if it would be possible for them to give us the solution, or perhaps, they knew that such a thing could not be done. We were supposed to understand that and basically withdraw our request, or just forget that we ever made it in the first place, which apparently was what Satoh San did. This somewhat hideous sound made by sucking air through one's teeth is mostly made by men; thankfully, it's not common for Japanese women to make such sounds. While I understood the custom, it didn't make much sense to me at that time. Interestingly, within a year or so, I would find myself making the same sound if I could not cater to a request instead of directly saying 'no'. I understand now how these gestures are a more polite way of refusing something, despite sounding hideous, at least from the perspective of the Japanese custom of being polite.

As it turned out, my stupid gaijin behaviour at Sony that day, violating the Japanese business norms, was going to pay off handsomely. Within the next couple of years, our business with them would grow from zero to over $100 million per year. But of course, I wasn't aware of this at that time and felt like I had really screwed up the meeting by asking directly for the designs. As the train approached Shinjuku Station, my worry started to grow that we had likely lost whatever chances we had to win business from Sony because of my stupid and arrogant behaviour. I didn't feel like discussing this any further, and we all remained quiet for the rest of the way.

My colleagues would later tell me that it's not uncommon for Japanese to use their foreign colleagues to ask such direct questions in meetings. They often invariably apologize for such directness by their ignorant gaijin teammate. But in some cases, such directness does bear fruit like it did in our case with Sony. If it doesn't, then it doesn't matter anyway; they have already apologized for the rude behaviour by their fellow *baka* gaijin (stupid foreigner) sarariman.

Chapter 6

All Quiet on the Home Front

As things seemed to be slowly progressing on the work front, having found our new home, we started to settle down in Tokyo. With the help and guidance of Miku San from IBM HR, we signed a two-year lease at the nice maanshon. It was a twenty minutes' drive from my office in Ebisu. The closest train station was Toritsu Daigaku, a fifteen-minute walk from our home, the same walk we had taken earlier with Miku San when we had first come to see the condo. Our local station was located twenty minutes from Shibuya Station, one of the two major stations in the Shibuya Ward.

The Tokyo metropolis is divided into twenty-three wards. Shibuya Ward is one of the major commercial and finance hubs of the city. Well-known for its trendy shopping outlets, it is also home to two of the busiest railway stations in the world, Shinjuku and Shibuya. Shibuya is most famous for its iconic multi-directional pedestrian crossing, known as the Shibuya Crossing. Vehicles stop at all five intersections to allow people to cross; it is the busiest pedestrian crossing in the world, with up to 3,000 people crossing at a time. Large TV screens and illuminated billboards give the place a futuristic aura. Shibuya Crossing provides a perfect visual representation of the density and energy of this dynamic city. It has been used as a backdrop for numerous movies, films and documentaries about Tokyo and Japan. It was good to be close to one of the most iconic places in the city but more importantly, to a major railway hub.

While we had found our new home, we didn't have any furniture, of course. Furnishing in our previous hill-top condo in Seoul was provided by our local office. They had offered to sell all of them at a discount before we moved out. But Sharmeen and I weren't very keen on the Korean furniture. So we decided not to accept their offer. We did acquire a few pieces of oriental furniture on our own, which included a very nice replica of a Korean step-chest, still one of our most treasured possessions. The office had arranged for these items to be shipped to Japan along with our other personal belongings.

Our company was very generous when it came to moving its expatriates around the world. They had provided a very reasonable moving allowance and I had not used all of it since we had relatively few items shipped from Seoul. So we had to buy most of the furniture for our new home locally; the allowance was for moving household goods, but not for buying them. To use it for this purpose, I would have to get my boss's approval. As Tom had readily approved my request to increase our housing allowance, I felt uncomfortable asking for another favour. Again, after much deliberation, I decided to just ask. This time, it wasn't as easy as last time. Tom said that he would have to confirm with the HR department. But after a few rounds of negotiations, my boss and HR agreed to my request, as long as I stayed within the budget. This was between me and our head office, and I didn't get any of the local HR folks involved.

Buying furniture for an entire home was not going to be cheap. The question was who was going to fork up the cash upfront. Typically, our local office would pay for it, which meant I had to bring it up with Toda San. The last thing I wanted was to have another long, drawn-out discussion and argument with her about our personal needs, especially when we were going around company policy, despite having got the special approval. With things picking up at work, I decided that this wasn't a good time to rock the boat. Instead, I decided to work it out with our head office, bypassing Toda San altogether. I would pay for it from my own pocket and then get it reimbursed by our head office. Our finance team seemed a little puzzled by my request but agreed to it, as long as I documented the purchases by keeping the receipts.

Now that we had our approval and knew what our home looked like, Sharmeen and I were ready to go furniture shopping. Miku San kindly agreed to help us with this. She picked us up in her car one Saturday and took us to various furniture stores around the city. Once again, we experienced another round of sticker-shock. While the selections were nice, they were all very expensive. Buying the living room sofa and a couple of chairs would blow our entire budget. I wasn't at all comfortable pushing my luck and asking for increasing the budget to buy home furniture for us.

Fupu and Fupa came to our rescue. They had navigated the same road when they first moved to Japan and seemed to be familiar with the process. They introduced us to a small furniture store in their neighbourhood of Azabu-Juban in Tokyo. The store was a small showroom that sold the majority of its furniture out of a warehouse at reasonable prices. We were quite surprised to be introduced to such a store in the otherwise high-rent district of Azabu-Juban. As we would find out over the course of our stay in the city, there are many similar outlets that are relatively inexpensive in otherwise expensive Tokyo. One has to know where to look. Of course, the local people are aware of these places, but new expatriates like us were clueless. Anyhow, we were glad to pick up a very nice Italian sofa set and a dining table from the warehouse at very reasonable prices. In fact, we ended up buying most of our furniture from that little store in Azabu-Juban. Fupa also introduced us to a store called Tokyo Hands, which is like a smaller and more upscale version of Home Depot. I fell in love with that hardware store and would visit it often. It had all sorts of trinkets that can only be found in Japan.

Fupu and Fupa would go on to introduce us to other places around the city. For example, through them, we discovered grocery shops with Western brands at reasonable prices. Finding a doctor or medical facility was on top of our to-do list, especially since we had a two-year-old. Fupa introduced us to the Tokyo International Clinic, located right by the famous landmark Tokyo Tower, where all the doctors and most of the nurses are from English-speaking countries like the US, UK, New Zealand and Australia. The clinic primarily catered to the expatriate community. We found a wonderful paediatrician from New Zealand for Farhana—another key accomplishment, as we were worried that if we had to go to a local doctor, we would have to use a translator.

Our personal items from Seoul arrived within a couple of weeks after we moved into our new home. I was surprised to see a small army of people arriving with the delivery truck as the size of our shipment was relatively small. The process of moving things from the truck to our third-floor maanshon turned out to be quite a production, quite different from what we had experienced during our previous international moves. All the movers were dressed in clean and neatly pressed uniforms. Everyone was wearing white gloves, identical to the white gloves worn by taxi drivers, bank tellers, people selling tickets and many other people in other service industries all over Japan. It symbolized the Japanese obsession with neatness and cleanliness, and we quite enjoyed it when a taxi driver wearing a suit handed us our change wearing these white gloves.

The moving team spent a significant amount of time inspecting, huddling and strategizing, then repeating the process a few times. They spent another hour preparing for the actual unloading and the moving process. To ensure that carrying the items didn't cause any accidental damage to any part of the building, they covered the entire floor of the lobby and part of our apartment entrance with a thick blue-coloured mat. All the walls, including the walls of our tiny elevator, were covered with heavily padded foam-like material. With all the floors and walls covered, finally, they started to move our items with extreme care. As they brought each item inside the building to the edge of the covered floors, they would take their shoes off to carry it to the final area. Each of them would neatly unwrap every little item. One would think that they were moving some precious museum pieces, not our relatively simple furniture, books, clothing and underwear.

After they finished bringing in all our stuff, they removed all the wall and floor coverings. Then to our astonishment, they quickly vacuumed and swept our apartment. The place seemed cleaner than when they had first arrived. As they left, they all bowed and thanked us in unison. Once again, the Japanese attention to detail, their neatness, their dedication to whatever task is at hand, and their politeness, were on full display. The whole process felt like an episode from a documentary about Japan. Sharmeen and I were thoroughly impressed and in awe.

* * *

Acquiring cable and Wi-Fi turned out to be uneventful, thanks to Miku San. Unlike in the States, the cable guy showed up within the one-hour window that they had originally scheduled with us.

Slowly, we began to explore our neighbourhood. There was a small Chinese restaurant on the way to the station, which we liked. We were pleased to find a grocery store close to the station, which turned out to be very convenient. Despite being small, it was well-stocked with essentials. To our pleasant surprise, they also had all sorts of American brands such as Kellogg's cereals, Thousand

Island dressing, Heinz ketchup and Tabasco, except that all the products were half the size and cost two to three times as much.

In all the grocery stores, every item, even the produce, seemed to be in pristine condition, as if they had been freshly plucked within the last hour. I was always amazed by the spotless bananas. I developed an interesting pastime of trying to find a 'bad' banana when visiting a grocery store, but I rarely succeeded during my four years in Tokyo. I am still not sure how this was possible. What I found even more intriguing was that most of the grocery stores, especially the convenience stores such as 7-Eleven (yes, there are 7-Elevens in Tokyo) sold a single banana, neatly wrapped in clear plastic with a golden bow, or a single egg in a neat, clear plastic box. What was that all about? I asked Miku San.

It turns out that the grocery shopping habits of the Japanese people are different from that of the Americans. Back home, most people would buy their groceries once a week or perhaps even once a month. Many prefer to buy household items in bulk from large warehouse stores like Costco, Sam's Club or Walmart. It is not uncommon for us to buy a large quantity of beef, poultry or fish, and put them in freezers in our home for cooking later.

The Japanese, on the other hand, do their grocery shopping daily or at least a few times a week. It is common for families to decide what they want to eat that day and go shopping for the main items such as fish, beef or chicken. The reason is not only that they want to buy things fresh, but also that most Japanese homes are small. They don't have enough room for a large freezer or room to store months' worth of supplies. That's why the sizes, the packaging and portions of almost everything are smaller. Exported items are packaged specially for the Japanese market. There is a well-known case study about how Pampers lost their market share in Japan for failing to understand this and forcing larger boxes of diapers into the Japanese market, which Japanese families were not keen on buying.[1] While these smaller packages and sizes look cute, the novelty disappears as soon as one notices their exorbitant prices.

* * *

Both Sharmeen and I were excited to be in Tokyo. We had already started to explore the city while living at the Hyatt, visiting places like the high-end shopping districts of Ginza and Omotesando, and of course, Shinjuku and Shibuya, various parks around the city (for a large concrete jungle, Tokyo has a lot of nice, large park areas), Akihabara, the electronic capital of the world, and so on. Everything looked nice, neat and novel to us: we invariably felt like kids in a candy store. As we got settled in our new place, we started to explore the Himoniya neighbourhood. For whatever reason, we had always chosen to explore the area towards the station, most likely because all the shops and restaurants seemed to be congregated close to and around the station. To go to the station from our house, we had to cross a major street called the Kannana Dori Avenue. It was a very busy street, and it didn't seem like there were a lot of things to do around there. One day, we decided to check out the other side, our side of the neighbourhood, without crossing the Kannana Dori. This part of the neighbourhood appeared quieter and less crowded. The narrow street was lined with nice houses and low-rise apartment buildings. There was a nice, small park with a small children's playground, which was perfect for Farhana. We came across a church and also discovered a five-storey department store within fifteen minutes from our home. The first floor of the department

---

[1] Margaret Shapiro, 'Changing Diapers for Japan's Moms', *The Washington Post*, 21 August 1990. Available at: https://www.washingtonpost.com/archive/business/1990/08/21/changing-diapers-for-japans-moms/0301ac0e-6417-4be6-9ecd-dfadc2e46101/. Accessed May 2022.

store was a large grocery shop, much larger than the one close by our station. The other floors had pretty much everything, from home repair to clothing. Sharmeen and I were delighted to make this important discovery. Clearly, it had been a wise decision to move into this neighbourhood.

Whenever we crossed Kannana Dori Ave. to go towards the station, we always saw this large billboard with pictures of delicious-looking Japanese food along the busy street, very close to our home. One evening, we decided to check out the place. It was literally five minutes from our home. As we walked towards the billboard, we came across a large building with very traditional-style architecture and a nice Japanese garden in the front yard. There was a small Koi Pond on one side of the garden. Farhana was very excited to see all the colourful Koi fish. There was a sign in Japanese we couldn't read, but the place indeed looked like a restaurant. It looked quite nice and we decided to give it a try.

The restaurant specialized in serving a popular Japanese dish called Shabu-Shabu. As we entered the restaurant, we were a little startled as all the employees yelled, '*irasshaimase*' or 'welcome'. This is a very common practice in Japan. When patrons enter a store or restaurant, all the employees welcome them, yelling at the top of their lungs. When the customers exit, all the employees will yell '*arigatou gozaimashita*' or 'thank you' in unison. It is rare to hear Japanese people speak in a loud voice, an integral part of their politeness. So yelling these phrases at every customer arriving and leaving seemed somewhat un-Japanese to me. It definitely made the nice surrounding of the restaurant unnecessarily noisy, in my opinion. I always found this dichotomy a little baffling— unnecessary yelling in a country where everyone speaks in a whisper.

As we entered the restaurant, a young lady wearing a beautiful orange-coloured kimono showed up, bowed and said a few lines in Japanese with what seemed to end with a question while holding three fingers towards us. I figured she must be confirming if we are a party of three, and I just replied 'hai' in Japanese. That seemed to work; she showed us to our table. In traditional Japanese style, all the sitting arrangements were on the floor, with low tables and cushions around them to sit on. The table had a built-in electric stove. The atmosphere felt very nice, warm and cozy. It was quite early in the evening so the large space inside was relatively empty. As we sat down, our waitress approached and started speaking in Japanese. She was also young and dressed in a similarly beautiful and bright kimono as the lady who had showed us to the table. This time, we had to admit that we didn't speak any Japanese at all and very slowly asked if she or someone perhaps did speak English. To our great surprise, it turned out that she spoke a little English, enough for us to be able to intelligently place our orders. In her broken English, she recommended that we order the house speciality the Shabu-Shabu. We asked if the dish contained any pork. Once she confirmed and assured us that it was all beef and vegetables, we went with her recommendation without having any idea what it was.

Soon, she showed up again with a large bowl of soup broth, put it on top of the stove in the middle of our table and turned it on. Then came a large plate containing all kinds of vegetables like sliced carrots, mushrooms, tofu and cabbage, followed by a plate full of beef, each piece sliced very thin. We confessed to the waitress that this was our first time trying Shabu-Shabu and we had no clue what to do. She smiled and told us not to worry, she would be happy to help us through the process—clearly taking pity on her gaijin customers. She told us to wait till the broth was about to boil and left. Sharmeen and I looked around the table full of beautifully chopped and sliced vegetables and raw meat, wondering how this would turn out. Farhana, completely oblivious to what was going on, luckily, was sitting down quietly playing with her toys, which we always carried with us.

Our young and beautifully dressed waitress showed up just as the broth was about to start to boil. Perfect timing, we thought.

There was a nice aroma coming from the boiling soup stock. She took one of the lean pieces of meat with a long pair of chopsticks, dipped it into the liquid moving it back and forth for about thirty seconds or so. Then she took out the fully cooked, thin slice of meat and put it on my wife's plate. There were a couple of small bowls with different kinds of sauces. She explained that one of the bowls contained a peanut-based yellow-coloured sauce, while the other bowl contained a sweet soya sauce, and we could choose any one of them to dip the meat in before eating it. Mimicking her, I picked up a piece of meat with my own chopsticks, dipped it into the boiling broth and swished it around just like she had done. Then, I took out the nicely cooked piece of meat, dipped it into the yellow sauce and put it in my mouth. It was very delicious, with the beef literally melting in my mouth, leaving a hint of the tasty peanut sauce in its wake. Sharmeen took a piece and I could tell from her expression that she found it equally delicious. We devoured the rest of the beef while taking turns feeding Farhana in between. She also seemed to like the tenderness of the meat. We ordered a second plate of beef, much to the surprise of our kind waitress.

After we were done finishing two plates of meat, our waitress poured all the vegetables into the broth. Then she told us that once they were ready, we could eat the rest at our leisure. The vegetables were also very tasty, and we ate every last piece. We thought that we were done but our waitress showed up again, this time with three small bowls and served the leftover broth as a soup to us. The Shabu-Shabu meal was not only delicious, but we also enjoyed the process. We found it quite entertaining. As we left the restaurant, we thanked our waitress for her kindness, the food, and the entertainment, while she kept on thanking us back. Shabu-Shabu remains one of our favourite Japanese foods till today.

* * *

One weekend, exhausted after unpacking and organizing, we decided to stay home and order pizza for dinner. That afternoon, we had found a flyer in our mailbox from a local branch of Pizza Hut. Even though it was in Japanese, we recognized the logo and the sign of the famous Pizza Hut, and it had pictures of various kinds of pizza with corresponding prices. Their phone number was printed in large font on both sides of the flyer. While we were thrilled about the possibility of getting a pizza from a Pizza Hut delivered to our new home in Tokyo, we wondered if we could order in English. Pizza Hut may be an American establishment, but I was quite sure that the local employees didn't speak any English.

After a few minutes of contemplation on how to do this, I called a fellow sarariman, Hasegawa San, and solicited his help. After the customary greetings and apologies, I told him what we were trying to do and asked him if he wouldn't mind teaching me some of the key Japanese vocabulary and phrases needed to order pizza. Hasegawa San was friendly on the phone, unlike in the office, and found my request amusing. He even offered to order the pizza for us, and in hindsight, I should have agreed. But I didn't want to trouble him and replied that if he could teach me some of the Japanese words, I would do it myself. He offered a few key words: *gyu-niku* (or beef), *oneeon* (or onion), *thino crusto* (or thin crust), *buta-niku wa dame* (no pork), etc. I jotted them down on a piece of paper. Armed with these limited but important phrases and beaming with confidence, I dialled the number printed on the flyer.

'*Moshi Moshi, Peeza Huto de gozaimas* (Hello, this is Pizza Hut)', some lady answered.

Almost immediately, I lost all my confidence, so I blurted out in English, 'Hello, may I order a large pizza?'

'*Hai, wakarimashita* (yes, I understand)', she replied.

She does understand English, I thought, feeling a little relieved. *This may not be as difficult as I had anticipated.* After all, pizza is a very international cuisine; if one can call it a cuisine at all.

'*Sumimasen, eigo wa ii desu ka?* (excuse me, is it okay to speak in English?)', I asked using one of the very few phrases that I had learnt, worried that she may not understand my heavy accent.

'Aaaahhh', she made a weird sound, making me nervous again. '*Eigo wa hanasa nai. Muri desu yo. Sumimasen.* (I can't speak any English, impossible, sorry).'

While I didn't understand what she said, it was clear that we would not be conversing in English. The little confidence I had managed to regain, soon disappeared.

'*Nanno pizza desu ka? Sorekara topping wa . . .*'

She asked a few questions, most of which sounded like gibberish to me. But I recognized two keywords in her long sentence, 'pizza' and 'topping'. She was asking what kind of pizza and what toppings we wanted. I pressed on, asking for a large pizza with cheese and certain toppings. In English, of course. After I stopped speaking, there was a long silence, and I thought she had hung up on me. I would have, if I were her.

'*Sumimasen, eigo wa zen zen wakaranai, sumimasen . . .* (Sorry, but I don't understand English at all, sorry).' Her voice kind of trailed off in frustration.

While I was glad that she hadn't hung up the phone, this ordering process was clearly not going well at all. What to do? Should I just hang up and try again? How would that change anything? I was getting mad at myself for no reason. Then I decided to try something. Clearly, she seemed to understand and speak some of the key words. So instead of speaking in full sentences, I decided to use only these key words and do so very slowly.

'*Laarrge peezzaa desu*, topping *beffu, oneeon, ooleeve, mushoroomu*', I said, trying to make my English words sound like Japanese, completely forgetting the Japanese words Hasegawa San had just taught me.

This seemed to do the trick. I was delighted to be back in the game again.

'*Hai, hai, wakaraimashita, laarge peezza de, befu toka, oneeoon toka, ooleevu, sorekara mushoroomu des ne*', she repeated with equal delight and some excitement.

Not bad for a gaijin ordering pizza for the first time in Tokyo, I thought, regaining my confidence. As I was about to hang up, thinking 'mission accomplished', the pizza lady asked me for something else.

'*Ja, denwa bango to jusho wa oshiete morae masu ka?*'

What maska? I thought we had both just succeeded in communicating even though none of us spoke the other's language. This was huge. Couldn't we just leave it at that? What else did she want to know?

I kept saying that I didn't understand while she kept repeating the same thing. I knew how to say 'I don't understand' in Japanese, so I tried that.

'*Sumimasen, wakarimasen.* (Sorry but I don't understand).'

'*Hai . . . so desu ka . . . aahhhh . . . pleaso teacho phone aand addresso.*'

Ah, she wanted to know our phone number and address. Why didn't she just say so? How the hell were they going to deliver the pizza without our address? Good thing that I hadn't hung up the phone in my excitement. As soon as I gave her my number and our address, the pizza lady said '*arigato gozaimas*', which I reciprocated and hung up, relieved. I am sure she was equally relieved that her ordeal with the baka gaijin was over.

As I hung up the phone, I saw Sharmeen laughing. She had been listening to my side of the conversation the whole time. Indeed, the whole thing was hilarious and I joined in laughing with her. But we were both pleased that I had succeeded in my quest and soon we would be eating pizza for dinner. The whole process had taken about twenty minutes and a lot of wind out of me. Despite my sense of accomplishment, I felt completely spent. Very hungry, we hoped that the local Pizza Hut would adhere to the Japanese efficiency practices and deliver our pizza on time or earlier. The pizza lady had probably mentioned how long the delivery would take, but of course, I hadn't understood. Sharmeen asked me what the odds were of getting what we wanted, especially the toppings. About fifty-fifty, I thought, but I didn't want to sound negative. I said 80 per cent and told her not to worry.

The pizza arrived within twenty minutes, right on time. We were very excited and got our plates and drinks ready. The box looked the same as back home. Inside, the large pizza looked fabulous with all the toppings that I had requested. *Not bad at all*, I thought.

'Looks like the pizza is full of pepperoni', my wife said.

Oh crap! In my confusion and excitement, I had forgotten to mention to the pizza lady not to include pepperoni, as we don't eat pork. We kept staring at the beautiful-looking pizza with our hungry eyes. It was very disappointing and frustrating. Well, at least I was able to get some of the toppings right. We headed for our neighbourhood Shabu-Shabu restaurant, throwing away the wonderful pizza on our way out.

There would be many such frustrating and often funny incidents during our stay in Tokyo. This was all part of our learning process as we adjusted to our new life here. While many of them were genuinely frustrating, for some reason, we didn't let the feeling linger and bother us too much. Our excitement and joy at being able to live in this vibrant capital and the opportunity to learn about and explore Japan made these relatively small incidents quite tolerable. Luckily, both Sharmeen and I shared this same positive attitude towards our assignment during most of our stay, even though at the end, things would start to get to us as well.

If the attitude is not right, it would be easy for a new expatriate to find Japan to be quite unbearable. These challenges seemed relatively minuscule to me, compared to the challenge I had at work to grow our Japan revenue. Especially since the Sony meeting at Hon-Atsugi had only just taken place, and I was very worried about how things were going to turn out.

Chapter 7

Acceptance

As I was driving to the office the day after the meeting with Sony, a sense of paranoia started to kick in. If I had indeed blown an important opportunity—which I was sure I had, at that point—it would not go well with anyone, including my boss, Tom. Satoh San's earlier prediction that I would be useless in Japan without the language skill, would prove to be true and my chances of becoming a part of the local team would diminish. I arrived with some trepidation and dashed towards my cubicle. I wanted to hide behind my desk and remain hidden for the rest of the day. But soon, people started to stop by my cubicle to say their 'ohayou gozaimasu' to me. Previously, the ritual of exchanging this morning greeting had been in passing in the hallways or in the pantry. No one would usually stop by my cubicle just to say their morning greetings. I was both surprised and curious. *Why are they specially popping in to say good morning?* Their usual monotonous and robotic voice seemed to have been replaced with a more jovial and friendly tone. At this positive sign, I summoned up the courage to walk towards the pantry for my morning coffee. As I passed a few other people, I noticed a change in their demeanour as well, when they greeted me. The usual cold shoulder I was used to receiving had been replaced with friendly gestures. Some even enquired about how my family was settling in. What was going on? Why was everyone so nice to me all of a sudden?

By the end of the week, the office environment had gotten so much better that I became suspicious. I suspected foul play; perhaps my sarariman colleagues were scheming to get rid of me. What were these guys up to? Were they happy to find out how I had screwed up the Sony meeting and perhaps figured that I would soon be sent back to Arizona? I didn't want to ask the local guys, including Satoh San. Instead, I decided to call Tom and see if he knew anything. Of course, I wasn't going to share with him my concern about a potential coup-d'etat by my fellow sarariman. Nor was I going to volunteer my screw-up at the Sony meeting. But I wanted to see if he perhaps had heard something about it.

We exchanged our usual greetings and Tom asked me how things were going. I didn't notice anything special in his voice. I cautiously brought up the subject of the Sony meeting. Immediately, Tom's voice perked up. He mentioned that he had indeed received a call from Satoh San about it. Apparently, Satoh San had been very impressed with my knowledge of our products and my ability to handle Japanese customers. *Really?* Satoh San had also reported to him that because of the positive way the meeting went, he felt confident that we now had a good chance to win their business. Tom seemed very pleased and told me to keep up the good work. I was very pleased as well, but somewhat shocked to receive such positive feedback, since I thought that the Sony meeting had been a disaster. So it hadn't gone badly at all, as I had feared. It seemed that I had been paranoid for nothing and I felt very relieved by this new piece of information.

Satoh San must have spread the word around the office, and that is why everyone was now being nice to me. It all made sense now. I couldn't be more pleased with this sudden knowledge of such a positive outcome.

After this, things started to change. My fellow sarariman slowly began to approach me with questions about our products, our quality system, or our capacity. I was able to address most of their enquiries right on the spot. When I didn't have the answer, I was able to advise them on how to get the information. Soon, our sarariman sales folks were lining up in front of my office with all sorts of enquiries. It was actually a complete 180-degree turn from what I had been used to.

Slowly but surely, these interactions led to broader business discussions among us. The sarariman sales folks started to share detailed information about their customers, current business status, future plans and potential opportunities. I realized that there were a lot of good opportunities to take advantage of. It was becoming obvious that my sarariman colleagues were also hungry for information and eager to grow our business. My role in the office started to gel, and I was very happy and excited to help the team in any way I could.

Through our interactions, I realized that many of our employees were not very well aware of how our larger organization worked and didn't exactly know who the key players and decision-makers were. As I continued to work with them, I was shocked to learn that they struggled to get even basic information or guidance, which was necessary to respond to most of our customers' enquiries. I was aware that the Japan office had been an afterthought for the management team at our head office, literally tucked away on some faraway island, cut off from the rest of the organization. The key people in the product groups based in Arizona paid little attention to this region. And the Japan team also lacked the knowledge on how to seek their attention. It was obvious that despite working for many years for the company, most of the local employees had had very little training. They worked more closely with our manufacturing sites in Korea and the Philippines, even though that's not where the key decision-makers resided. While the sarariman visited these facilities regularly, most of them had never been to our head office and had not met most of the management and key players in our product teams. It was no wonder that our Japan business had been stagnant for the past decade.

The language barrier was also an issue. It seemed like most of the sarariman had difficulty writing e-mails in English. They would struggle even more with interpreting the responses. What normally could be achieved through a simple e-mail exchange, or by a five-minute phone conversation, took the local team a few days and a few rounds of back-and-forth e-mailing to accomplish. The team relied heavily on e-mail communication and hardly ever made any enquiries through phone calls to our product groups, worried about their English skills. However, the more I read their e-mails, the more I realized that the cultural difference was playing a bigger role in the communication gap—more so than the language barrier.

I noticed a consistent tone of gratitude on almost every e-mail sent by the sarariman to the product group or to people at our manufacturing sites. Each e-mail was written in the politest way possible, even though their requests were being routinely ignored. Almost every e-mail would start with an apology and a note of gratitude. They would start with something like, 'Dear so and so, I am very sorry to bother you and thanks for your kind support . . .' despite the lack of support. Then the following paragraphs would contain the main issue or enquiries. The e-mails would invariably end with further apologies, 'Again, so sorry to bother you with such a request.' As I read e-mails after e-mails, all written in the same apologetic and thankful manner, I was somewhat baffled. From our many discussions, it was apparent that the local team was quite frustrated with the lack of or delayed responses to their enquiries. Yet, that frustration didn't come across in any of their e-mails. In fact, it was quite the opposite. What the hell was going on? Why wouldn't the team be more demanding?

As I would soon discover, apology and gratitude play big parts in everyday life and serve as the fundamental pillars of all Japanese communications, both formal and informal. For example, sumimasen, meaning 'I am sorry' or *'gomennasai'*, meaning 'my apologies', are regularly used in daily conversations. Especially in formal communications, sarariman routinely used these terms, even though no apology or gratitude may be warranted. For example, it is very common to start a phone conversation with something like this: 'Moshi-moshi (hello). I am so sorry to bother you for no good reason but . . .'

Further apologies would likely be exchanged a few times during the conversation for no apparent reason, and the call will likely end with a final apology, sounding something like this: 'My sincere apologies to bother you with such a trivial matter . . .' even though the matter may not be trivial at all.

Most of our American and European sales teams would be kicking, screaming and chasing our product groups if the responses were even half as slow. I had dealt with them when I was at the headquarters. Compared to them, these sarariman were like angels. No wonder they were not being taken seriously and the support was so poor. As the saying goes, 'the squeaking wheel gets the oil', and our guys in Japan were not making even the slightest noise.

I explained this to the sales representative and pushed them to sound more demanding. They would smile and agree with me while promising to sound more aggressive. Unfortunately, I failed to see any kind of improvement in this area and their e-mails continued to sound polite. Even their most aggressive e-mails would sound reasonably pleasant to us. I found such behaviour ironic from the descendants of the samurai, when generations after generations were mired in brutal and bloody feudal warfare

for centuries. What happened to the sword-wielding samurai spirit
of the past? Where were the samurai sarariman? After coaching,
coaxing and pushing for months, trying to bring out that samurai
spirit in them, I realized that they were not going to change. It
would be easier to train my American colleagues to basically
ignore or overlook the polite tone of the e-mails. It was time
to provide our American product managers with some cultural
training. I started to have informal calls with my colleagues and
friends in Arizona office, where I explained the situation to them.
I would tell them to try to ignore the politeness in the e-mails
from the Japanese folks and really try to understand what they
wanted. The people in our Arizona office were quite receptive.
They also seemed a little amused by these cultural differences and
nuances, even though most of them were well-travelled.

* * *

It took me some time to assess what was needed to bring the
capability of the team up to par with other sales offices. The first
course of action was to make our Japan office and the sarariman
more visible to our product groups and management teams.
I arranged conference calls with our local team and the business
units at the headquarters instead of e-mails. This not only allowed
us to achieve faster resolutions, but also provided an opportunity
for people to get to know each other. During the calls, our
sarariman would remain quiet and I did most of the talking, but I
would encourage them to participate in the discussion whenever
possible. Over time, especially with me present, they became
more comfortable with such interactions.

I arranged training sessions for the team and planned trips
to Arizona. The fact that I was reporting directly to Tom turned
out to be quite advantageous in getting broader support for these
training sessions. Over the next six months, a key member of the

Japan team spent a week in the US interacting with the people from various teams at our head office. I also invited our product group managers to Japan. I knew that most of them were making multiple trips to Asia to visit our manufacturing sites. Many of them were using the Narita Airport as a transit, as I had been doing in my previous role. I was also aware that many of them loved Japan, especially Japanese food. Over time, we saw a revolving door of product group people visiting our office and our sarariman would take them on customer visits.

Eventually, I started to notice an improvement in the overall capability and the confidence levels of our employees. Despite this, the tone of their e-mails continued to remain polite with the usual apologies and gratitude. But they were getting responses much faster. The Japan office was migrating from being an afterthought to becoming the main radar of our business unit and management team. The folks in the office were quite happy with such progress. Even Satoh San seemed to have come around, despite his occasional remarks reminding me that I was still a gaijin sarariman. I felt like I had made progress when even Toda San loosened her military-like demeanour and started being nicer to me.

Chapter 8

Planes, Trains and Automobiles

With the progress in the office, the amount of work started to increase and our life in Japan began to change. Along with the daily meetings and various training sessions, our sales folks started to invite me to meet customers on a regular basis. They were mostly with the top Japanese semiconductor companies such as Toshiba, Panasonic, Sony, Mitsubishi, Ricoh, Renesas and Sharp. The number of potential opportunities also started to grow, but they were still just 'potentials'. We were not actually winning many new businesses and hence, were not making any meaningful impact on our growth targets. I began to feel frustrated with the lack of actual business wins.

For example, we would go to numerous meetings, dinners and drinking sessions with the same customer, talk about opportunities at length, but no business was ever awarded. It felt like we were going in circles, presenting the same materials, and answering the same questions, talking about the same business potentials at each of those meetings. When I would press my fellow sarariman about it, they would advise me to have patience. 'It's not so easy to win business from Japanese companies, and it might take a long time before we see any real business', they would warn. And there lay another very important lesson in the process of successfully engaging with Japanese entities.

In most business transactions, relationships play an important role. Most companies around the world prefer to have good relationships with their clients and suppliers, or anyone with whom they do business. Japan Inc. takes this to a whole new level. To them, the relationship plays a very important role in engaging with potential business partners and serves as an essential pillar for any meaningful new business engagement. At the same time, once such a relationship is established, business is awarded and successfully executed on both sides and Japanese companies rarely abandon their partners, even during the toughest of times. So they tend to take their time to forge the relationship first, to assess and ensure that the potential supplier or partner is indeed worthy of a long-term commitment.

Forming such relationships can take a significant amount of time, patience and persistence. Multiple visits to various customer sites, numerous meetings with people from different departments and various levels of management, along with many expensive dinners, late-night drinking sessions, often accompanied by entertaining karaoke parties with occasional rounds of golf— these are all integral parts of the sarariman lifestyle. The process can also include joint visits to overseas manufacturing plants for the Japanese firms to visit and audit these sites, but more importantly, for them to become comfortable with overseas outsourcing. For us, all our factories were outside Japan. Potential partners must pass the hurdle of these initial phases of relationship-building before moving on to the next phase of actual business engagement. While such relationships can be difficult and time-consuming to form, once established, they can pay dividends for years. This was explained to me many times by my sarariman colleagues.

Additionally, Japanese companies tend to think in longer terms compared to their Western counterparts. Sarariman today still enjoy lifetime employment to a large extent, even though things have become more competitive. The Japanese perception remains that their Western counterparts are not quite as focused on long-term relationships. So they tend to put potential international partners through an even more rigorous initiation process before awarding new business. It is not uncommon for foreign entities to court Japanese firms for long periods of time without success, giving up too early, and losing any possibility to engage in new and meaningful opportunities. A company with a business culture that values transactions over relationships will find it difficult to be successful in Japan.

We were right in the midst of this initial phase of relationship-building with most of our customers. So there were numerous and repeated engagements with almost all the semiconductor companies. And our sales team wanted me to be a part of all those engagements, since I had started to make meaningful impact with the customers with my detailed knowledge of our company and services. At first, it started with one to two customer visits a week, around the Tokyo area. Our sales folks would introduce me to the key management team of these companies in their respective head offices located in Tokyo. But most of these companies have manufacturing plants scattered all over the country, many of them located in *inaka* or in rural villages, far away from the big cities. Some of their key stakeholders and decision-makers were in these satellite locations, which, I would find out, is an important detail to keep in mind when building a rapport with these companies. Soon, I found myself travelling to all these sites all over the country along with our sarariman sales folks.

* * *

Japan is made up of four main islands. The main and the biggest island is Honshu, where the capital Tokyo and other big cities such as Osaka, Kyoto and Nagoya are located. North of the main island is the island of Hokkaido—a nature's paradise, like northern Canada or Alaska, with pristine wilderness, ski resorts and a sparse population. South of Honshu are the islands of Kyushu and Shikoku. There are hundreds of smaller islands, but these four islands, forming a narrow north-to-south elongated landscape, form the country of Japan. While Hokkaido can be a winter wonderland, the southern parts of Kyushu feel like a tropical paradise. Okinawa, one of the smaller southernmost islands, is famous for its tropical weather and scenes. Showcased in many American movies, the island is well-known for its strategic US military base. And the semiconductor companies had their manufacturing units located all over this Japanese archipelago.

But the southern island of Kyushu is where many semiconductor-manufacturing plants are located, and it is known as the Silicon Valley of Japan. Soon, I found myself travelling to all these places multiple times a week, especially to the island of Kyushu, in our quest to form the required broader relationships. My travels required planes, trains and automobiles, and sometimes all of them during the same trip. Many days, we would start early and go to faraway places but I would be back home for dinner. And this was possible due to the amazing transportation system of the country.

If I was impressed with the train and subway systems in Tokyo, I was mesmerized by how the whole country is connected by a super-efficient network of railways. The large cities are connected via high-speed *Shinkansen*, more popularly known as bullet trains. Smaller cities are connected by networks of local trains. Then, each city has its own transit system, consisting of trains, subways and buses. One can travel to all corners of Japan via this extensive railway system. All of these transports run precisely on time. So we were able to schedule meetings in a manner where we would go maybe three hours away by train, have our meetings and then return to Tokyo by evening time.

I will be remiss if I don't talk about the Japanese bullet trains. Introduced during the first Tokyo Olympics in 1964, the

Shinkansen is an amazing Japanese invention, introduced way ahead of its time. The first such service, known as Tokaido Shinkansen, was designed with the world's most advanced technologies, capable of operating at speeds up to 210 kilometres per hour, a world record when it first began service. It was also the world's first inter-city, high-speed railway system, connecting the 500 kilometres between Tokyo and Osaka. Today, various types of Shinkansen, with speed up to 300 kilometres per hour connect all the major cities of Japan across all the four islands. Since its introduction, the bullet trains have carried 1.5 billion people with an impeccable safety record: there has not been a single accident in its fifty-seven years of service. Allowing sarariman and others to efficiently travel all over Japan, the Shinkansen has made a major contribution to Japan's rapid post-war economic growth and is the country's principal transportation artery. During my four-year sarariman adventure and on numerous trips to Japan afterwards, I have taken the Shinkansen countless times. Yet every time, I am awed to see one of these very futuristic-looking trains rolling into Tokyo Station. I can't help but feel that I was somehow transported into a sci-fi movie.

* * *

My acceptance as a sarariman marked the beginning of my four-year, jet-set life, shuttling all over Japan, as well as making extensive travels to our Asian locations in Korea, the Philippines, Taiwan, China and of course, a few trips annually to our head office in Arizona. There would hardly be a week when I didn't take the Shinkansen on a *shuchcho* (business trip) to visit customers, unless I was travelling outside the country. In my last year in Japan, I flew 140,000 miles between American Airlines and Japan Airlines (JAL), making it into the highest tiers of their mileage programmes.

After our arrival in Tokyo, my life had been relatively quiet and slow-paced, commuting to the office and being ignored by my fellow sarariman. I would be back home by six o'clock in the evening, in time for dinner with Sharmeen and Farhana. Once my schedule filled with customer engagements, I worried that I would become a true sarariman and rarely see my family. When I was living in the US and taking regular business trips to Asia, I spent two weekends away from home because of the long travel time and the need to visit all the sites across several Asian countries. By living in Japan, most of my trips were within the country or in another part of Asia. This meant that most of my business travels were either day trips or overnight trips. I rarely had to stay away from home over the weekend. So while I dedicated my weekdays to work, I dedicated my weekends to my family. It turned out that I could be a sarariman during the weekdays while being a family man on the weekends. My fellow sarariman seemed to be quite okay with my request to return home after meetings, even if it was late, instead of staying overnight.

Frankly, I was enjoying all the attention, along with my elevated status in the office, a complete flip from the months of indifference. I now looked forward to going to the office, for a change. I also enjoyed the business trips, meeting all the customers, and making deals, delighted to be able to contribute to our business growth in Japan. I was hopeful that all the travels, dinners, drinks, and karaoke sessions would start to pay off and business growth would soon follow.

Chapter 9

A *Gaijin* in a *Ginko*

Sharmeen and I slowly became accustomed to my busy schedule. By now, we had been in Japan for about six months and Sharmeen had been exploring the city on her own. She seemed to know more about where to find things than I did. We were happy that despite the busy weeks, I was home during the weekends. We were now familiar gaijin faces in our neighbourhood and people not only started to recognize us, but would also nod and smile at us. We started to feel like we were part of the neighbourhood, much to our delight. Some would even wave at us. Our neighbourhood laundry shop was located close to the train station and owned by an elderly couple, neither of whom spoke any English at all. They were one of the store owners who would always wave at us whenever we passed by their shop.

One Saturday afternoon, I decided to walk to the grocery store to do some shopping. Sharmeen had decided to stay home, but Farhana wanted to come with her dad. I really enjoyed that my baby girl was willing to go everywhere with me and I never had to ask twice. We were enjoying our father–daughter chat as we were walking towards the station; my two-year-old seemed to have a lot of things to share about her little world with me. I was listening intently and asking all sorts of questions to keep her going.

As we passed by the laundry shop, I saw one of the owners inside, and we waved at each other, just as we always would. Suddenly, I heard someone yelling from behind us. I turned around to see what the fuss was all about and saw the owner of the laundry shop, waving something in his right hand and yelling something in Japanese to get our attention. Did I forget to pick up our laundry or something? I was worried about what the old man might want, especially when we would struggle to communicate. For a split second, I thought about ignoring him and wanted to keep walking. But on second thought, I realized it would be rude to do so and decided against it. Reluctantly, I walked back towards him with Farhana in tow. As I got closer, I noticed that he was holding what looked like a colourful lollipop in his hand. When we approached him, he politely bowed and said '*konnichiwa* (good afternoon)' to me with a broad smile and then handed the lollipop to Farhana with an even broader smile on his face. I was pleasantly surprised, and Farhana was clearly happy. As I thanked him for his kindness, I realized that I was also bowing in Japanese style. I noticed that Farhana was also bowing, and to my surprise, she even said '*arigatou* (thanks)' in Japanese. I wondered where she had learnt that from. For the first time, I truly felt that we were part of our little community and realized that Tokyo had become our new home.

After that day, Farhana would always look forward to visiting the laundry shop with us. Each time, the older couple would give her a treat while speaking to us in Japanese. Even though I didn't understand much of what they said, the love and the affection in their voices were easily detectable and warmed our hearts. I wondered if Farhana reminded them of their own daughter, or perhaps their granddaughter.

* * *

To have our aunt and uncle living in Tokyo was a blessing. They lived about thirty minutes away from us, and we would spend many weekends together, having dinner or watching old movies at our place. Sometimes, we would all go around Tokyo, visiting some of the popular spots and scenes. My aunt was fond of the upscale fashion district of Omotesando. It is like the Fifth Avenue of New York. We would often go there on weekends for coffee and walk around, window shopping at all the designer shops and trendy stores.

Another place we liked to visit was the Odaiba area. Situated along the Tokyo Bay, Odaiba provides a magnificent view of the beautiful Rainbow Bridge, one of the key landmarks of the city, similar to the Golden Gate Bridge in San Francisco. The area is built on reclaimed land and resembles a futuristic city. Odaiba has its own transit service, a fully autonomous train, running on tracks high above the city, providing nice views of the Tokyo Bay and the surrounding area. We enjoyed Odaiba's many unique stores and great restaurants. Interestingly, there is a smaller version of the Statue of Liberty in a park in Odaiba. I never learnt what purpose it served in the middle of a Japanese park devoid of any other structures. Still, it was good to see this little replica of our famous Lady Liberty. Odaiba has the only beach inside the city of Tokyo. Farhana loved to play on the beach, so we would often take her there during the summer days.

It was wise to have negotiated our Toyota as part of my expatriate assignment. Thanks to its extensive network of commuter systems, consisting of trains, subways, taxis and buses, it is easy to travel around Tokyo without owning a car. In fact, many people who live in the city do not own cars. At times, it can be a burden with expensive and relatively limited parking facilities available around the city. Many times, we had to wait for thirty minutes or more to get a parking spot, especially during peak hours. Nevertheless, it was good to have our little

Toyota as it was nice to be able to go places without having to walk ten minutes to the station, then waiting for the train to arrive, struggling to get on if it was crowded, transferring to a different train or subway line, and finally walking to our final destination. This was especially challenging to navigate with a stroller, a diaper bag, often a camera bag, and of course, our baby Farhana. Our little Toyota provided an added lifestyle advantage we would not have otherwise.

In Japan, driving is done on the wrong side of the road—everyone drives on the left side, opposite to what we are used to in the US. It was quite scary at first, as I always worried that I would look at the wrong side of the road when merging into traffic at an intersection. Every now and then, I would find myself driving on the wrong side of the road, especially if the road was empty. With no cars in sight, I would lose my bearing and intuitively but mistakenly start driving on the right-hand side, only to come to my senses when I would be scared out of my wits to see a car coming straight at me, all of a sudden, and quickly moving to the left side. But slowly, I got accustomed to this. As I became more comfortable with driving on the wrong side of the road, we began to take day trips outside Tokyo. There are three main highways that radially lead out of the city, connecting the capital to other big cities such as Nagoya and Kyoto in the west, Nagano (where the 2004 Winter Olympics were held) to the northeast, and Nigata and Sendai in the north. Driving an hour or so on any of those highways, the scenery quickly changes from the concrete jungle of a busy city to pristine and quiet countryside, nestled between small mountains around beautiful, green and lush valleys. We loved this change of scenery and enjoyed visiting some of the smaller towns, especially around Mount Fuji, or as they call it in Japan, Fuji San. Located close to the five lakes surrounding the wider area of the mountain, these small towns offer some of the most scenic beauties in Japan. During each trip, we would discover something new or a new spot to see the majestic Fuji San from. We would often stop by a small, local, hole-in-the-wall place for lunch, a delicious bowl of ramen or some fresh sushi, and then sit in a nice café afterwards, near one of the lakes with a gorgeous view of the mountain. Located by Lake Ashinoko, we loved to visit Hakone. The small city is famous for its iconic and breathtaking views of Fuji and natural hot springs, known as '*onsen*' in Japanese. We would venture out to other areas outside Tokyo as well. Taking these day trips became a part of our routine, and we really enjoyed them. Sometimes, Fupu and Fupa would join us, making these day excursions even more fun.

* * *

We started to meet people and make friends outside of work. Our uncle and aunt introduced us to quite a few people, and we became particularly close with four families. Azad Bhai and Renu Apa were the kindest couple we met in Japan. They had migrated to Japan in the early sixties and both of their sons were born in Tokyo. They taught language at an international institute run by the Japan International Cooperation Agency (JAICA), which is chartered with providing economic assistance and training for growth in developing nations. On top of that, they also ran a cultural school in Tokyo called Shorolipi, promoting Bangla art, culture and language. Once a year, they would put together a cultural function showcasing traditional Bangla songs, dances and other performances. A unique part of the show was the performance by the Japanese wives of Bangladeshi residents, all wearing traditional saris,[2] singing old folk songs from Bangladesh.

---

[2] 'Sari' or 'shari' is the traditional garment worn by women in India, Bangladesh and Pakistan.

Kamal Bhai and Roshni Apa lived relatively close to us. Kamal Bhai was the Economic Minister at the Bangladesh embassy. Roshni Apa and Sharmeen became quite close. Their two kids were going to international schools in Tokyo; one was in middle school and the other one was in high school. Unfortunately, they left within a year and a half after we moved to Japan.

Like Azad Bhai and his family, Rahman Bhai and Nazneen Apa had also been living in Japan since the sixties. Their only son was born in Tokyo as well. Interestingly, Rahman Bhai was also a gaijin sarariman, working for the Tokyo branch of an American Fortune 500 company. Nazneen Apa worked at the Japanese broadcasting company, Nippon Hōsō Kyōkai or as it is more commonly known, NHK. They were also very nice and sweet; there for us whenever we needed them.

Finally, there were Syed Bhai and Nurjahan Apa, who lived close to us. Syed Bhai was working for a Japanese international organization chartered to help developing nations in the Southeast Asia region. So he was constantly on the road, travelling all over Asia. Nurjahan Apa, a medical doctor, was doing her PhD at the Waseda University in Tokyo. They had the cutest five-year-old daughter, who was in kindergarten, and a son, who was in middle school, attending an international school. Syed Bhai and Nurjahan Apa were also very kind. They migrated to the US during our final year in Japan.

We typically connected with all of them once a month or so, where we would all get together for a nice dinner, which Sharmeen and I always looked forward to. We also met a few expat families in our neighbourhood, with whom we became close. It was good to have a circle of friends, and it was especially good for Sharmeen to have these friends, as I was busy with my work.

* * *

Invariably, there were hiccups every now and then, like my pizza-ordering fiasco, which is to be expected due to the cultural and language barriers.

One such incident involved the simple act of withdrawing money from our local bank. With the help of our friendly Miku San from IBM, we had opened an account at a small neighbourhood branch of the large Sumitomo Ginko ('*ginko*' meaning bank). It was located very close to our local train station. There were a couple of ATM machines, but the instructions were all in Japanese. Since I didn't understand any of it, I had memorized which buttons to press and in what sequence to press them, to retrieve cash. Having mastered the Japanese ATM machines, I always withdrew money for both of us.

One late evening, Sharmeen told me that she needed some Japanese Yen for some activity the following day, and she had just realized that she didn't have enough cash. Luck would have it that I had also run out of cash. It was quite late, and I had to be in the office early, the next morning. So I told Sharmeen to withdraw the money from our account at the local branch. I told her that she could also use one of the ATM machines, perhaps with assistance from someone from the branch. Since it was very likely that none of the employees would be able to communicate in English, she wasn't comfortable with this idea. 'But how hard could it be to ask a banker to show you how to use an ATM machine?' I argued. Sharmeen agreed and said that she would give it a try.

The next morning, in the middle of my meeting, I got a frantic call from Sharmeen. Apparently, her enquiry in our local ginko had created quite a commotion at the bank. It turned out that we were the first gaijin family to bank at that branch. The possibility of failing to satisfy the enquiry of this gaijin customer due to their inability to speak English or understand the hand gestures of my wife had almost created a panic-like situation among its few employees, especially the branch manager. Their nervousness had made Sharmeen even more nervous. In fact, she sounded so aggravated and was speaking so fast that it took me some time to understand what the issue was. Once I understood what was going on, I realized that we needed a translator quickly. So, I walked to our finance office and requested one of the employees to help her out. She kindly obliged and spoke to the branch manager, translating that Sharmeen was simply trying to get some cash from her account. Finally, the manager did help her out with the ATM machine. After hanging up the phone, the finance employee told me that the manager would like to apologize to us for all the inconvenience. I felt guilty for stirring such a commotion and told her that we were the ones who should be apologizing for not being able to speak Japanese.

With more faces become increasingly familiar in our quiet neighbourhood, our weekend excursions around and outside the city, having occasional get-togethers not only with our aunt and uncle, but also with our new friends, my expanding workload, and Sharmeen's new study schedule, Tokyo had now become our home

Chapter 10

The Alien Concept of *Tanshin-funin*

During my numerous business travels in Japan, I met with many sarariman from various top Japanese conglomerates. I got to know a few of them well, as I would meet them several times to discuss a particular business engagement, particularly from Sony. Things with Sony were progressing well. With my boss's blessings, I had managed to form a multinational team to support the potentially big opportunity with them. The team consisted of members from our product group in the US, our engineering team in the Korean factory, and our local sales folks.

Even though the team was performing the detailed technical due diligence, Satoh San and I had decided to remain involved due to the importance of this project. We were having regular follow-up meetings with various teams from Sony. We learnt that while they were planning to outsource the manufacturing of this new product to us, they nevertheless planned to have a limited manufacturing capacity for the product internally. We also found out that for whatever reason, Sony had decided that their plant located in Oita prefecture on Kyushu Island would be the site for this limited production. Oita, one of the larger cities in Kyushu, is about an hour's flight from Tokyo's Haneda Airport. The factory is located about forty miles north of Oita City, in a small village, or '*machi*', called Kunisaki. As a result of this, the task of outsourcing this project was transferred from their R&D centre in Hon-Atsugi, to the Sony folks at the Oita manufacturing site.

We started to make weekly trips to their plant in Kunisaki, instead of Hon-Atsugi. During most of our trips, we would stay overnight, so that we could take the Sony folks out to dinner: it was very important to establish a good relationship and trust with them.

Tucked far away from the bustling Oita city, Kunisaki Machi is a small, sleepy coastal village. The Sony factory was the most prestigious thing that had happened to the town. Rice paddies surround the two-lane road that leads into this small village from Oita International Airport. A few traditional-style farmhouses are scattered here and there, some distance from the road. It is all only farmland, as far as the eye can see. It was a common sight to see farmers attending to their rice fields, seemingly oblivious to all worldly problems. Every now and then, the road would snake around the coast, providing a glimpse of the blue waters of the Pacific Ocean. As the road turned into the main street of the village, it narrowed, lined with traditional-style Japanese homes on both sides. Visiting this quaint machi, I always felt like I was travelling back in time, to some scene from an old Japanese movie. I couldn't figure out why Sony would establish such a large manufacturing site in the middle of this farmland, but I was always pleased to visit Kunisaki, which was worlds apart from the hustle and bustle of Tokyo.

We always stayed at a business hotel located not too far from the Sony plant. These business hotels are commonly found all over Japan and primarily cater to the sarariman during their business trips. These simple but functional hotels provide no-frills accommodation at very reasonable prices. The rooms are invariably clean and very functional, but are often very small with even smaller, attached, prefabricated bathrooms. Any six-foot-tall Western visitor will have a hard time being comfortable in such

a cramped space. I heard many stories—more like complaints—
from visitors and other expats about how they could not shut
the bathroom door while sitting down on the toilet. Being of
relatively small stature, I didn't have that problem, but the rooms
were indeed quite tiny. But they were also very affordable, at only
50,000 Yen (~ $45) to 100,000 Yen (~ $90) per night, and served
as homes away from home for the travelling sarariman.

These business hotels make travel within Japan relatively easy
for the sarariman. Basic amenities, such as soap, towels, shaving
kits and combs are all provided. A sarariman can just take his
office bag and a change of clothes for an overnight business trip.
But I found out that for some reason, shampoo and conditioner
were rarely provided, especially if the business hotel was located
in the countryside. The business hotel in Kunisaki didn't provide
these simple amenities. I wondered if the sarariman preferred not
to wash their hair during their business travels. But most of them
didn't seem to care much about what amenities were provided.
That wasn't the case with me. I preferred my own set of toiletries,
especially a deodorant, a must-have for hot and humid days. But
two things are always available at any of these business hotels—
free ice machines and pay-per-view adult movie channels. After
all, why not allow the sarariman to cool off with a cold drink and
enjoy their stay while on business trips?

* * *

Through multiple meetings, we had got to know several Sony
sarariman in the Oita plant quite well. We would always invite
them out for dinner after our meetings if they had time, and
they seemed to always be available. These were pretty elaborate
Japanese-style dinners and often ended with drunken karaoke
sessions. Perhaps primarily to cater to the Sony sarariman, there
were quite a few nice Japanese-style restaurants and karaoke

bars in Kunisaki. Even though most of the sarariman from Sony didn't speak much English, they were always eager to have a conversation with me with the help of some of my colleagues translating back and forth. Almost on every occasion, they had a ton of questions for me, some regarding business and others about my life. When did I move to America? Why did I move? How long have I been with the company? How did I like living in Japan? Was I here alone or with my family? There were always many enquiries like this. For some reason, when I answered 'yes' to the last question, they would be a little surprised. I was also equally interested in their backgrounds and would reciprocate by asking similar questions about their lives and families.

We had our own favourite karaoke bar and after dinner, we would invariably end up there. The place had a large collection of both Japanese and English songs. The Beatles seemed to be very popular. With most of the sarariman a little tipsy, we would sing all the popular Beatles songs, in our out-of-tune voices, at different pitches, late into the night. I started to understand the importance of these regular social interminglings. It was through these dinners and karaoke sessions, more than the business meetings, that we formed some sort of a bond and friendship among the team members. It helped to build a level of trust, which in turn made the difficult meetings and negotiations a little easier to transact and navigate. Over the course of a few of these social events, two key members of the Sony team, Sakamoto San and Mistumata San became our close friends and trusted partners.

As our dinner and karaoke sessions were either after our meetings or on the evenings before, they almost always took place on weeknights. I couldn't help but feel a little guilty taking the Sony folks away from their families for the evenings, even though I was aware that such activities are an integral part of every sarariman's life. I had also been wondering how Sony had been able to get so many smart and talented people to stay in such a small machi like

Kunisaki. I was sure that all their sarariman were not from this small town, but had probably been transferred from Tokyo or other locations. I wondered how their families liked living in such a small town, especially if they were from big cities.

During one of our dinners, I decided to bring up the subject with the Sony folks. Mitsumata San mentioned that he was living by himself in Kunisaki; his wife and two young kids were back in Tokyo. I was sorry to hear that they were in this small town by themselves without their families. When I mentioned this to him, I was a little taken aback by his answer.

'I am tanshin-funin, Asif San, married but single', he said while laughing out loud.

Tanshin-funin? This was the first time I heard this Japanese term. *What does that mean?* My inquisitive mind wanted to know more. Everyone around the table seemed amused at my interest and after a few chuckles among themselves, as always, Satoh San took the lead to explain what it meant.

Apparently, it is quite common for Japanese companies to transfer their sarariman to various locations away from their home offices for two to three years at a time. It can happen multiple times during a sarariman's career. However, the transfer involves only the employees and not their families. The spouse and the kids stay back in their hometowns. Unlike in American and other Western organizations, the sarariman's opinion on the transfer matters little. They are rarely asked if they are okay with the transfer, or if they might have some personal or family constraints, or if they have any issues with the new location. Typically, the company mandates the transfer and the sarariman are expected to follow. Depending on how far away the new location is, they may visit their families once a week or once a month, and sometimes less frequently if the transfer is outside of Japan. This phenomenon is so common that there is a special term for these sarariman. They are known as tanshin-funin.

As others were chatting away, enjoying the very tasty assorted sushi with sake, I got my handy, intelligent Casio English-Japanese-English electronic translator out of my bag. I had found this piece of intelligent technology during one of our family excursions to the electronic shopping area of Akihabara in Tokyo. The small device was about the size of a pocket calculator and could translate not only words but also certain phrases. I had started to use it to learn a little Japanese. Anyhow, I typed in tanshin-funin in it to see if the gadget would provide me with the equivalent English word or meaning. It translated the term as 'business bachelor'. I found the translation strange, and it piqued my interest even further. Later, I would come across a few other interesting English translations of tanshin-funin during my Google searches. The most accurate one is 'an employee who moves away from his or her family for extended periods of time due to job transfer'. Even though it says his or her, it's rarely applicable to female employees; I am yet to meet a female tanshin-funin. Interestingly, another translation read 'commuter marriage'.

Sakamoto San and Mitsumata San pointed out that the people working at the Oita site, especially in management and operations, were all mostly tanshin-funins. I found it difficult to imagine that so many of them would agree to such transfers away from their wives and kids. After all, I had moved all the way from America with my wife and my two-year-old daughter. I couldn't even fathom moving to Japan and leaving them behind. Especially missing out on seeing Farhana grow up was simply unthinkable.

Curious, I started to ask more detailed questions about being tanshin-funin. How did their wives like such arrangements? Was it an easy sell to the family or was there a lot of resistance? How about the kids? Wasn't it tough not to see them grow? Did the kids miss them and want them back? I went on with my enquiries, much to my fellow sarariman's amusement.

'This is the Japanese way, Asif San', Sakamoto San said. '*Shouga nai ne.*' 'Shouga nai' or '*shikata ga nai*' are very popular Japanese expressions, meaning 'it can't be helped'. I had heard it before and would hear it many times during my four years in Japan. If something couldn't be done, the expression 'shoga nai' would conveniently put an end to the conversation. Satoh San explained that tanshin-funin is a common Japanese practice and has been for decades. Companies prefer to move the employee by himself.

But as we discussed it more, some other peripheral reasons emerged for not moving the family. One of them was the kids' education. Since these transfers are usually for two to three years, families are reluctant to uproot their kids from school for such a short period of time. Often, these transfers are to rural areas and the family may not like the local schools. Secondly, real estate in Japan is neither cheap nor readily available. Selling one's house and buying a new one in a new location for a temporary transfer is not wise. Renting can also be difficult and is an added expense. Sometimes, housing is provided by the company, but these are often like dormitories, which may not be convenient for families. Additionally, it's common for Japanese families to take care of their elderly parents and relatives. Leaving them behind by themselves may not be a good option. But all of them agreed that regardless of these reasons, it is simply not customary for sarariman to bring along their families to their new assignment locations.

I sometimes felt that there might be another not-so-commonly-publicized reason for this. Japan is well-known for its long working hours. During my conversation with many of the tanshin-funins, I discovered that since they are relocated to small towns where the factories are located, they don't have much to do outside of work. With nothing to do and no family distractions, they end up working long hours, way into the night. The companies clearly get more productivity out of their tanshin-funins. The tanshin-funin sarariman focuses on work, while their wives focus on taking care of their households and families. I wondered if there were such ulterior motives of effective division of labour lurking beneath the surface of the tanshin-funin philosophy and practice.

Once I learnt about this practice, I was surprised to find that many of our employees were also tanshin-funins. For example, Satoh San himself was a tanshin-funin living in Tokyo. His wife was living in Nagano, about two hours away by car. Shibata San (whom we would soon hire to head our Japan sales during my second year there, and who would become my good friend; but more about him in the coming chapters) was also a tanshin-funin. His family lived in Hakodate, a beautiful coastal city on the northern island of Hokkaido. He had been working in Tokyo alone for many years. Shibata San would go home once a month since Hakodate was a couple of hours away by plane.

Typically, larger corporations, national and local government agencies engage in this kind of employee transfer practice. Most sarariman are likely to be tanshin-funins at some point in their lives. Some estimates suggest that one in every fifty workers live away from their families due to being transferred to branch offices and factories.[3]

I also encountered some extreme cases of tanshin-funins, where the husbands had been away for work almost all their married lives. During my third year in Japan, we would engage in a joint venture with Toshiba. Through the joint venture, we would acquire a manufacturing facility in a town called Iwate in northern Japan. The Managing Director of the facility was a gentleman named Satoshi Suzuki. As I would talk to him about his career, I was a little surprised to find out that he had lived as a

[3] Yoshio Sugimoto, *An Introduction to Japanese Society* (Cambridge: Cambridge University Press, 2014).

tanshin-funin for over thirty-five years, most of his married life. He would visit his wife and kids every so often and would typically spend some weekends with them. How was the marriage? I would ask. Suzuki San would always claim that they were very happily married, which I found difficult to comprehend. I was even more surprised to hear that his wife rarely complained about him being gone most of their married lives.

'She is happy as long as she gets my paycheck every month, Asif San', Suzuki San would tell me, laughing. I thought he was joking but he told me that his salary went directly to his wife's bank account. His wife then would provide him with a monthly allowance. Apparently, it is a common practice for the sarariman husband to hand over their entire paycheck to their wife at the end of the month. It is the wife's job to manage the money, including all the family expenses, such as paying bills and saving for the future. She would then provide a monthly allowance to her sarariman husband. While this may seem surprising in a male-dominated country like Japan, there is some historical precedence for such practice. For centuries during the Samurai era, feudal lords and men in powerful positions were expected not to worry about running households, including finances. This was left to the matriarch of the family. The idea being that this would free up the men's time and minds to do more important things. I often wonder if the traditional Japanese women, even though always walking a few steps behind their men, wield the true power in most families.

There have been many studies done to see the effects of tanshin-funin on individuals and families, and not surprisingly, most of them show negative results. Tanshin-funins are more prone to suffer from higher levels of stress and related health issues.[4] Children also suffer from the long-term absence of their

---

[4] Hiroto Nakadaira et al., 'Mental and Physical Effects of Tanshin funin, Posting without Family, on Married Male Workers in Japan', *Journal of Occupational Health*, 2006.

tanshin-funin fathers. One study found that many of these children suffer from mental stress, and there is a higher delinquency rate among them.[5] Also, years of living separately, despite the weekly or monthly visits to the family, can damage a marriage. In spite of these social costs, the practice of tanshin-funin remains a common practice today.

Sitting at dinner that evening, I genuinely felt bad for my new friends at Sony, living all alone in Kunisaki without their families. When I expressed my concern, Mitsumata San replied, 'Ahh, no problem, Asif San. This is very common in Japan. *Shinpai shinaide kudasai* (don't worry). I go visit my family almost every weekend.' Then he emptied a quarter of his beer and added with a wink, 'I am happy to be tanshin-funin helping my company.'

Such personal sacrifice for the benefit of the company and ultimately, the nation, has always been a hallmark of the sarariman. No wonder they are referred to as Japanese foot-soldiers, playing an integral part in the country's post-war economic miracle.

Over the course of my assignment in Japan, I met many tanshin-funin sarariman from all walks of life. Regardless of some of the social issues, they all seemed to be generally okay with such assignments. Perhaps, the broader society has accepted and adjusted to the practice of tanshin-funin: it seems to work for Japan, however strange it may seem to some of us.

---

[5] J. Nakazawa, Y. Tanaka, S. Nakazawa, 'Tanshinfunin: Effects of Father Absence on Children's Socioemotional Development', 2000.

Chapter 11

Anpanman!

As summer rolled in, Sharmeen was getting ready to start her studies at the Tokyo Kaplan Centre for her US medical licensing exam. The exam consists of three separate tests, each requiring an extensive amount of studying. Sharmeen would need to be at the Tokyo Kaplan Centre for ten hours a day, seven days a week. This meant that someone had to look after Farhana on the weekdays; I was already quite busy visiting customers, especially Sony in Oita. With the help of some of our new expat acquaintances, we located an international daycare centre fairly close to our local station. As we looked into the centre, we realized that despite the name, it was very much a local *hoikuen* or a daycare centre, except few of the teachers spoke English. We visited the place multiple times and we were impressed with how they managed the babies and toddlers. We also figured that it would be good for Farhana to pick up some Japanese.

This was the first time Farhana would go to a daycare centre; while we were a little worried as to how she would do, we were also excited for this new phase of her life. At first, both of us—but especially Sharmeen—found it difficult to leave her at the centre. As we dropped her off, Farhana would cry and cling to us, refusing to let us go. Her *sensei* assured us that everything was going to be fine and not to worry. Of course, we knew that it would be fine, but it took us a few weeks to graduate into this new phase of our lives, where our little baby girl was now going to spend a considerable time of the day without any of us around. Sure enough, within a few weeks, Farhana's weeping turned to a few tears, and then soon, the crying stopped altogether even though we always sensed some reluctance to let us go in the morning. Her teacher would tell us that Farhana was eager to play with her newfound friends. Just to make sure, Sharmeen and I once went to take a peek at how she was doing, fifteen minutes after we dropped her off. We were pleased to find that Farhana was happily participating in the day's activity along with the other toddlers. With Farhana settled, Sharmeen started her studies at Kaplan, but we were soon faced with an issue neither of us had anticipated. With Farhana going to a hoikuen for the first time, she also started to get sick once a month or so, primarily with a cold or ear infections. I had to take off from work in the middle of the week or Sharmeen had to cut short her studies to take care of her. We needed another solution to mitigate this issue. We decided that it was time to seek help from one of our parents. We figured that we would ask one of them to come and stay with us for a few months, till Farhana got used to the daycare centre. Both our parents were retired, so perhaps one of them would agree.

Back in Texas, my parents were busy taking care of my youngest sister's twin daughters, who were Farhana's age. Even if they were able to visit us, they could only stay with us for a couple of weeks. So my parents were not able to help us out. Luckily, Sharmeen's parents were available. Despite some commitments to her own family, my mother-in-law agreed to come and spend most of the summer with us. With her looking after Farhana, Sharmeen could focus on her studies, while I was able to focus on my work. We would still put Farhana in the hoikuen a couple of days a week, but on most other days, she stayed home with her Nani. The best part was that her Nani was kind enough to cook all sorts of wonderful and delicious dishes for us, an added plus to coming home after a long day at the office.

This was my mother-in-law's first visit to Japan. So she was just as excited to visit us as we were to have her, and I wanted to make sure that she got to see as much of Tokyo and its surrounding areas as possible. Almost every weekend, Farhana, her Nani and I would drive to some of the places we had already discovered so far, such as Fuji San, Hakone, the surrounding lakes and so on. Every now and then, we would find a new place to visit. Unfortunately, Sharmeen wasn't able to join us most of the time, as she was busy studying for her licensing exams. One of our visits was to the Meiji Jingu or Shrine, located in the heart of Tokyo in the Harajuku district. Built in 1920, it is a Shinto shrine dedicated to Emperor Meiji.[6] We would spend hours walking around the 170 acres of forest containing 120,000 trees of 365 different species. It was hard to believe that we were right in the middle of a bustling city. The place provided a glimpse into the traditional Japanese architecture and gardens, which my mother-in-law seemed to especially enjoy.

Another place we often visited was Yokohama city in the next prefecture, which we went to for the first time with her. Yokohama has a promenade and a nice park right by the ocean, only about a forty-minute drive from our place. Japan's largest China Town is also located here. I would take Farhana's little pink tricycle with us and she loved riding it all around the park. We enjoyed watching her pedal away as fast as she could against the backdrop of the Pacific Ocean and the pristine Yokohama skyline. During one of our excursions to Yokohama, Sharmeen decided to join us. It turned out that there was a festival going on, and we got to watch some wonderful floats and dragon dances. Farhana really

---

[6] Emperor Meiji was the 122nd emperor of Japan. He ruled during the Meiji Period from 1852 to 1912.

got a kick out of a long colourful paper dragon dancing along with the procession. We all had a wonderful time and before we knew it, it was almost the end of summer and time for her Nani to go back.

* * *

In the fall, Sharmeen cleared the first part of the licensing exam, and she was going to take a long break before starting to get ready for the second exam. As winter started to roll in, we decided that it was time to take some trips outside the Tokyo area. We decided that we would take a trip to Nagano. Nestled amidst a snowcapped mountain range known as the Japanese Alps, Nagano is a very scenic place and a skier's paradise. In 1998, Nagano was host to the Winter Olympics and the place is easily accessible from Tokyo, either by a three hours' drive or an hour and a half by Shinkansen (in fact, the Shinkansen service from Tokyo to Nagano was established for the Winter Olympic games). I had heard that the place turns into a winter wonderland due to heavy snowfall during the winter season.

I had already visited Nagano a couple of times with Satoh San to meet with Hitachi, but they were just business trips. During one of those trips, Satoh San and I got to talk about how Nagano is a great place to go sightseeing, especially for skiing. During our conversation, I found out that Satoh San had a summer home in the mountains of Nagano, and he often spent his weekends there. *Must be nice*, I thought. I shared with him that Sharmeen and I were planning to take a short vacation there. Satoh San said that we would definitely enjoy the place and then surprised me by inviting us to his summer home. He mentioned that there was already some snow on the mountains close to where his house was located, and that he could take us skiing. Sharmeen didn't ski and I wasn't a great skier either, but I loved being around the ski

slopes, especially on sunny winter days. Satoh San surprised me
even further by revealing that both he and his wife used to be
ski instructors, and he wouldn't mind giving us some free lessons
if we were interested. But we didn't have any skis, I said. Satoh
San said not to worry. Apparently, they had quite a few pairs of
skis and boots of various sizes so we most likely would not need
to buy or rent any. He added that he surely didn't have a pair of
skis for Farhana, in case we wanted her to learn to ski as well.
I wasn't very keen on putting my three-year-old on ski slopes,
since I wasn't a good skier by any means myself. But Satoh San
said that this was the best age to learn and encouraged me to get
a pair of skis for Farhana. His invitation was simply too good to
pass up and the timing was perfect. I readily accepted.

During the next couple of weekends, we went shopping for
our ski gear. Since Satoh San offered us the skis and boots from
his collection, Sharmeen and I splurged and got nice pairs of ski
pants and jackets. We bought the entire set of ski gear for Farhana.
She wasn't keen on trying it on, but after being coaxed for five
minutes and bribed with ice cream, she agreed. She looked simply
adorable in the orange, one-piece ski suit, with yellow boots and
red skis. With all our gear purchased, we were ready for our ski
adventure with Satoh San.

It took us three hours to get to Satoh San's house by
car. I enjoyed the drive as it took us through some beautiful
mountainous areas with tall pine trees. Satoh San's summer
cottage looked like a typical New England winter home from
the outside. As we got off the car, his wife invited us in; it was
our first time meeting her. She didn't speak much English but
seemed very welcoming. The house wasn't huge, though certainly
big by Tokyo standards, but it seemed to have a nice and warm
atmosphere. The main living room was relatively large and had
a gas stove right in the centre with a kettle sitting on top, and
a couple of rocking chairs around it. There was a small office

room and also a Japanese-style room downstairs. The bedrooms were upstairs. By the time we arrived, it was already past 8 p.m. After dinner, we all gathered around the stove with cups of hot chocolate just chit-chatting, with Satoh San occasionally translating for his wife in Japanese. Then we noticed that it had started to snow outside. It was very relaxing to be out of Tokyo, feeling very cozy and comfortable around the warm stove in the mountains of Nagano, surrounded by forest and watching the powdery snow coming down outside.

The next morning, after a hot breakfast, we went to Satoh San's attic on top of his garage to try out the skis. I was surprised to see their large collection of skis of all shapes and sizes. We found a couple of pairs that fit us perfectly. With our skis on top of our cars, we headed for the slopes.

It was a bright sunny day with clear blue skies and the temperature right around the freezing point—a perfect day for skiing. Satoh San tried to give us lessons on the bunny hill. After thirty minutes, and a few falls, Sharmeen said that she had had about enough and went inside the ski lodge to enjoy the warmth and hot coffee. I had never taken any formal lessons, so my techniques were apparently all wrong, according to a very frustrated Satoh San. He gave me a few tips and showed me some tricks to improve my skiing. While some I was able to master quickly, I struggled with some of the other techniques. After a while, he gave up on me and switched his focus to Farhana. He would take her up the bunny slope and hold her as they skied down together. I was quite moved by the care and attention he gave to my daughter's skiing for the remainder of the afternoon. I saw a very different side of him that weekend. Farhana seemed to be able to catch on much faster than her parents. After an enjoyable afternoon on the slopes, we came back to his house. That evening, we invited Satoh San and his wife out to dinner to thank them for their kindness and hospitality.

* * *

After the Nagano trip, our appetite for travel grew and we couldn't wait to take another long trip outside Tokyo. Since I had been to Oita a few times, I decided to take Sharmeen and Farhana there on a long weekend. We flew down to Oita on a Thursday afternoon. We stayed at a nice resort right by the Pacific Ocean in Oita City. Fully comfortable with driving on the wrong side of the road by then, I decided to rent a car so that we could drive around and visit the tourist attractions of the area. For the next few days, we drove all around the Oita prefecture. The countryside in northern Kyushu is also very mountainous, with tall and lush evergreen pine trees. The best part was the lack of crowd and traffic. It was wonderful and a welcome change to be able to drive for miles on empty highways without seeing another vehicle. We stopped by a small town called Beppu, the hot-spring capital of Japan. Sharmeen wasn't too keen to get in those hot springs in her birthday suit, so we decided against it. One place Farhana really enjoyed was a park on Mount Takasaki, known as the 'monkey mountain'. The feeding of monkeys here is a very popular tourist attraction; hundreds of monkeys zoom past the visitors to get to the feeding area. It seemed like Farhana enjoyed watching the monkeys from afar. As the feeding time arrived and hundreds of monkeys started to run past us, she got really scared. It is indeed a little scary to see so many monkeys aggressively running towards food. Before we left Oita, I decided that I must take Sharmeen to the Sony plant. We drove to Kunisaki, and I showed her the place I had been visiting quite regularly for the past few months. Sharmeen was also surprised to see the large Sony factory in the middle of a small, sleepy fishing village.

The long weekend was over, and it was time for us to fly back home. After returning the rental car, we checked in at the JAL counter at Oita airport. We grabbed some dinner at a restaurant close to our gate, as it was getting a little late. Just as our boarding announcement came through the loudspeaker, Farhana declared that she had to go the bathroom. Seeing a long queue at the gate, we decided it was best to take her to the bathroom before boarding the flight. On our way back from the restroom, we passed a few gift shops. Suddenly, Farhana stopped walking, pointed at something inside one of the gift shops, and tried to pull me inside. She screamed what sounded like, 'ampanmaan'. Normally, I would follow her lead to see what she wanted, but I could see that our boarding was almost complete. I tried to explain to her that we had to go, but she kept saying the same thing over and over again quite loudly, while trying to pull me by my hand, refusing to follow me to the gate. Clearly, something had caught her attention, but I couldn't tell what it was. But there was no time for any last-minute shopping. As she refused to budge, I picked her up and carried her to the gate, much to her dismay. She threw a temper tantrum for the next ten minutes. The flight attendants were very nice and patient, trying to calm her down. Other passengers seemed to be getting annoyed while we were feeling embarrassed. One of the flight attendants brought her some toys, which she tossed aside while continuing to yell 'ampanmaan'. Finally, we managed to calm her down soon after we took off, much to our relief as well as to the relief of the surrounding passengers. In another few minutes, she had forgotten all about whatever it was that she had wanted at the airport and started to play with her new toy from the kind flight attendant.

Two weeks later, Farhana was watching TV in the living room while Sharmeen and I were getting dinner ready. Suddenly, she yelled 'ampanmaan'. In the next moment, she ran up to me and pulled me by my finger to the living room. She pointed at the screen where there was a Japanese cartoon I had never seen before. It looked like some kind of a superhero character wearing a red cape, with a very round face. She ran to the TV screen pointed at it and said, 'Daddy, ampanmaan.' So, the character must be called Ampanmaan, I thought. It also looked familiar.

Then I remembered that I had seen the same toy character being sold at various gift shops. Farhana must have seen such a figurine and wanted me to buy it for her at the Oita airport.

The next day, I asked Satoh San about it. Turns out that there is indeed a very famous Japanese superhero cartoon character known as Anpanman. Its head is based on a bread filled with red bean paste, while the rest of his body is dressed like any other superhero. The red-bean-filled bread is known as *anpan* in Japanese, hence the name Anpanman. It seemed like Farhana was perhaps learning more about Japan than either of her parents.

Chapter 12

Commuting Sarariman Style

By the beginning of my second year in Japan, everyone in the office was busy, as the number of our engagements and meetings with customers had grown significantly. We had also started to win a few new businesses, much to my delight. Along with my frequent trips to Oita, I was now visiting manufacturing plants of various semiconductor companies located all over the country. Kyoto and surrounding towns were other areas we started to visit frequently, as there are a few semiconductors companies headquartered there.

One winter morning, a few of us sarariman were scheduled to take the 8 a.m. Tokaido Shinkansen to visit one of those customers, Panasonic, in Kyoto, for an *ippotsu* or a one-day business trip. I had been to Kyoto a couple of times before with my colleagues, but previously, we had taken the Shinkansen in the late afternoon, stayed overnight in Kyoto and returned to Tokyo the following day. This was my first time taking the bullet train service so early in the morning. We agreed to meet on the Shinkansen platform at the Tokyo Station around 7.45 a.m. By now, I had a decent understanding of the Tokyo transit system, so my fellow sarariman had stopped guiding me as to how to navigate it.

Tokyo rush hour is well-known for its insane number of commuters; some 2.4 million workers commute into Tokyo every day.[7] Even with the increased number of services, the trains are jampacked during peak hours. I preferred not to ride in these super-crowded trains wearing a suit and was lucky to have avoided taking them so far. And I rarely had to commute by train to the office because of our wonderful little Toyota. Whenever there was a business trip and we left from the office, I would splurge and take an expensive taxi to the office in the morning, since I didn't want to leave my car. I wanted to take a taxi that morning as well, but decided against it. Tokyo Station was a forty-five minutes' drive from my home during normal hours. With the morning traffic, God only knows how long it would take to reach there. I couldn't afford to be late: it would not be good if the gaijin sarariman missed the Shinkansen. I planned to take the series of commuter trains instead. I knew that they would be crowded, but I had a very good chance of getting into Tokyo Station on time as trains are hardly ever late in Japan.

I knew what I had to do. First, I would have to take the local train, the Tokyu Line, to Shibuya Station and then change to the Yamanote Line, which would take me all the way to Tokyo Station. To ensure on-time arrival, I started very early, giving myself enough time, and walked leisurely to our local Toritsudaigku Station. Despite being quite early, the station was already very crowded with long lines of sarariman,s ready for the day's battle, all of them armoured in suits and ties, and armed with their faithful office bags. Despite being a gaijin, I fit in quite well into the scene, also in a tie and suit with my office briefcase.

In all the stations in Japan, the locations of the doors of a particular train line are clearly marked on the platform. When the train stops, all its exits always line up perfectly with those markings. This happens without fail for every train, every time.

---

[7] 'Tokyo Population 2022', World Population Review, https://worldpopulationreview.com/world-cities/tokyo-population. Accessed May 2022.

In my four years of living and subsequent extensive travel within Japan, I never experienced a time when the doors of a train did not perfectly align with its designated marking on the platform when it came to a stop. So commuters always line up in front of these markings. It was no different that morning, except that all the lines were very long. I tried to see if there was a shorter queue somewhere, but all of them seemed to be equally long. So, I just lined in one of them. The train arrived right on schedule, and surprisingly, despite the long queue, I managed to get on this very crowded Tokyu Line, which would take me to my first stop, Shibuya Station.

The train was already fully packed when I got on. And as it started to take on more passengers at each subsequent stop, I kept getting shoved towards the middle of the compartment, away from the door. By the time the train was approaching Shibuya Station, I found myself squeezed among a sea of sarariman commuters and as far away from both the exits as possible. The train stopped for less than a minute at each of the stops. I started to panic, thinking that I might not be able to make it to the door on time to get off at Shibuya Station. If I failed to get off, I would have to get off at the next station and turn around, which would make me late for the Shinkansen. I could just imagine the satisfied look on Satoh San's face. His devilish smirk subtly reminded me that, naturally, the gaijin sarariman had failed to successfully navigate the complex Tokyo railway system, and then he gave me a lecture on the subject. Even though we were on good terms by now, he would remind me that I am gaijin, every now and then. There was no way I was letting him have that satisfaction that morning.

So I prepared myself for the ultimate battle of pushing past all the sarariman and a few women who stood between me and the exit. I was ready to pull, push and shove—whatever was necessary to ensure that I made it out that door. The train pulled into the station exactly on time, and as soon as the door opened,

I sprang into action, ready to implement my plan. As I started to push, I was surprised to see that everyone seemed to be getting off as well. I stopped pushing almost as soon as I had started it, but in those few seconds, I seemed to have managed to piss off a few sarariman around me, clear from the disdained looks they were giving me. In my somewhat paranoid state of mind, it had completely escaped me that Shibuya Station was the last stop for this line—no wonder everyone was getting off here. At any rate, I was relieved to get off, and started getting ready for the next battle—changing to the famous Yamanote Line that would take me to Tokyo Station.

The iconic Yamanote Line with green stripes on each of its trains is essentially a loop encircling Tokyo. Named after the hilly western part of the city, it is one of Tokyo's busiest and most important lines, connecting its major stations and urban centres such as Shibuya, Shinjuku, Harajuku, Shinagawa, Ueno and Tokyo. Forming a thirty-four-kilometre-long chain with twenty-nine stops, Yamanote Line is one of the best ways to get around the city. The whole line is above ground, sometimes on elevated tracks. A journey around the whole loop takes an hour. I had become very familiar with the Yamanote Line, as we would use it almost every time we visited a customer.

While not as busy as the Tokyo or Shinjuku stations, Shibuya Station still serves as a major train and subway junction, and the place was packed that morning. I slowly managed to make my way through the sea of sarariman to the Yamanote Line platform. I was shocked to see how crowded the platform was. Navigating the crowd at Toritsudaigaku Station seemed like a cakewalk compared to this.

When the train arrived, I was horrified to see hardly any room inside any of the passenger coaches. How in the world was it going to take on more passengers? A few people did get off, but far fewer than the number of passengers waiting to get on.

Despite this and I am not sure exactly how, our queue moved quite a bit. But I was still far away from the door. It was clear that I wasn't going to make it on this train. I wasn't too worried, encouraged by how much the queue had moved, and especially as I was aware that the trains in Yamanote Line were scheduled almost every two or three minutes during peak hours.

As the next train arrived, it looked like it was also very full. Just like the last one, a few number passengers got off, but once again the line moved quite a bit. That's when I noticed the 'big guy' close to the door. These employees of Japan Railway have only one job—to push and pack people inside the trains during rush hour. It is essentially like pushing down your fluffy clothes in a suitcase to make room for more clothes, except for the fact that the commuters are not fluffy. The 'train pushers' tend to be big guys, kind of like the sumo wrestlers and this guy was no different. As the train compartment looked full, I saw him spread both his arms on his sides and push the people inside, making room for a few more commuters before the door finally closed. I had heard about these 'train pushers' and even seen them in documentaries. But this was the first time I was witnessing it in person, and I started to sweat a little as I realized that I was about to experience this infamous Japanese commuter tradition.

The next train arrived in less than five minutes and right on schedule. This time, I managed to make it inside the train along with a bunch of sarariman. It was more like I was autonomically pushed into moving along with the crowd towards the open door. My back was against the door, so I didn't see the big guy in action, but I felt him as he packed us all in. Luckily, I wasn't the guy closest to the door, so I didn't feel his wrath directly, but I definitely experienced the 'packing in'. As I heard the door close, I found myself squeezed among the other sarariman, completely unable to move. Moreover, both my arms seemed to be stuck in between other commuters with my office bag tucked somewhere among them. The only movement was swaying along with the crowd in unison in sync with the swaying of the train.

I remained stuck in that position until we arrived at the next station, which felt like an eternity; but took less than five minutes. As some people got off, I was finally able to free myself and was relieved to be able to feel my arms and legs again for a few seconds. At each subsequent station, the train kept taking in more and more people, and it got even more crowded. Soon, the train rolled into Shinagawa Station, where many of the sarariman got off as Shinagawa is a fairly large office district. The rest of the way to Tokyo Station wasn't as crowded, and it was good to be out of the great squeeze. I was happy when we finally rolled into Tokyo Station.

During any weekday morning, Tokyo Station, just like the Shinjuku Station, is a sight to behold. Almost all major train and subway lines have stops here. Its thousand-feet long corridors are packed with millions of marching commuters transiting through the station. It is a sea of morning commuters as far as the eye can see, mostly sarariman. No one is speaking, no one seems to be looking at anyone else, yet no one is bumping into each other, no pushing or shoving, each in his or her quest to catch the next train. In the moments of silence in between the sweet and melodious announcements from the stations' loudspeakers announcing the imminent arrival or departure of a train, one can hear nothing but a roaring sound. It's the sound of the thousands of the sarariman's feet, marching on their way to their daily battles. A first-time visitor can be easily overwhelmed by such sights and sounds. To this day, I always find observing these morning commutes, either at Tokyo or Shinjuku station, fascinating, even though I don't necessarily always enjoy being a part of it.

I was indeed overwhelmed that morning as it was the first time I was experiencing Tokyo Station in its grandeur of peak-hour commute. Navigating my way through that sea of sarariman, exhausted from my first Tokyo morning commute, I was happy that I had managed to arrive at the right Shinkansen platform. And it was only 7.40 in the morning. I still had a whole day of the business trip ahead of me. I was even happier to see Satoh San and others at the platform, having successfully made it on time for our bullet train to Kyoto.

I realized that I had just gone through what millions of sarariman are used to experiencing every morning in Tokyo as they commute to their workplaces. Then they get to do it again during their evening commute. I wondered if that's why the sarariman regularly prefer to going to dinner and drinking with their colleagues after work, instead of going back home to their families—to avoid such insane rush hours. I was grateful that I had managed to avoid the morning rush hour train commute so far, thanks to our little Toyota, and made a mental note to try to avoid it in the future, if possible. My appreciation and love for our little Toyota deepened that morning.

Chapter 13

Growing Gains

Within the next few months, it became clear to us that the company's business growth potential had become quite real. For almost over a year now, the team had been working hard, spending a significant amount of time on planes, trains and automobiles, travelling all over Japan, meeting and establishing relationships with sarariman from the top Japanese semiconductor companies. We had already been awarded several new opportunities, and the team felt that we were in a good position to win more significant new business. However, with all the hard work and continual business travels, some people were on the verge of burning out. It was clear that we needed to expand the number of our local resources.

We had spent the Christmas holidays back home in Texas, on an extended home leave. While Tokyo had now become our new home, it was wonderful to be back in our 'real' home, being able to spend time with my parents, sisters and their families. It felt good to go to our local grocery store and buy a regular-sized bottle of Tabasco or Thousand Island dressing without forking up an exuberant amount of money. These home leaves always made me realize how precious our families are, how good we have it back home, and how we often take these things for granted.

Towards the end of our break, Tom called and asked if I wouldn't mind stopping by Arizona for a few days before heading back to Tokyo. He mentioned that it would be good if I presented all the good work that we had been doing along with some of the positive results achieved thus far. There were a few things that I wanted to discuss with him as well, especially regarding the possibility of expanding the team in Japan. This was the perfect opportunity to do so, and I readily agreed to come see him.

I ended up working for a week from our head office before returning to Tokyo. As per Tom's suggestion, I presented a summary of the progress we had made in Japan. Our management folks, including our CEO, Steve Sullivan, seemed quite satisfied with the progress and asked if there was anything we needed. This was the opening I had been waiting for. I informed them that considering these potential growth opportunities, we were extremely short-staffed and needed to immediately start the process of hiring and training competent people. The management was in agreement with my assessment. They promised to support us with whatever was needed to achieve growth and sustain the new business. I also took the opportunity to meet some of the key stakeholders in our business unit, thanking them for their improved cooperation and support. Satisfied, I returned to Tokyo with Sharmeen and Farhana.

Within the next month or so, Tom and our global head of sales, Robert Green, visited the Tokyo office. We had a few very productive sessions and came up with a detailed plan to expand our staff and reorganize the team to ensure improved customer support. One of the key recommendations from them was to find a new head of sales—a seasoned Japanese sales leader with significant experience in and exposure to the local semiconductor industry. When I asked about the plan for Satoh San, Tom and Robert told me that while he was very knowledgeable about the industry, they both felt that Satoh San just wasn't the right guy to lead the sales team to our next growth phase. What we needed was a seasoned salesperson, a veteran, who was well-connected with the key people within the Japanese semiconductor industry.

Even though I was somewhat shocked to hear this, I had to agree with their assessment. Indeed, Satoh San had good technical knowledge about our products, but I felt that his expertise didn't include sales or managing the business side of things. While I had started to enjoy working with him, at times, he did come across as more of a hindrance to our business growth. For example, whenever we would propose a necessary change or try to think outside the box, his tendency was to bring up all sorts of barriers to our proposals. Yet, without these changes, our growth would surely stall.

Tom also mentioned that he would like me to take the lead of the business unit and technical team in Japan, and act as a consultant for the sales team. He also wanted me to ensure that we hired the right people and that the training for the new hires was well-planned and executed.

That all sounded good to me, but I was still a little taken aback by this sudden decision to move Satoh San out of his role, even though I agreed with them that it was the right thing to do. As I was trying to process this new piece of information, Tom added that he thought Satoh San should work in my team. I couldn't believe what I had just heard.

'Did you just say that Satoh San should work for me?' I repeated incuriously.

'Yes. He is good technically and would be better off being a member of the technical team', Tom replied firmly.

'But you mean that he will be working under me? You realize that he is currently the head of our office here?' I reminded Tom, still in disbelief at what I had just heard.

Tom confirmed once again that it was exactly what he meant.

I felt very uncomfortable with this sudden suggestion of becoming Satoh San's boss. I was sure Satoh San wasn't going to be happy about this. *What if he quits? We do need all his tribal knowledge to grow our business.* Sensing my discomfort, clearly visible from my demeanour, Tom assured me that it was the right decision.

'You both may find it difficult at first, Asif, but it is the right decision for us to go forward', Tom assured me.

I asked him if he could give me a couple of days to think about it. Tom agreed.

Even though I had asked for some time to mull over it, there didn't seem much to think about. The way Tom and Robert had put it to me, it seemed like the decision had already been made. Still, I couldn't help but worry about how Satoh San might react or how the office people might feel regarding such a change and how difficult it might prove to manage Satoh San. After giving it some thought, I decided that it should be done in an appropriate manner. Instead of making the change relatively quickly, it would be best if we first bring in the head of our Japan sales, and then have him make this change. This way, the local folks won't feel that such a decision was shoved down their throats by the folks at the head office. The next day when I suggested this to Tom, he agreed with me. But he cautioned that we shouldn't wait indefinitely to implement these much-needed changes.

The plan we had put together was to hire several sales guys, engineers and customer service people. Essentially, we were going to almost double the number of staff in less than six months, which was not going to be an easy task. Then, of course, we would have to make sure that they were all properly trained. It was quite exciting to move on to this new phase. Even though it had been a little over a year since I had first arrived in the office, I felt like we had come a long way and things were moving in the right direction.

As we started our interview process, it occurred to us that our current office in Ebisu had no space for all these new hires. Our office suite in Ebisu was quite small with barely enough cubicles for everyone, a very small meeting room and one office; we were already kind of bursting at the seams. It was clear that we would need to move into a larger office space. So, after some discussion and deliberation, Satoh San, Toda San and I decided that we needed to find a new and bigger office, but at a different location. The rent at the Ebisu office building was exuberant. They mentioned that if we moved to another location in a slightly older building, we might be able to find a much larger office for just a small increase in rent. As luck would have it, the timing was almost perfect as our current office lease was about to expire. A small team was formed to look for our new office location with the help of a property management agent. One thing we all agreed on was that it was best to be in one of the key office districts of Tokyo, such as Shinagawa, Shimbashi or Shinjuku, close to a major train or subway station, in order to attract new hires.

Within a few weeks, we were informed that the team had found a new office in Shinjuku, on the tenth floor of Dai-Ichi Seimei Biru (*biru* is 'building' in Japanese). The building was not as new and glitzy as the one in Ebisu, but it was at a great location, close to the Shinjuku station and right on top of one of the key subway stations. It turned out that the building was right next to the very Hyatt Hotel we had stayed for almost two months when we had first moved to Japan. Of course, I had some familiarity with the area, which made me feel good, but I wondered how bad my commute was going to be since I was the only one driving to the office every day. Our current office was only a twenty-minute drive from my home in Himoniya, and there wasn't much traffic, as Ebisu is not a major office district. This was a precious gift in a city where the average one-way commute can easily take over an hour. I figured that my driving time would now double, at least, but the fact that I would still be within driving distance and would avoid fighting the morning commute by train with the millions of sarariman brought me some comfort.

Within two months, we relocated to our new office in Shinjuku. The move itself was painless, other than having to pack our personal items in boxes. All items were moved over one weekend and by the time we showed up in the new office on a Monday, our computers and Wi-Fi were all set up and running.

We had taken up one side of the entire tenth floor of the Dai-Ichi Semi Biru. It was much more spacious than our Ebisu office. One side of the entire wall was made of floor-to-ceiling windows, providing ample sunlight and nice views of the Shinjuku area. The cubicles were also larger, providing a lot more working space. We had three separate meeting rooms, compared to only one tiny one at our Ebisu office.

My morning commute turned out to be about an hour during the morning rush hour, but the location was much more convenient, compared to our office in Ebisu. Shinjuku Station was only a ten-minute walk from the office. The Tochomae subway station was accessible from the basement of the building. In addition to being next door to the Hyatt, the Tokyo Hilton was across the street from this office. Both the hotels had some nice restaurants, and most of them offered great choices of Western food as part of their lunch menu at reasonable prices. There were also plenty of other choices for lunch outside those hotels and around the office. More importantly, there was a Starbucks right across the street. I felt right at home, despite the longer commute. Everyone also seemed to be pleased with the new place.

A problem did arise for me, personally, when I was told that the building required a monthly parking fee. It was 50,000 Yen or about $500 per month for each parking spot. I figured that this might not go well with Toda San, and it reminded me of my earlier days in the office when I was facing all sorts of uphill battles to get anything done. Just as I had expected, Toda San's stand was that this was my own issue, since I was the only employee who was driving to the office. My position was that the office should be paying for this sudden expense as no one had informed me of this before our move. But I was glad to notice a much weaker resistance from Toda San, this time around: she said that if my boss approved the expense, she would take care of it. After a few rounds of negotiations and a couple of phone calls with Tom, I got the approval, and Toda San readily agreed.

In the meantime, we had been actively hiring and by the time we moved into our new office, we had already brought a few new salespeople on board. My primary role in the hiring process was to assess their English skills. I was also in the process of strengthening my technical team, so I was looking for good engineers with semiconductor experience. While there were quite a few good candidates, the primary challenge was to find people with a reasonable level of English skills, who also had experience working with international organizations. Luckily, some of the US semiconductor companies were in the process of downsizing their local offices, and we were able to hire some of their talented employees.

One of these was Norito Umehara, who joined us from Texas Instruments. With his long working experience at one of the Texas Instruments factories in southern Japan and then later at their sales office, he was well-versed in the ways of American companies. We were the same age, and both of us had daughters who were also of the same age. He would soon become my right-hand man in Japan, and we went on to become very good friends despite the fact that I was his boss.

We also found a senior salesperson named Ken Shibata, to run our most valuable Sony account. He had worked as a sarariman at Hitachi for over twenty years. Having served on a four-year expatriate assignment in Germany, and later as the lead of their global outsourced manufacturing service, Shibata San was one of the most international sarariman I had ever met in Japan. Because of his business development role, both locally and globally, Shibata San seemed to be relatively well-known in the industry, both in and outside Japan. He had a very good sense of humour and a great personality, compared to the usual serious and stoic sarariman. For the next three years, Shibata San, Umehara San and I would have a very productive and wonderful experience growing our business together, travelling all over Japan as well as to our overseas facilities.

A senior gentleman named Takashi Fujita soon joined as the head of our Japan office. He was a seasoned leader, even though he didn't have any direct experience working in the semiconductor industry. I initially had some concerns about his lack of experience in our industry but what we needed was for someone to lead, encourage and mentor the team. Fujita San fit well into this role. Within a month of his arrival, he made the organizational changes that Tom, Robert and I had discussed a few months earlier. In our new Japan organization, the sales leaders reported to him. Each sales leader was responsible for certain customers, and they had a small team of people working for them as junior-level salespeople and customer service managers to better manage the accounts. While all the sales guys and engineers were sarariman, the customer service managers were all women. I was in charge of the technical team and the business unit, representing our product units in Arizona, and continued to be the de facto consultant to the sales teams. While I continued to report directly to Tom, I now had a dotted line reporting structure to Fujita San. Initially, I was a little worried about it. Would it limit my influence and ability to help the team if Fujita San started to negatively intervene in my affairs? But for the most part, he left me alone with respect to what I was doing and, in fact, often consulted with me on various business decisions and proposals. He also made the change I was kind of dreading for a while. He assigned Satoh San to my team, and now he was going to report to me.

Needless to say, Satoh San wasn't very pleased with this new arrangement. I wasn't feeling very comfortable with it either. After all, he had helped me become part of the local sarariman landscape, despite his initial pushbacks. Also, he was considerably older than me. It's not easy for anyone to accept a boss much younger than themselves. Especially in Japanese culture, as in many Asian countries, age and position tend to have a relatively strong positive correlation. One's promotion typically comes when one has worked for a period of time, gaining experience, knowledge and wisdom in the process. In this hierarchical system, it is not common to have a boss who is much younger. It started out quite awkward at first, for a couple of months. Our daily discussion and interactions were reduced to a bare minimum. Obviously, he had to sit in my staff meeting and report his updates to me and the team, but in general, Satoh San seemed to be avoiding me. His response to me often seemed to be curt, but I just ignored it as long as I got what was needed. And I was quite okay not having to deal with him unless absolutely necessary. Luckily, Satoh San knew what to do and rarely needed any instruction or guidance from me. I was worried that he would be demotivated and stop pursuing some of the key programmes with the effort required. While I am sure that there was a level of demotivation, clear in his demeanour, it didn't seem to affect his work, which was a relief. My other worry about a possible negative impact on other sarariman in our office turned out to be unwarranted. If there was any gossip or negative feeling about this reversal of position, it never reached my ears or affected my working relationship with anyone. Over the course of a few months, the feeling of awkwardness slowly started to dissipate, and things started to become more normal between us. In hindsight, one thing that might have helped this transition to go relatively smoothly was that I continued to treat Satoh San with the same respect as I had been treating him over the last year. I rarely acted like the boss if it wasn't absolutely necessary, and gave him the time and space to come to terms with his new predicament. I continued to discuss matters with him, building consensus regarding most decisions, as we had been doing all along. Over time, his initial, somewhat hostile attitude started to soften. While it wasn't quite like before, we established a pleasant working relationship, much to my relief.

Soon, Fujita San soon decided that Shibata San and I should move into offices from our cubicles, since we had broader responsibilities. I was glad to have my own office with a door again. We also hired a few administrative assistants or 'office ladies', as they are known in Japan. Fujita San agreed to provide me with my own administrative assistants who would support me and my team to help manage our meeting schedules, travels and other needs. This turned out to be very helpful—delegating those tasks allowed me more time to focus on the actual business of growing our revenue. My new administrative assistant was a very capable and attractive woman named Kyoko Takamiyagi, from the island of Okinawa. Her cubicle was close to my office.

Soon after she joined the company, I noticed that many of my fellow sarariman were stopping by my office more frequently, even though they didn't seem to have anything in particular to discuss with me. I found this a little strange and started to wonder why suddenly there was a surge in interest to stop by my office. Within a few weeks, I realized that their main objective was not to talk to me, but to get a chance to look at and, if the opportunity presented itself, talk to Takamiyagi San on their way to my office. I found this to be both amusing and irritating. I guess sarariman will always be sarariman. Despite such loutish behaviour, Takamiyagi San handled the attention with grace. I soon had to tell them to stop bothering her unnecessarily.

There was an added benefit of our office expansion that I didn't foresee. When I joined the office in Tokyo, I was the new gaijin employee and struggled to get acceptance. For these new sarariman, *they* were the newcomers. Even though I was still a gaijin, for them, I was already a part of the local sarariman scene and as a result, they simply accepted my sarariman status without ever questioning it. I felt like my place as a gaijin sarariman was further solidified by our office growth.

One of the key tasks that Tom and Robert had entrusted me with was to ensure that the new hires were trained properly. Since I had already done this for our current employees, I used the same playbook for the new hires. As a key part of their training, I took the new team of sarariman to Arizona, and introduced them to our key people there. As all of them were industry veterans, with most having some level of international experience, most of them were able to hit the ground running. With the new hires on board and properly trained, I felt that we were now ready for the second phase of our growth.

Chapter 14

Getting Naked with Fellow Sarariman

With the help of the expanded team's members, we started to aggressively pursue new business. We were either engaged in new business or in discussion for new opportunities with most of the Japanese semiconductor companies. In the meantime, our work with Sony was progressing well. We continued to make multiple trips a month to their facility in Oita. Our new sales guy and soon to be my friend, Shibata San, had started to take the lead from the sales side, replacing Satoh San. Umehara San was taking the lead for technical matters. But since this was one of the most important projects for us, I ensured that Satoh San was involved, especially to maintain continuity.

One evening, Shibata San, Umehara San, Hasegawa and I met at the Haneda Airport for an evening flight to Oita, for another meeting with Sony. This was my first business trip with Shibata San and Umehara San. Satoh San was unable to travel with us that evening as he had some prior engagement. Instead of taking the evening flight with us, he had decided to take the early flight the next morning, and was planning on joining us directly at the Sony plant for our meeting. I couldn't help but wonder if this was part of his scheme to avoid me due to the organizational changes, even though everyone, including Satoh San and I, had by now fully embraced and grown comfortable with the arrangement.

On the flight, Shibata San, Umehara San and I chatted about various things, including our backgrounds, our past jobs, our families and, of course, the semiconductor business. I discovered that Shibata San and I had quite a few common acquaintances in the industry, especially in the US. He also knew Yamazaki San of Sony (with whom we had the first weird meeting in Hon-Atsugi) from his previous job. Also, Umehara San and I also knew some of the same people at his previous employer, Texas Instruments. I asked Shibata San about his expatriate assignment in Germany, and he seemed to talk fondly about his four-year assignment in Munich. I asked if he was a tanshin-funin while there, but to my great surprise, he said that he was there with his wife and kids. How was that possible, I wondered? Shibata San said that indeed it was an exception that his previous employer made. It was clear that he had thoroughly enjoyed his overseas assignments. While we were talking, he mentioned that he could even speak a little German.

'Really, that's awesome', I said. 'So you speak English, German and Japanese? Very talented, Shibata San.'

'Eins, zwei, drie, vier', he said, showing off his German speaking skills to us.

'Wow, that's great. What does that mean?' I asked.

'One, two, three, four', he answered, laughing.

What a change these new sarariman will bring to the team, I thought. Even though they were relatively new, it felt like we had known each other for years. With the previous group of people, I rarely had such relaxed, friendly and casual chats, either in the office or during our business trips.

In the middle of our conversation, Hasegawa San suddenly announced that the business hotel we usually stayed at was completely booked. Apparently, all other business hotels in the area were also not available. So he had reserved us rooms at a *ryokan* instead. Apparently, this place was also near Sony Oita, and he apologized to us for the inconvenience. I was a little surprised to hear this. I had heard about ryokans before. They are traditional Japanese-style inns or hotels. I was told that it is a must to stay at a ryokan before leaving Japan, to experience these old and authentic traditional-style inns. But I had also heard some mixed reviews. For example, some foreigners may not find ryokans very pleasant, with their floor sleeping arrangements and communal toilets, etc. I had been wanting to experience a ryokan stay, so it seemed like a great opportunity to do so. But I wondered why Hasegawa San apologized for the change. Was this a run-down ryokan or something? I couldn't also help but feel somewhat paranoid. Also, why didn't my new admin, Takamiyagi San, inform me of this change? I felt a little disappointed with her. In Arizona, we had Tracey Kovach, our group administrative assistant. She had learnt some of the nuances and details of our travel patterns and always took care of us. Where was Tracey when I needed her?

Anyhow, for the rest of the trip, I couldn't help but worry about this ryokan. I hoped that the place wasn't a dump or some shady joint that Hasegawa San had booked in desperation. However, in Japan, everything was always neat, clean and tidy, so even a 'dump' would not be too bad, I thought. Shibata San and Umehara San didn't seem to care at all, and even seemed a little delighted to hear about the ryokan arrangement, which gave me some sense of comfort. I started to miss Satoh San; he would have surely given me all sorts of information about ryokan by now.

By the time we landed in Oita, it was about 6.30 in the evening. The ryokan was a little far away from the Sony plant, towards the Oita city. We took a taxi and rolled into the large driveway of the ryokan, which looked remarkably different from our regular business hotel. The structure of the ryokan resembled a mini-Japanese palace designed in traditional architecture, reminiscent of the samurai era. There was a beautiful Japanese garden around the premises. The driveway was paved with small pebbles. The entrance to the hotel lobby was also designed in a very traditional style, with sliding doors made of *shoji* screens. (Shoji screens are the traditional Japanese-style doors and windows made of opaque white paper.) This certainly didn't look anything like a dump. In fact, quite the opposite; it looked too extravagant to stay in, for a business trip. I was already very happy with what I had seen from the outside. My slight paranoia was completely replaced by pleasure. For some reason, the facade and the grandeur of the ryokan reminded me of something that could belong to the yakuza.

Yakuza is the Japanese mafia and can be dangerous. They have their own sets of codes, rituals and lifestyles that they strictly adhere to. One of their interesting rituals is to cut off half of their little fingers as atonement for any wrongdoing. The yakuza are also well-known for having tattoos all over their bodies. The women in the yakuza families are also known to have elaborate and colourful tattoos. The yakuza members always dress in sharp black suits with neatly brushed, slick hair. They are also known to drive in large black Mercedes Benz sedans with tinted windows. The top yakuza members are usually very rich and engaged in all kinds of business, both legal and illegal, from owning taxi companies to hotels (and I am sure, ryokans) to operating shady nightclubs and hostess bars. While there has been a steady decline in their numbers, the yakuza still is very much in existence today, and the Japanese people remain fearful of them. While walking into the ryokan thinking about the Japanese yakuza for no apparent reason, I remembered that Toda San had once warned me about them when I first got to Japan. As she was telling me about the Shinjuku district, where I was staying at the Hyatt, she had cautioned me not to venture around in certain areas by myself, especially in the entertainment district known as Kabuki-Cho. Apparently, many of the clubs in that place were owned by the yakuza. I am not sure why I started to think about the yakuza looking at this beautiful ryokan—perhaps because I had seen one too many gory movies like Quentin Tarantino's *Kill Bill*.

As we entered the lobby area, we were greeted by a couple of young lady attendants wearing very beautiful and colourful kimonos, at the main entrance. They offered us slippers in exchange for our shoes. Taking your shoes off to enter homes or some offices, especially manufacturing sites, was common. I figured this being a traditional inn, it was natural to leave our shoes in the lobby. But I wondered what would happen if they accidentally misplaced some of our shoes. I imagined all of us going into the Sony meeting the next morning in suits, ties and socks only. They placed our footwear in the wooden shoe lockers on the right side of the entrance and handed us the keys to our respective shoe lockers.

The lobby area was small and sparsely decorated. The place was well-lit by lamps resembling old-style Japanese lanterns. Two different ladies, equally immaculately clad in colourful kimonos, checked us in. Once we were all checked in, Hasegawa San announced that he had made a special dinner reservation for us. He seemed to be full of surprises that evening, hoarding information and enjoying dispensing it on a need-to-know basis, I thought. We all agreed to meet back at the lobby in about thirty minutes.

My room was on the second floor of the two-storey ryokan, and instead of the elevator, I took the traditional-looking wooden staircase from the lobby area, lugging my small carry-on with me. It was quite spacious, much larger than the tiny rooms of the business hotels. The floor was made of *tatami* mats. These traditional mats are made of tightly woven straw, and the Japanese seem to really like tatami flooring. It is common for Japanese homes to have a traditional tatami room (with its floor made of these tatami mats). Just like the lobby, the room was also very sparsely decorated, almost devoid of any furniture.

There was a thick futon laid out on one side of the room with very comfortable-looking white blankets on top. Clearly, this was going to be my bed for the night. A small, rectangular coffee table was placed in the middle of the room. Instead of chairs, it was surrounded by four cushions meant for floor sitting. A very tall and intricate flower arrangement on one side of the wall, inside a small, raised alcove, caught my attention. There was a bright light on the ceiling almost on top of it, shining down on the flower arrangement, highlighting its elegance. This was the only piece of decoration in the room. I would later learn that these alcoves with traditional flower arrangements or a piece of Japanese art are known as *tokonoma*, and are common features of tatami rooms. The Japanese mantra of beauty in simplicity was on clear display everywhere. To my great delight, the room had an attached bathroom, small yet functional, with all the usual amenities. I noticed a set of sliding shoji doors across the room, slightly ajar. I walked towards them and slid them open to find a small patio with two very low, Western-style chairs and a small sidetable, facing a well-lit Japanese garden. Impressed with this upgrade from our usual business hotel, I made a mental note to thank Hasegawa San later.

After a quick inspection of my room, I headed downstairs to meet up with our sarariman team for dinner; everyone was already gathered in the lobby. Exactly on schedule, an older lady, also wearing a bright and colourful kimono, ushered us into what seemed like a private dining area with tatami floors. I wasn't a big fan of floor sitting, as I am unable to fold my legs comfortably like most of the contortionist Japanese sarariman. Whenever I sat on the floor on such occasions, I would find myself almost constantly changing sitting positions to feel comfortable. This, in turn, would make me self-conscious, causing further discomfort. I had been to some Japanese restaurants that offered the look of floor-sitting, but with a hole under the table. So the guests didn't have to fold their legs and were essentially sitting like they would on chairs. I quickly took a peek under our low and long dining table, but realized that there would be no such luck that night.

While I was very pleased with our accommodation at the ryokan, the ten-course dinner was simply out of this world. It started with a flavoured miso soup, a traditional and staple Japanese soup, and assorted sashimi so fresh that each one melted in my mouth. After the appetizers, there was a parade of delightful and tasty Japanese delicacies, consisting of a variety of pickled vegetables, various tempura, fried fish, small bites of tender beef steaks and so on. All the dishes were served in traditional Japanese colourful plates and bowls. We were also served an egg-based pudding-type dish in a cup called *chawanmushi*. I fell in love with this dish that night and would eat it every chance I got from then on. There was also a very tasty, mildly sour Umeboshi or pickled Japanese plums ('ume' is a type of Japanese plum) along with local sake. Our waitresses were very attentive to all our needs, pouring our drinks as soon as our glasses were empty. Each time they brought in a new dish, they would introduce it in Japanese and Shibata San would translate it for me.

'Asif San, these umeboshi are from a local farm. Typically, they can be very sour, but the chef pickled the ume in his own mild vinegar-based mixture and so it has a very nice, sweet-and-sour taste', he informed me.

'Ahh, she explained that this fish was caught this afternoon by a local fisherman, so it is very fresh, Asif San, please try it', and so on. The whole experience was just wonderful and satisfying.

I wanted to show my gratitude to Hasegawa San for such lovely arrangements.

'Thanks a lot, Hasegawa San. This looks like a lovely nice place. And the dinner was simply exquisite. By the way, my room is quite spacious and nicer than the business hotels. Thanks for such excellent arrangements.'

Before Hasegawa San got a chance to answer, Shibata San chimed in, 'Of course this is better than a business hotel, Asif San. This is a Japanese ryokan, after all.'

'I am happy you like it, Asif San', Hasegawa San replied.

'May I ask why you said you were sorry at the airport for making reservations here? This is clearly a better place to stay', I enquired.

'I think some foreigners may not like ryokans because it is too Japanese-style. So I was not sure if you would like it here.'

'I love it, Hasegawa San. No worries', I assured him. 'By the way, why don't we stay here from now on. Is it very expensive?'

'Yes, it is a little more expensive, but depends on season', Hasegawa San said. 'Currently the price is a little higher than the business hotel. No problem to stay here next time.'

'Let's do that, Hasegawa San. In fact, let's try to stay here whenever we travel to Oita', I said.

Shibata San and Umehara San were in full agreement with me. They both expressed their surprise that I hadn't stayed at a ryokan before, even though I had been in Japan for over a year and a half.

'You have to be more adventurous, Asif San. This is a great chance to experience Japan. You must take advantage of it', Shibata San recommended.

I had to agree with him. Indeed, we should take advantage of it. In fact, we *were* taking advantage of it, but perhaps not as much, with me being busy with work and Sharmeen attending her classes almost seven days a week. Also, it wasn't always so easy to travel around with a toddler.

As I was about to bid my goodnight in the lobby, Shibata San mentioned that they were all heading for the onsen or the public bath, and he invited me to join them. I was very tired after the long day and politely declined.

'I thought you just agreed to experience Japan. What happened, Asif San?' Shibata San asked with a smile.

'Ahh sure, true, Shibata San, perhaps tomorrow', I said, smiling back, trying to wiggle out of the situation. I apologized and quickly headed for my room.

The next morning, we met for breakfast and the topic of ryokan came up again. Shibata San took over the role of Satoh San and proceeded to give me a detailed introduction. These traditional Japanese-style inns are apparently very popular among both Japanese and foreign tourists. They can be found all over the country, and there are even vacation spots built around some of the more famous ryokans. While design and decor may vary, ryokans generally follow traditional Japanese architecture and design, such as shoji sliding doors, tatami floors, and a Japanese garden. They incorporate many traditional elements of Japanese life, like sleeping on the floor, offering local cuisines, onsens and so on.

'Staying at a ryokan is the best way to experience true Japan, Asif San', Shibata San added. After this experience, I couldn't agree more. Language can be an issue for foreign guests as most ryokan employees can't speak English. I couldn't help but think that perhaps it is by design to keep the gaijins away.

Shibata San said the best thing he enjoyed about ryokans was the onsen. The closest thing to an onsen in the West would be a spa with large hot tubs. Almost all ryokans offer this communal bathing facility. While some of them are just regular baths with hot water, like a jacuzzi, most of them use hot-spring water. Unfortunately, Japan lies in an area known as the Ring of Fire, where more than 10 per cent of the world's active volcanos are located, making it prone to natural disasters. Throughout its long history, the country has suffered numerous natural disasters related to volcanic eruptions and earthquakes, the latest one being the unfortunate incident at the Fukushima

Daiichi Nuclear Power Plant in 2011. However, one benefit of being close to the Ring of Fire is that it has an abundance of natural hot springs filled with minerals, some with therapeutic qualities. Most onsens pipe in water from their local hot springs. Visiting onsens is an extremely popular pastime among Japanese people of all ages. Some areas of the country are particularly famous for onsens, and it turned out that we were very close to one. Oita is near a city called Beppu, apparently one of the top onsen spots in Japan, Shibata San said. Our ryokan also had a very nice onsen, and that's where the team went after our dinner the night before. I had heard that all guests were required to be naked inside these public baths. As much as I would have loved a good soak in a hot bath and wanted to bask in this Japanese tradition, I didn't feel comfortable bathing in the nude with a whole bunch of sarariman.

After our breakfast and learning many things about the Japanese onsen tradition, we all headed to Sony for our meeting. When we arrived at the plant, Satoh San was already in the lobby, waiting for us. As always, we had a very long and tiring but fruitful meeting with the Sony folks. It was clear from their tone that they were very pleased with all progress the team had made so far. Usually, we would always invite the team to dinner after our meetings. But this time, before we got a chance to invite them, my two friends from Sony, Sakamoto San and Mitsumata San, invited us to dinner. Apparently, this was going to be their treat for a change. I was a little surprised by this as Sony had never invited us to dinner before; it had always been the other way around. I looked around to see if there was any reaction from any of our sarariman. If there was, they didn't show it and no one mentioned anything. We politely accepted their gracious offer and agreed to meet at the restaurant before taking our leave.

As we got into the taxi to head towards the restaurant, almost at once, all of us expressed our surprise at their dinner invitation.

We couldn't help but wonder if they were now officially ready to declare us the recipient of their big business. While we were pretty sure that we were going to get the business, Sony hadn't officially announced it to us yet. We all happily agreed that such a decision was forthcoming.

It was another elaborate and tasty Japanese meal, served with similar attention and care as the night before. Everyone seemed to be in a great mood, and as usual, we were all having a good time eating all the delicious food, drinking the local sake, chatting away. Shibata San and Satoh San were helping with all the necessary translations to ensure that I was participating in the conversation as well. Towards the end of our meal, after most of us had had quite a few rounds of sake, Sakamoto San stood up and announced that apparently Sony had made a decision about awarding the business to us. Then he put his finger on his lips, indicating that it was still a secret, even though he said it quite loudly for everyone to hear. He added that Sony would soon officially inform us of this good news. Of course, we were all ecstatic to hear this. All our efforts over the many months, all the extensive travel, hours of meetings and scores of dinners and karaoke sessions, were about to pay off. We ended our dinner party on that good note, hugging each other as we said our sayonaras for the night.

When we returned to the hotel, Shibata San said that the team was heading for the onsen and insisted that I join them this time. I tried to wiggle my way out of it again, but this time, he seemed quite adamant.

'You must experience onsen while in Japan, Asif San. Especially this place is famous for it', he insisted.

'How can you be a sarariman if you haven't taken naked baths with other sarariman?' he questioned, bursting out laughing. *Well, he has a point*, I thought. Perhaps this is an official part of the initiation process to be defined as a sarariman. I agreed to join them.

'Please change into the *yukata* in your room and come down', Satoh San instructed and then pointed in the direction of the onsen.

'By the way, you will see two entrances. Please use the one with the blue curtain. Do not use the one with the red curtain, Asif San', Satoh San cautioned me.

Apparently, the blue-curtained entrance led to the men's area of the onsen, while the red curtain led to the women's area. It was good to know that the bath area was separated by gender.

'But don't worry if you enter through the red curtain, Asif San. You will enjoy it more. And they will forgive you since you are a gaijin', Shibata San said with another of his boisterous laughs.

Glad to be armed with this very important piece of intelligence to prevent any possible embarrassment, I headed to my room to change into my yukata to join them at the onsen. Before that, I quickly asked Satoh San where I would find this yukata, whatever it was. Apparently, yukata is a Japanese kimono-style attire. One wears it like a robe. A yukata is tied with a wide and long colourful piece of cloth known as an *obi*. Satoh San said that there should be a yukata in my room. Indeed, I had seen it the previous night, laid on top of the futon.

Once I got back into my room and changed into my yukata, I regretted my decision to join the team in the onsen, worried about having to appear in my birthday suit. What the hell was I thinking? But it was too late to back down now. Part of me wanted to partake in the onsen experience but having to do so in the nude with a bunch of sarariman dampened my enthusiasm a little. I walked down the wooden stairs, each step more reluctant than the next, and after a long couple of minutes, arrived at the entrance. Sure enough, there were two entrances, one with a blue curtain on the right and the other with a red one on the left side. There was something written in Japanese on each of the curtains in Japanese, but no sign or diagram to indicate which one was the male or female entrance. For a split second, the devil on my left shoulder made me recall what Shibata San had said about acting like an ignorant gaijin and encouraged me to take a sneak peek. But luckily, the pleading from the angel on my right shoulder and the image of a very angry Sharmeen were enough to make me stop at the thought of such an indecent act. Besides, surely, the women inside the onsen would not appreciate such intrusion.

As I went through the set of blue curtains, I immediately arrived at what looked like a men's locker room. An attendant passed me two sets of towels almost right at the entrance—one large and a small one. There were a few people drying themselves and changing in the area. I saw a sliding glass door on the opposite side of the room, which I figured was the entrance to the main bath area. Not knowing the exact onsen custom, I tried to see what others were doing. Following some of them, I took off my yukata and slid it inside one of the lockers. I wrapped myself with the larger towel and bravely walked towards the sliding door. As soon as I went through the doors, I was greeted by a whiff of very warm and humid air. There was also a faint smell of sulfur, most likely coming from the volcanic spring water, I thought. I was surprised to see how large the bath area was. I was expecting a single large tub, but there were several of them, all containing bodies of warm water. There was also a large area with rows of handheld showers pretty low on the floor with small and very low sitting stools. Not knowing exactly what to do first, I started to look for my sarariman colleagues. Out of nowhere, a fully naked Satoh San appeared and almost immediately and thankfully started to provide some guidance regarding the proper onsen etiquette. Satoh San explained that before getting into any of the baths, I would first have to shower and rinse myself thoroughly with the soap and shampoo provided in the shower area. Once I had cleaned myself, only then was I allowed to enter the hot baths. He explained that the different baths are kept at different temperature levels, some hotter than others, and I could use whichever one I wanted to. He pointed at one of the baths where the rest of the gang were soaking. Then he left me almost as suddenly as he had appeared, quickly walking towards one of the baths.

There were quite a few naked sarariman going through the ritualistic cleansing process, essentially taking a shower, just as Satoh San has asked me to do. They were all sitting down on the small plastic stool while using the handheld shower heads. I sat down in one of the empty spaces, showered and shampooed, as instructed by Satoh San. I had never showered sitting down; it actually felt very comfortable. Once I was cleansed, I looked for my sarariman colleagues again. I found them inside one of the larger baths in the middle of the room. Before I got in, Satoh San advised me to first splash myself with the water from the bath using a small wooden bucket that was next to it. This would help the body to adjust to the sudden warmth of the water, he said. I did as I was told and then sank into the bath, a little bit at a time, allowing my body to adjust to what felt like boiling hot water. Soon, my body acclimated to the heat, and it started to feel great. Within a minute or so, I felt completely relaxed as all my muscles seemed to really enjoy and embrace the hot volcanic water. It seemed to wash away all the stress and pain from the day. Everyone else also seemed to be relaxed, completely uninhibited and oblivious of the nakedness all around, enjoying the hot baths, accompanied by the soothing sound of continually splashing water. Soon, I also forgot that I was not only naked in public but also taking a bath with a whole bunch of other naked sarariman.

Ever the senpai, Satoh San explained that the Japanese people always take hot baths at night before going to bed. This is known as *ofuro*, and almost every home in Japan is equipped with a deep bathtub for this purpose, some quite sophisticated with electric gadgets to automatically control the level and temperature of the water. I could relate to this as we had one in our home in Tokyo, and I had seen all the digital switches and the display. But we had never used it. Once the ofuro is filled, the same bath is used by all the family members. Just as in the onsen, each person takes a shower and after cleaning themselves, soaks in the ofuro for twenty or thirty minutes. Sitting chin-deep inside the hot bath in our onsen, I felt that this nightly ofuro ritual was a very good idea.

The next day, we flew back to Tokyo. I felt extremely satisfied, not only with our imminent success with Sony but also with the rewarding experience of the traditional ryokan and the onsen. They were just added bonuses. I made a mental note to ensure that I take Sharmeen and Farhana for a ryokan and onsen experience at some point in the near future. I was sure that Sharmeen would love the ryokan, but I wondered how she would feel about the onsen, taking a naked bath with a bunch of other naked ladies. As gaijins, we were not very comfortable with such surroundings, but heaven awaits on the other side if one can overcome one's inhibitions. Having achieved that it felt like I had passed a crucial sarariman initiation process.

Chapter 15

Kyoto

With the Sony business win behind me, I started to focus on similar big business opportunities from some of the other top semiconductor companies. While the southern island of Kyushu is considered to be the Silicon Valley of Japan, there are a few well-known semiconductor and electronics companies with headquarters located in the Kansai region of Japan, such as Matsushita (parent company of Panasonic) and Mitsubishi, particularly in and around Kyoto and Nagoya area. As our business potential started to grow, so did our number of shuchchos or business trips to these cities in the Kansai area.

The main island of Honshu is made up of five regions. The Kanto Plain is located in the middle and eastern part of the island. With big cities like Tokyo and Yokohama located in this region, it is the most densely populated area of the island. The Kansai region lies about 300 miles west of Tokyo. Since the ancient cities and old capitals of Nara and Kyoto are in this region, Kansai serves as the heart of Japan's history and culture. Osaka and Kobe are two other big cities located in this region of the main island.

One day, exhausted after a gruelling four-hour morning meeting with a very demanding customer in Kyoto, Shibata San and I decided to relax over a nice Japanese lunch. He took me to one of his favourite sushi places inside the Kyoto station.

With its vast open atrium in the centre, Kyoto Station includes a couple of hotels, a multi-storey shopping mall and numerous restaurants. The seamless design makes it difficult to realize where the elaborate shopping area ends and the station begins. The open atrium has one of the highest and longest series of escalators laid out in a series that I have seen anywhere in the world. As Shibata San and I rode the series of escalators to the top floor, I was standing next to him on the left side. Shibata San leaned towards me and whispered that I should move and stand on his right side, instead. I looked up and down the long series of escalators and realized that everyone was indeed standing on the right-hand side and people who were walking up the escalator were doing so from the left side. Something about the whole setup regarding this standing protocol seemed a little different to me, even though I quite couldn't figure out what it was.

'In Kansai, people stand on the right side of the escalator, allowing people to pass on the left', Shibata San told me in a very low voice. 'This is only in Kansai area, Asif San. In all other places in Japan, people stand on the left. You see, Kansai people are a little different from Tokyo people. They also speak in a special dialect, by the way.'

Now I understood why things looked a little different to me. Having lived in Tokyo, I was used to standing on the left side when taking escalators. This is a courtesy that I found almost all Japanese to follow everywhere I went. So I had been following the same polite protocol and was used to standing on the left on escalators. Indeed, everyone was following the opposite of what I was used to. I also learnt that aside from this unique escalator etiquette, the overall characteristics of the people from the Kansai region can be quite different from those of the Kanto Plain and other parts of Japan. People from the Kansai region tends to be more direct, open, cheerful, boisterous and gregarious, compared to the rest of Japan. It is not uncommon for them to engage in small talk or strike up a conversation with a complete stranger, which is rare in other parts of the country, especially in Tokyo. Kansai people are also known for their business acumen. A common form of greetings in the Kansai region is '*mo kare makka*', which literally translates to 'are you making money?' I was glad to learn about the uniqueness of the people from the Kansai region. After Shibata San mentioned it to me, I started to notice these distinct characteristics in them as I met many people from this area during my many visits.

As we rode up the escalator, there were large billboards and digital screens all around us, advertising some of the top tourist attractions in Kyoto. One of its most recognizable landmarks seemed to be commonly displayed in all these advertisements—a picture of the Kinkaku-ji or Temple of the Golden Pavilion under clear blue skies, with its magnificent reflection on the very still waters of a pond. I have seen this picture hundreds of times in many Japanese calendars, travel brochures and books. Shibata San saw me looking at the picture and asked, 'Have you ever been there when it snows? It's really gorgeous.'

'What snow, I have never been there, period. I would love to visit, though. One of these days . . .'

Shibata San was shocked that I had never visited Kinkaku-ji.

'Unbelievable, Asif San. You have been to Kyoto so many times and never visited this most famous temple? I can't believe it', he said, sounding genuinely disappointed.

I explained to him that, indeed, I had visited Kyoto multiple times, but it was always on business trips with the schedule usually packed with meetings and many times, followed by dinners with customers. Alternatively, we always returned to Tokyo right after our meetings were over. 'So, I never got a chance to do any sightseeing here. And I haven't had the time to take a vacation, it has been so busy', I admitted.

As we were chatting away during our sushi lunch, suddenly Shibata San enquired if I needed to return to Tokyo right away.

'Even if we leave after lunch, we will arrive around 4 p.m. so we won't be able to return to the office', he seemed to want to remind me for some reason.

'That's true. By the time we arrive at the office, it will be past five o'clock. No point in doing that. I am planning to head straight home from Tokyo Station. But no, I don't have anything special planned.'

'Great, I am taking you for a quick tour of Kyoto today', Shibata San declared. 'I know the city well. I guarantee that it will be worth your while.'

Shibata San did have a point, I thought. Even if we left now, we wouldn't arrive till very late in the afternoon in Tokyo. Besides, what was the point of spending two and a half hours inside the Shinkansen, especially on such a gorgeous day? The key benefit, of course, was being able to return home to Sharmeen and Farhana in the evening. But I decided that a tour of Kyoto with Shibata San was worth missing an evening at home. *It would be good for me to experience Kyoto with an experienced Japanese person so that I could guide Sharmeen when we visit the city*, I justified to myself. I didn't need any further convincing; I readily agreed to Shibata San's proposal.

Of course, I was well aware of the historic significance of Kyoto. It is one of the most historic cities and served as the capital of Japan for over a thousand years (from 794 to 1868), before Tokyo was established as the new capital during the Meiji Restoration.[8] There are seventeen UNESCO World Heritage Sites in this ancient capital and it is one of the most visited

---

[8] In 1868, the Japanese political system was restored under the emperor, shifting power to Emperor Meiji and ending the 250-year reign of the Tokugawa Shogunate. It is a significant event in Japanese history and is known as the Meiji Restoration.

cities in Japan by foreign tourists. I was well-informed about the city, including its famous historic spots. I was very excited that afternoon to be able to finally visit some of these sites.

Shibata San took me to the Kinkaku-ji first, perhaps because he saw me gazing at its photos at the station. Despite seeing numerous photos and videos of the place since my childhood in calendars, books, movies and documentaries, I was simply awestruck as I stood across the small pond and found myself staring at the magnificent Zen Buddhist temple with its gold-plated roof. From across the small pond with its full bright reflection in the calm water, it looked just magical. The temple was established in the late fourteenth century. Unfortunately, like many historic buildings in Japan, the original and subsequent rebuild constructions burnt down several times due to earthquakes and other natural disasters. The current structure that I was staring at was built in 1955, but apparently it resembles how it originally looked. The temple is surrounded by a lush Japanese garden. After spending an hour strolling around the beautiful garden of Kinkaku-ji, we decided to leave for our next sightseeing spot. Shibata San said that it wouldn't be wise for me to leave Kyoto without paying a visit to Nijo Castle. So we took a taxi and off we went to our next destination.

Our taxi let us out right outside the castle area. Again, I knew the history of this famous castle well and I couldn't believe that I was standing right in front of it. The castle compound was over an area of sixty-nine acres. There was a lot of ground to cover and it would take hours if we really wanted to soak in the whole place. Shibata San recommended that he get me a taste of the place by taking me to some of the key historic parts of the castle. This way, I would have an incentive to come back again to really see the place, he justified, smiling. Built in the seventeenth century, Nijo Castle served as the residence of the Tokugawa Shogunate.[9] Shibata San seemed to know the place relatively well and whisked me around some of the best parts of it. The highlight was seeing some of the main halls with large mural-like paintings all around, depicting cherry blossoms, scenes from olden Japan, and exotic animals. *Indeed, I must come back to really see this place*, I thought as we left Nijo Castle after only an hour.

By the time we left the castle, it was 4.30 p.m. and I was ready to head back to Tokyo. But Shibata San seemed to have other plans. He said that we would now head towards one of the most famous Buddhist temples known as Kyomizu-dera. I had never heard of the place before, but Shibata San insisted that it was a must-see before we finished our whirlwind tour of the city. I had no objection whatsoever as I was quite enjoying visiting all these famous historic sites.

Kyomizu-dera sits along a wooded hillside next to a small waterfall on the outskirts of Kyoto. Indeed, it is one of the famous Buddhist temples in Japan and people from all over the country come to visit the place all year round. Originally founded over 1,200 years ago, the current structures of Kyomizu-dera were built in 1633. The taxi dropped us off a little way from the temple. We had to walk up a relatively crowded narrow path with all kinds of souvenir and gift shops, as well as small stores selling local delicacies. After walking for about ten minutes, we arrived at the main entrance of the temple. Shibata San said that he planned to show me something very special. But he wouldn't tell me what

---

[9] The Tokugawa Shogunate were the military rulers or Shoguns of Japan, during the Edo Period from 1603 to 1867. It was established by Tokugawa Ieyasu after winning the famous Battle of Sekigahara. This period is known for a time of political stability, relative calm, internal peace and economic growth after hundreds of years of continual feudal rivalry. This final period of a traditional Japanese political system lasted till the Meiji Restoration.

it was: apparently, he wanted it to be a surprise. It turned out that Kinkaku-ji wasn't just one temple but a compound with series of temples, all built in traditional Japanese style, each probably having its own significance. As we walked through the compound, I couldn't enjoy the place as Shibata San rushed me through most of it, much to my annoyance. Finally, as we arrived at the far end of the temple, I noticed a long wooden walkway resembling a broadwalk, which appeared to jut out from one of the temple's main halls along the hillside. The place seemed very crowded compared to the rest of the temple compound. As we managed to make our way through the crowd and reach the long railing along the edge of the walkway, I realized that we were about three or four storeys high along the adjacent hillside. It was then that I realized why Shibata San had been rushing me all this time. There was a clear and unobstructed view of Kyoto city in front of us with the beautiful red coloured temples of the Kyomizu-dera on our right, and the sun was about to set on the horizon. No wonder this particular spot was so crowded. We stood there silently among the others, watching the sun slowly set on Kyoto city. It was a remarkable sight.

'Wow, that was really spectacular. Thanks, Shibata San. Seems like a perfect ending to our mini Kyoto tour', I said.

'But our tour is not over yet, Asif San. You can't leave Kyoto without visiting Gion', Shibata San replied.

'You mean you really want to continue? But its already dark, Shibata San.' I was eager to head back home. I didn't want to arrive home too late.

'I Understand, but it is best to visit Gion during the evening. Let's go have dinner there before we head back. If you are lucky, you may even see a *geisha*', Shibata San replied, trying to entice me.

And it worked. My ears perked up when I heard him say 'geisha'. I had just finished reading the book *Memoirs of a Geisha* by Arthur Golden in the Shinkansen on our way over to Kyoto.

I found the story in the book about how a little girl became a geisha in Kyoto and the detailed account of the geisha culture and customs, simply fascinating. I realized why the name Gion sounded so familiar. Gion of Kyoto is the most famous geisha district in all of Japan. There was no way I was about to pass up Shibata San's offer to visit Gion.

Geishas are traditional Japanese performance artists who, for centuries, had provided entertainment and companionship to the lords, *daimyos*, and nobles of Japan. The tradition continues to this day. Geisha or *geiko* and *maiko* (apprentice geisha) as they are known in Kyoto, remain an enigma to the outside world, made even more popular by Golden's book, which was later made into a movie. The story in the book takes place in Gion and it describes the area in detail. Established as an entertainment district during the Sengoku period[10] in the fifteenth century, Gion remained the geisha capital of Japan for centuries. While the geisha tradition continues to this day in Gion, albeit at a much smaller scale, this famous district now houses some of the city's most expensive dining establishments and traditional *ochaya* or teahouses.

By the time we took a taxi from the Kyomizu-dera, it was totally dark. The taxi dropped us off at a beautifully well-lit and wide street. Shibata San said that it was known as the Hanami-Koji Street. It is the most popular area of the Gion district, which was obvious from the crowd and the number of foreign visitors walking around. I couldn't believe that I was standing in Gion on the same day I had finished reading Arthur Golden's well-known book about the geisha tradition.

We walked along the Hanami-Koji Street for five minutes, then I followed Shibata San, turning left into a small alleyway. Immediately, the scenery changed from the modern, busy city

---

[10] The Sengoku Period from 1467 to 1615 is considered to be Japan's most tumultuous period in terms of continual civil wars all over the country. It is also known as the 'Warring States Period'.

street to old traditional Japan. The concrete buildings with modern shops on the main street were replaced with small traditional wooden homes on both sides of the narrow alleyway. Shibata San explained that these traditional wooden homes were known as *machiyas*. Apparently, Gion has the most concentration of machiyas in all of Japan. Most of them have been turned into expensive and exclusive restaurants or teahouses. I was hoping to run into a couple of geikos or maikos, but unfortunately, we didn't see any. After exploring the alleyways for about thirty minutes, we emerged again at one end of the Hanami-Koji Street. I noticed another traditional shrine across from where we were. Seeing the shrine, Shibata San said, 'Ah, this is also a very famous shrine, Asif San. Let's make a quick stop.' He immediately started to cross the street before I got a chance to answer. It was already late, and I decided that there was no harm in touring another famous site in Kyoto when we were so close to it. I followed Shibata San through the main gate into the temple compound. While it was nothing like the Kyomizu-dera temple, I could tell that it was also a fairly old shrine, apparently originally established in the seventh century. Shibata San led me to the main hall of the temple. Then, to my surprise, without saying a word, he went into prayer mode with his eyes shut and hands clasped together. After thirty seconds or so, he opened his eyes and clapped twice.

'I just wanted to say a prayer to Kami Sama (god)', Shibata San said, smiling.

'Good. I didn't realize that you are a religious man.'

'I just prayed so that we can find a good restaurant in Gion to eat, Asif San', Shibata San said and burst out laughing.

Well, I was hungry and hoped that his Kami Sama would grant him his prayers. We took another taxi to what looked like a narrow road along a canal lined with willow trees. There were restaurants alongside the canal with outside seating. Apparently, this was a well-known area of Gion, known as Shirakawa with many traditional restaurants. Shibata San's prayer paid off, and we were able to find a nice restaurant that specialized in Kyo-ryori, or food cooked in traditional Kyoto style. After yet another delicious Japanese dinner, as we left the restaurant, I saw two women wearing beautiful kimonos walking towards us. What got my attention was their footwear. They were wearing the traditional wooden Japanese sandals known as *geta*.

'Asif San, geikos!' Shibata San leaned towards me and whispered in excitement. 'Your tour of Kyoto is now really complete.'

It was exactly like the hundreds of pictures I had seen in many places. It was easy to tell who they were as their whole faces were painted white, and both of them were wearing bright red lipstick. I realized that the people around me were also kind of staring at them, clearly impressed by this historic Japanese novelty.

Shibata San was right. I felt like my brief tour of Kyoto was quite complete now. Fully satisfied, we made our way to Kyoto station to take the Shinkansen back to Tokyo.

Chapter 16

Where are the *Sarariwoman*?

Headquartered in the outskirts of Tokyo area, Ricoh was another one of our target customers. Our team had been working them for a few months. The main salesperson for Ricoh was Y.C. Park. Originally from Korea, he had been living in Japan for a long time and spoke Japanese fluently. I had got to know him well in the last year and a half. He always seemed like a perfect gentleman. One day YC informed me that Ricoh's procurement team, responsible for the outsourcing, had requested a top-level meeting between our companies. He mentioned that we were at a pivotal point with them; apparently, Ricoh was at the final stage of deciding to award a new business. Hence, this meeting was very important, he added. Some of the senior members of Ricoh were planning on joining the meeting. YC requested that it would be good if we reciprocated and the management joined the meeting, which essentially meant Fujita San, Shibata San and I. We all agreed that it would be good to attend the Ricoh meeting to show our full support. I also invited Satoh San to be a part of it as he had worked with Ricoh before. By this time, I had attended, participated in and presented at many such meetings in Japan, so I was quite used to it. In fact, I felt quite excited at the possibility of winning another big business.

On the day of the meeting, we all took the local trains to get to the closest station to the Ricoh head office. We arrived early and decided to stop by a nearby coffee shop to do some last-minute strategizing on how to best handle the meeting. Then we took a ten-minute cab ride to their office.

In the lobby, we met up with the rest of our sarariman team, who had arrived before us. We were greeted by a polite, immaculately dressed and well-groomed receptionist. We signed in, were given visitors' badges, and escorted to our designated meeting room. The room was quite large with a long executive-style table in the middle, which could easily accommodate more than fifty people. I wondered why they had put us in such a big room and how many people from Ricoh were going to join. I had come to realize that sometimes we could tell how meaningful some of these meetings were depending on the number of attendees. Higher number of attendees invariably meant a higher level of interest. As we settled in, the sarariman from Ricoh started to arrive, each politely bowing as they entered the room. I noticed that there were two women among the Ricoh sarariman. This was new, I thought. We began the important and ritualistic process of exchanging our meishi. As I exchanged meishi with the two women, I paid particular attention to the information on their business cards as I wanted to know what their roles were. I was pleasantly surprised to learn that both of them were engineering managers. They both looked like they were in their late thirties or early forties.

It suddenly occurred to me that all the meetings and encounters I had had so far with Japanese companies, had been with sarariman only. Never once there was a woman present at any of them. The only time women participated was when it was time to bring in refreshments, which were provided by the office ladies. Indeed, the semiconductor industry is more male-dominated, globally, but in the US and Europe, it is not at all uncommon to have female engineers or procurement managers. But I had never experienced this in Japan during my last year and a half of encounters with various semiconductor companies. Indeed, how come I hadn't encountered even one sarariwoman before? Where had they been hiding? Of course, I was aware that by definition, sarariman are men. But it was refreshing to see the two ladies participating in our meeting that morning.

After our brief greeting session, we all sat down and the meeting started promptly. As I was up first, I stood up, thanked Ricoh San (yes, the honorific San is used even for company names) and started to present our company profile. Halfway through my presentation, two elderly office ladies arrived with refreshments. Then I noticed something very strange. As soon as the office ladies entered the room, the two lady engineering managers stood up and assisted the two office ladies in serving the refreshments to the rest of the sarariman. Not one of the men offered to help similarly. After everyone was served, the office ladies left the room, bowing politely and the two lady managers assumed their seats, and we continued with the meeting.

I was no stranger to the male-chauvinistic Japanese culture. Yet, I was a little stunned and had a hard time believing what I had just witnessed. As the two ladies were serving the sarariman along with the office ladies, I could not help but feel a certain sense of annoyance and discomfort. I felt a strong urge to stop presenting and help them serve the refreshments, just to make a statement. Luckily, I managed to control myself, hoping that my disappointment with the situation wasn't apparent in my voice and demeanour. But I found this kind of behaviour quite disappointing.

After this incident, I started to notice an attitude of servitude by our female employees towards our sarariman. For example, whenever we would go to lunch or dinner, I noticed that the ladies would 'take care' of us without fail. It was as if we were visiting their home and they were playing hosts, instead of all of us being out at a restaurant. Most of the time, they would take charge of the ordering and reordering process, and ensure that our glasses were full by refilling our drinks. Whenever I would try to be the gentleman and pour drinks for any of the ladies, I would sense discomfort on their part. Whoever's glass I was trying to fill, would almost invariably try to take the bottle away from me and pour the drink for me first, and then fill her own glass afterwards. In general, it seemed that our female employees would rather serve than be served. It is possible that they were doing that as most of the ladies in the office were junior to most of us, at least in ranks. Regardless, I found myself being very conscious about these kinds of behaviours after what I saw at the meeting at Ricoh. I did bring up the subject with Shibata San and Umehara San, a few times. From my discussions with them, I gathered that it is not uncommon for the Japanese female colleagues to 'take care' of the sarariman at work this way. I mentioned to them that I thought this was a little strange, but as always, they reminded me that this was the Japanese way.

* * *

Traditionally, the majority of Japanese women tend to get into the workforce early in their lives, get married at some point, and then quit their jobs and careers to take care of their husbands and families. The wives are expected to do all the housework and take care of the kids and the family, while the husbands stay focused on work. The pressure and expectation from the wives to perform these duties seem more acute in Japan, compared to most other countries. Because of this, some of them think of marriage more like a prison sentence, which forces them into family commitments and allows very little personal time or freedom. During the past decades, there has been a growing number of women who are bucking the trend by choosing not to get married at all.[11] In fact, this trend is one of the key contributors to the current problem of declining population in Japan.[12]

Our own office was a good sample of this new trend. Most of the female employees were single, and many of them were in their thirties, which is considered a late age for marriage in Japan. They would readily admit that they had no plans to get married and were quite happy to be single. But they are the same group of people who would gladly take care of the sarariman when we were out at lunch or dinner. I would sometimes ask them about their thoughts on this gender issue, complaining about the broader subject of Japanese male-dominated society. My expectation was that they would join in with me in complaining about it as well. But I rarely heard any of them complain. The typical answer was to write it off as a Japanese custom, or resignation. 'This is the Japanese way, Asif San. Shouga nai ne', was the common response, almost all the time.

* * *

Ryoko Yonekura San and Keiko Kitagawa San were two of our best customer service representatives in the office. Kyoko Arimura was Shibata San's administrative assistant, and the three of them seemed to be good friends. Yonekura San had joined the company a year before I had moved to the Japan office. Both Kitagawa San and Kyoko San were new hires. All of them had a good command of English. Over time, they had also become good friends with Shibata San, and through him, Umehara San and I had also got to know them well. We quickly became lunch

[11] https://theconversation.com/as-japan-undergoes-social-change-single-women-are-in-the-firing-line-96636.

[12] https://www.asahi.com/ajw/articles/14365588.

partners, and would all go to lunch a few times a month. The lunch sessions turned out to be opportunities for me to expand my understanding and knowledge of Japanese customs and cultures. With Kyoko San, Kitagawa San and Yonekura San, I also got a sense of the women's perspective on things. They also seemed pleased as these lunches were good opportunities for them to practice their English skills with me. It was a win-win for everyone.

During one of these lunch sessions, Yonekura San suddenly announced that she was getting married in a couple of months. I had heard rumours that she had been dating someone but I didn't enquire about it as it was a personal matter. I figured that others, especially Kitagawa San and Kyoko San, knew more about it. So I was somewhat surprised to see their surprise at this sudden good news. Turns out that for whatever reason, Yonekura San had never discussed her boyfriend with any of them. But we were all very happy for her. That day in the afternoon, Shibata San stopped by my office.

'*Zannen des ne*, Asif San (it's too bad, Asif San).'

What was too bad? I thought perhaps we had lost some business or something.

'Yonekura San is getting married. She is one of our best employees in the customer service department', Shibata San continued.

'What do you mean, Shibata San? You sounded very happy for her during our lunch', I said. I was wondering as to where Shibata San was going with this conversation.

'Well, she will surely quit after she gets married. Don't get me wrong. I am very happy for her, but it will be difficult to replace her.'

'Really? I didn't realize that she was planning on quitting. Yeah, that's too bad. She is really good at what she does. When is she planning on leaving?' I asked.

'Oh, I don't know. Hopefully, not too soon.'

'Did she give you any idea about the timing?'

'No, Asif San, she didn't say anything.'

'But can you find out when she plans to do so, Shibata San? It will be good to know so we can start thinking about hiring her replacement.'

'Not a good idea, Asif San. She never mentioned anything about leaving. So I can't ask her anything about it. If she does, then I will ask.'

I was confused.

'But you said that Yonekura San told you that she was going to quit.'

'No, she didn't say anything. But in Japan, most women quit after getting married. Her husband is a sarariman and works for a large company. I am almost sure that she will quit. Zannen des ne . . .'

It is so common for women to quit working after they get married that Shibata San seemed very confident about his prediction.

Once the news of Yonekura San's wedding became public, I spoke to a few other people about it, and all the sarariman had the same assessment: we would most likely lose her very soon.

I felt bad for Yonekura San, as she was not only a hard worker, contributing to our business growth, but she seemed to enjoy her work. Plus, it was a pleasure to work with her and she was fun to be around. *If she quit on her own, then it would be fine*, I thought. I hoped that she wouldn't be forced to quit just because she was getting married.

Yonekura San invited a few of us from the office to her wedding reception. The venue was a nice restaurant close to the Omotesando, my aunt's favourite high-end shopping district. Shibata San and I decided to go together, since spouses were not invited—quite common in Japanese companies. I contemplated pushing my luck and asking for an exception to bring Sharmeen along as I thought that it would be nice for her to experience a Japanese wedding ceremony. But I decided against it as Yonekura San might find it difficult to say 'no' to me, and I didn't want to put her in that awkward position unnecessarily.

It was a relatively small gathering at a nice upscale restaurant in Omotesando. Most of the invitees seemed to be friends and families of the bride and groom, other than a few of us from the office. While the couple looked gorgeous in their respective wedding gown and tuxedo, I felt a little disappointed that they were not wearing traditional Japanese kimonos. When I got a chance to talk to Yonekura San, I asked her about it. She said that they held the traditional Japanese ceremony earlier that day, where they had indeed worn the traditional clothes, but that was a family-only affair. Then she apologized for not being able to invite me to that ceremony. It's common for Japanese couples to hold Western-style marriage ceremonies where the bride walks down the aisle in a typical Western-style wedding dress. These ceremonies often have no religious significance but have become more of a social norm to follow the Western style of weddings. Some prefer a traditional Shinto-style wedding, where both the bride and groom are dressed in traditional Japanese costumes. Many couples may hold both ceremonies separately—a Shinto-style wedding with close family members, followed by a Western-style reception with broader family members and friends, just like Yonekura San had done.

After the wedding and a week-long honeymoon in Hawaii (a common destination for Japanese newlyweds), Yonekura San returned to work. She seemed very happy, and we were all happy for her. A couple of months passed, and she didn't mention anything about leaving work. We all felt relieved thinking that perhaps she wasn't going to quit after all. Replacing her was not going to be easy, and her talents would be missed, especially when our business was through the roof.

However, after a couple of months, we started to notice some changes in her mood and behaviour. She became very quiet and aloof, and increasingly started to keep to herself. She continued to join us for our monthly lunches, but would rarely speak. Soon, she stopped joining us altogether, each time offering some excuse. We decided that it was best to let her be as she might be going through some personal issues. As long as it wasn't affecting her work, it was none of our business anyway. Both Shibata San and I were a little concerned, thinking that whatever it was, it could lead to her leaving the company. It took another couple of months to find out what was going on.

Office year-end parties, known as *bonenkai*, are big events in Japan. The team decided that we should have a big bonenkai at a nice place to celebrate our business growth. The plan was to have the party towards the end of December at a quaint jazz bar in Shinjuku, not far from the office. The bonenkai was a nice affair with good food and nice wine, great music, some dancing, along with karaoke sessions. Even though I had participated in karaoke with customers before, especially Sony, I always avoided singing because I thought that my singing was best confined within my bathroom walls. With our own team, I didn't feel as inhibited and discovered that I had a natural talent for singing in karaoke bars. To our pleasant surprise, Yonekura San did show up at the party, and it seemed like she was back to her old self again, friendly, jovial, singing along with us into the night. The part ended pretty late, around 2 a.m., and we all went home.

One rule all sarariman live by is no matter how late they party till, or how hungover they are, they must show up to work on time the following morning. How effective and efficient they will be, given their hangover, is another matter. Sure enough, despite partying late into the night, everyone was back in the office the next morning right on time, including me. Everyone except Yonekura San. No one had heard from her or could get a hold of her. The following day, she was once again missing in action. Later that afternoon, Shibata San stopped by my office to inform me that apparently, after the party, Yonekura San had gone to a different bar alone and had got quite drunk. When she didn't return home, her husband got very worried. He finally somehow located her at one of the train stations around Tokyo at around five in the morning and took her home. Yonekura San was too hungover to come to work that day, or even the next day.

On the third day, Yonekura San showed up at the office. She worked quietly for the next couple of days. Then, late one morning, she stopped by my office to apologize for missing work. I wasn't her boss, so I wasn't quite sure why she was apologizing to me, but then again, Japanese people apologize for no reason sometimes, so I didn't think anything of it. I told her not to worry about it and that we were all just worried about her well-being. I also blurted out that we had been particularly concerned recently, because of the change we noticed in her behaviour. Hearing this, Yonekura San sat down and started to cry. I didn't know what to do or say, other than to hand my box of tissue papers to her. In a few minutes, she stopped crying. Then out of nowhere, she poured her heart out to me for the next thirty minutes. I just listened and tried to follow as best I could. The story went as follows.

Yonekura San's husband was a sarariman and was working for a well-known Japanese conglomerate. Like any other sararimans, he would routinely work late and then go out drinking with his colleagues every night. Yonekura San was also working full-time, but she was expected to take care of him. This included the regular chores, such as cooking, cleaning and doing the laundry, etc., which was okay with her. What bothered her was that she was expected to stay up late at night and take care of her husband when he returned home drunk. Even though she was aware of her duties as a Japanese wife and knew what she was getting into, she still had a hard time accepting the reality of this newly married lifestyle.

Yonekura San admitted that she missed her freedom. And to make things worse, her husband had been pressing her to quit her job, and she was expected to comply. She had been trying her best to act like a good wife all these months, but for whatever reason, after the bonenkai party, all her bottled-up frustration had come out. In a show of rebellion, she went to a bar all by herself, got really drunk and got lost till her husband came to her rescue. She refused to go back home with him and ended up having a big fight in public.

While Yonekura San had stopped crying, she still seemed a little distraught as she narrated her story. Of course, I was in no position to give her any kind of marital advice or tell her what to do about her job. Frankly, I was a little taken aback that she had shared all these details with me and felt really bad about her predicament. I didn't know quite what to say or how to respond. Her story seemed to be following the typical Japanese wedding playbook for the wife. Not having any solution for her, I asked if she perhaps wanted to take some time off to think about things. She thanked me and said that it wouldn't be necessary as she had already decided to quit. Before she left my office, she turned around and said, 'Shouga nai, Asif San.'

Yonekura San indeed quit her job a few months later.

* * *

Chapter 17

The Accident

Spring is a beautiful season in Japan, especially during the short two weeks when sakura is in full bloom. The entire country gets into a festive mood as anticipation starts to build for the traditional cherry blossom festival of Hanami. Depending on the location, the sakura season can start anywhere from late March on the southern island of Kyushu to early May on the northern island of Hokkaido. In Tokyo and the surrounding areas, for a week around late March to early April, streets, parks and neighbourhoods seem to come to life with rows and rows of fully blossomed sakura flowers. Sharmeen and I always enjoyed this magical transformation of the whole city and, like the Japanese people, looked forward to this season every year.

Hanami, literally meaning 'flower viewing', is an ancient tradition of enjoying the blooming of sakura.[13] This traditional festival is believed to date back more than 1,000 years, when emperors, nobles and aristocrats spent this short week viewing the sakura blossoms and wrote poems inspired by this mystical

---

[13] There are two kinds of flowers that are part of the Hanami festival. The most popular is the cherry or sakura blossoms found all over Japan, a common sight in cities and urban areas. But there is also the blossoming of plums or ume, which can be found mostly in parks and throughout the Japanese countryside. The white sakura and pink ume blossoms are easily distinguishable due to their colour differences.

and transient scene of natural beauty. The season has a significant place in Japanese culture, symbolizing the fleeting beauty of life. There have been scores of haikus,[14] poems, stories and paintings created around the sakura blossom throughout Japanese history.

These days, Hanami is more like a mass picnic with friends and families sitting underneath sakura trees eating, drinking, singing and relaxing during the festivities. Parks and the countryside fill with crowds as thousands of families and friends search for the perfect spots to gather and enjoy these flowers in full bloom. Many people go early in the morning or even a day earlier, to stake out and claim these coveted spots. Some bring homecooked meals accompanied by wine and sake, while others prefer to have barbecues. Certain parts of the city are well-known for Hanami festivities, such as Ueno Park, which is the most popular site, with about a thousand sakura trees along its main promenade.

During our first year, we were quite mesmerized to see how the neighbourhoods in and around Tokyo seemed to be magically transformed with these sakura trees in full bloom. Even boring, dull and drab alleyways and neighbourhoods become unrecognizably beautiful. We visited the Ueno park to enjoy Hanami during our first year. The following year, we learnt to enjoy this special week at less crowded but equally beautiful venues. Our own neighbourhood street was lined with sakura trees. While we couldn't have a picnic there, we enjoyed taking long walks underneath the rows and rows of sakura trees during this brief period, with Farhana in her stroller. It was during our third sakura season that I got into an unfortunate accident.

Our friends, Azad Bhai and Renu Apa, as I mentioned before, had established and ran a cultural group called Shorolipi

---

[14] Orginating in ancient Japan, haiku is a form of short poetry, consisting of three lines or phrases which follow a certain pattern. It is common to have references to seasons and nature in traditional haikus.

to promote the language, traditions and culture of Bangladesh. Local Bengali expatriates and immigrants were a big part of this group. Typically, during the sakura season, they would hold their annual cultural programme showcasing traditional dances, folk songs, drama and so forth. We got invited to their programme and were looking forward to attending their cultural show. On the day of the programme, we started a little early to first enjoy the hundreds of sakura trees located in Chiyoda-Ku district at the heart of the city, around and alongside the moat of the Tokyo Imperial Palace ground. We walked along the periphery of the Imperial Palace, soaking up the delightfully bright and cool afternoon, among the hundreds of beautiful sakura trees. After hanging out there for a couple of hours, we started for the venue of the cultural show. With the heavy Tokyo traffic due to Hanami festival, and after spending about ten minutes finding a good parking spot, by the time we arrived at the venue, the programme had already started.

After apologizing to the attendant at the entrance for our tardiness, we handed him our tickets and entered the large auditorium. As soon as we made our way in, we were awestruck by what we saw on the well-lit stage at the very front. There were rows of Japanese women, all wearing very colourful Indian traditional saris, singing old folk songs from Bangladesh in Bangla. Having never seen any Japanese woman wearing a sari before, let alone ten of them, and especially hearing them singing in a different language, my brain struggled for a few seconds to make sense of it all. The whole thing seemed surreal, but it was great to see these Japanese women immersed in the Bangla culture. We were later told that most of them were the wives of local expats.

The show continued with many traditional performances. Since we had rushed to see the cultural show after our sakura viewing, we didn't have any time to have our dinner and unfortunately, there was no food available at the venue. Farhana said that she was hungry and wanted some McNuggets from the McDonald's she had apparently seen as we were walking here from the parking lot. I asked one of the volunteers when the programme was supposed to end, and she told me that it wasn't for another couple of hours. Farhana would have a hard time waiting that long for her dinner. Even though I didn't want to miss any of it, I decided that it would be best to quickly go and buy some food before we got too hungry to enjoy the rest of the show. Farhana wanted to come with me to McDonald's, but it was drizzling and a little chilly outside. Besides, I wasn't sure exactly where the outlet was. So I decided not to take her along this time, a decision that would turn out to be one of the luckiest and smartest decisions I have ever made in my life. As Sharmeen distracted our daughter, I snuck out of the auditorium in my quest for Chicken McNuggets.

As I got out of the auditorium into the chilly and crisp spring evening, the drizzling had subsided. I saw the large sign of the McDonald's down the street. It took me about ten minutes to reach the place. I picked up Farhana's favourite chicken nuggets and a couple of Big Macs for me and Sharmeen. I started to walk back along the pedestrian path towards the auditorium hall minding my own business and wondering what programmes I might have missed. I was lamenting not eating dinner earlier, so that I didn't have to miss parts of the show. Suddenly, I heard a loud screeching sound from the small parking lot across the narrow street. My eyes followed the sound, and I saw a small car jerking to a stop, almost hitting the barrier as it tried to exit the parking lot. I paused, trying to understand what was going on. I looked at the vehicle and noticed that it was facing right towards me. Everyone else in the narrow alleyway had also stopped to see what was going on. The car jerked forward again, stopped for a second or so and then rapidly accelerated, coming right at me, breaking the barrier in the process. Realizing what was about to happen, I tried to get out of the way, but before I could, the raging car had crashed into the wall next to me. The whole thing happened so fast that it took me some time to fully understand what had just transpired. The first thing I realized was that I was kind of in between the car and the wall. Then I noticed that part of my left leg was kind of stuck in between. I tried to break free but seemed unable to do it. After jiggling it for a few seconds, I managed to get my left leg free. As I glanced down, I noticed that my pants were torn, and there was blood coming out of my left calf area. At first, I felt no pain. It felt as if I was watching a scene from a movie in slow motion. Despite the blood, my left leg seemed intact. Then I felt it—an excruciating pain in my left leg. The next few moments were a blur. All I remember was that I was lying in the middle of the street, screaming, while a whole bunch of bystanders watched me. No one offered any help, though someone must have called an ambulance as one arrived shortly afterwards. Somehow, the news of the accident had also reached the people inside the auditorium. Soon, I saw Azad Bhai, Sharmeen and Farhana running towards me. While I don't fully remember what happened next, I do remember how happy I was to see them. I was whisked away to the hospital in the ambulance, with Azad Bhai, Sharmeen and Farhana riding with me.

Once I arrived at the hospital, the doctors ran a series of x-rays. I had a deep cut in my calf requiring multiple stitches, bruises all over my left leg and a minor fracture, but luckily, nothing was broken. The doctors still decided to put my left leg in a cast. Still in a state of shock, I don't recall what happened, other than the fact that I was in quite a bit of pain still and kept asking for painkillers. At around two in the morning, they discharged me, and Azad Bhai drove us home. It was very kind of him to abandon his once-a-year cultural show and accompany me during my time of crisis. He was very helpful not only with the translations at the hospital, but also tried to take care of me almost like a brother would, for the next month or so till I got better. He would often call to ensure that I was doing okay. I remain grateful to him for his kindness.

The morning after the accident, when I woke up, it occurred to me what might have happened if I had taken Farhana with me to the McDonald's that evening. If I had taken her in her stroller, it would be in front of me, exactly in between the car and the wall. More often than not, Farhana would accompany me whenever I was out and about, running errands. I thank God for the bad weather that evening, which made me decide not to bring her along to buy our dinner. It turned out to be a blessing in disguise. A chill and sense of fear still run down my spine whenever I think about the accident.

I was homebound for the next two weeks. Toda San called and enquired about the accident, wanting to know every detail. She called me back a couple of days later and said that she had talked to the police about it. She mentioned that clearly, the accident was the driver's fault, and he would most likely pay for all the doctor's fees and any other incidental costs that I might incur. I wondered if the guy was driving drunk. When I asked Toda San about the details of the driver, she said that he wasn't driving drunk or anything like that. He was apparently a young man in his late twenties and did have a driver's licence.

'But he is a *pepaa driva*, Asif San', Toda San added.

'What the hell is a peppa driva?' I asked, feeling quite angry. I had a hard time understanding how someone could get into such a stupid accident.

Toda San said there are thousands of 'paper drivers' all over Japan, especially in big cities like Tokyo. These people go through the required training and tests to get their driver's licence but they hardly ever drive. Most of them don't even own cars. In my case, the guy who hit me had rarely driven, despite having a valid driver's licence. *So what happened that night?* Toda San said that as the driver was trying to exit the parking, he got nervous, for some reason. In his nervous state of mind, instead of putting his foot on the brake to stop for the automatic barrier to open, he had slammed down the gas pedal instead, breaking the parking lot barrier and hitting me. *What an idiot*, I thought. Before hanging up, Toda San said that the police would like to talk to me when I was feeling better.

I was still on crutches after two weeks, but the doctor said that it was okay to be out and about, as long as I didn't put too much strain on my left leg. So I returned to the office. One day, Toda San asked me to join her to visit the Shinjuku Police Station regarding the accident. We met with the officer-in-charge. He was a man of small stature and in his fifties, but something about him sent out an aura of a very capable officer. At first, he wanted to hear my side of the story and then asked me a lot of questions about the accident, trying to verify all the facts. I answered as best as I could, with Toda San helping with the translation. At the end, the officer repeated what Toda San had already told me, that the man was a 'paper driver', and he was clearly at fault. *Great, this should pave the way for me to sue the bastard*, I thought. Then, as we were about to leave, he asked Toda San something. Toda San turned to look at me and asked, 'By the way, has the driver called you or visited you to apologize yet?'

'No, I didn't receive any call from him', I confirmed. I added that I didn't care much about his apology. I was more worried that he would bail on paying my bills related to the accident. When Toda San conveyed this information to the officer, all hell broke loose. The officer seemed outraged and started to yell something in Japanese. I had no clue what he was saying or what was going on, but it was obvious that, for some reason, he was angry. After a minute of ranting, he calmed down, said something to Toda San, and she gestured for me to leave with her.

As soon as we left the police station, I asked her why the officer was so upset. Toda San explained that the officer could not believe that it had been more than two weeks since the accident and the driver hadn't yet apologized to me. Toda San mentioned that she was also a little surprised and upset to hear this. The officer was quite angry at such impertinence and impolite behaviour, and planned to give the driver a piece of his mind.

'What about paying for the medical bills and all? Do you know what is the status of that? Does the driver even have insurance?' I inquired, my American mind more interested in dollars and sense, than the apology.

My question almost seemed to have offended Toda San.

'Of course he will pay, Asif San. That is not the problem. For us Japanese, a real apology is more important than the compensation.'

'Not to me, Toda San', I said. 'Please make sure that the gentleman takes care of the bills.'

Toda San seemed displeased with my priorities but agreed to help me.

This was yet another good example of the important role apologies play in Japanese culture and society. It is common for even a corporate CEO to publicly apologize if his (female CEOs are rare in Japan) company causes some sort of problem for the general consumers and the public. In 2010, when Toyota had to recall 8.5 million cars due to a deadly flaw, Akio Toyoda, the CEO of Toyota, publicly apologized on national TV. When he flew to the US to appear before the Congressional House Committee investigating the issues, the first thing he did was to apologize with his head in a deep bow. Very rarely do we see CEOs of US companies doing anything similar. In America and most other nations and cultures, for that matter, we think of an apology as an admission of guilt, which can lead losing a potential lawsuit. In the polite Japanese culture, an apology doesn't always imply an automatic admission of guilt but that they value the relationship more than their egos.

The next day, Toda San came to see me in my office and said that someone representing the driver had reached out to her and that he wanted to stop by my place as soon as possible.

'For what?' I asked.

'To apologize, of course, Asif San.'

'Really? Does the guy speak any English? I really feel like this will be a waste of time.'

'Asif San, he must apologize to you for all the problems and inconvenience he has caused you. It is okay to apologize in Japanese.'

Somewhat reluctantly, I agreed to see him over the weekend, not sure what exactly this was supposed to solve. 'But if this is part of the culture and something that must be done, best to put this behind us as soon as possible so that we can move on to more important things', I said to myself.

'By the way, the driver sends his apologies for not apologizing sooner', Toda San said, smiling, as she was leaving my office.

I guess even she saw the humour in what she had just said. *All righty then*, I thought. That angry police officer must have given the driver a piece of his mind.

The following Saturday morning, exactly on time, the guilty party appeared at our house. A tall, skinny young man, who looked like he was in his early twenties, and another gentleman with him; I thought that perhaps he was there as a translator. The second guy said something in Japanese, while both of them bowed deeply. I stood there with the door open for a minute, not knowing what to say. They were also quiet, clearly at a loss for words as well. Then I decided to invite them in. They sat down on the couch in our living room, while I took my seat on a sofa across from them. Once again, there were a few minutes of awkward silence. Then, both the driver and the other man stood up suddenly, and almost yelled,

'*Sumimasen, moushiwake arimasen deshita* (I am sorry, and I have no excuse)', bowing at a ninety-degree angle. The other gentleman had stood up as well and was also bowing, but at a less of an angle. It happened so abruptly that I didn't know what to do or say. Both of them remained that way, making me a little uncomfortable. I wondered if I didn't say anything, how long would they remain in those positions. After a couple of minutes, feeling really uncomfortable, I told them in English to take a seat. They seemed to understand and sat back down on our couch. I couldn't help but give an angry lecture to him about his civic duties, reminding him how his carelessness could have caused a fatal accident, and how he should be more careful in the future. I said all this in English, of course, and none of them probably understood a single word I was saying. Besides, in my anger, I was speaking very fast. But they seemed to be listening to me intently, even though both of them had their heads down, looking guilty. At any rate, I felt much better after getting all that anger off my chest.

After a few minutes, again not knowing what to say, I decided that it would be best to try to end this somewhat awkward encounter. So I stood up and thanked them, speaking very slowly, ensuring that they understood that it was time to leave. They seemed to get the message as both of them stood up again. But before leaving, the driver bowed down deeply again, this time holding out both of his arms extended towards me, offering me a very decorative envelope. I wasn't sure what to do. Was he offering me the compensation for my medical expenses? Or was it some sort of a bribe so that I don't sue him? *Should I just take the envelope? What if the compensation isn't enough? Would it be rude to open the envelope and see if indeed there was money inside?* As all these thoughts were going through my head, Sharmeen nudged me to take the envelope from him. I quickly did so to ensure that he regained his posture and left. As soon as I did that, both of them apologized one last time and dashed out of our apartment. To this day, I still don't know who that second guy was.

Curious, I opened the envelope and was surprised to find 50,000 Yen (about $400) worth of shopping vouchers from Mitsukoshi, one of the top Japanese department stores. *What was this about?*

Monday morning, I told Toda San about the visit by the driver and his companion, and about the shopping vouchers.

'But did he apologize, Asif San?' Toda San wanted to confirm.

I confirmed that he did apologize, even though there were significant shortcomings in our communications. Toda San seemed relieved to hear this.

'What's with the vouchers, Toda San?' I asked.

'Those are just a gift, a token of his apology for you and your family, Asif San. It would be rude if he didn't bring anything. I am very glad that it went well. It is good to know that he has finally apologized. I will inform the police officer.'

Toda San also had no idea who the guy that accompanied him was. Perhaps his friend or agent, we gathered.

I wasn't very pleased about the whole thing. Everyone seemed to be focused on the apology part. I didn't have a problem with that, except that no one was talking about ensuring that the driver's insurance company was going to pay for the medical expenses. It had been a few weeks since I had submitted all the related receipts to Toda San. The possibility of suing the driver was still at the back of my mind. It wasn't about any monetary compensation, but for some reason, I felt quite angry at the driver, perhaps because the whole thing seemed so stupid to me. The anger could also be due to fact that I had a hard time shaking the idea that Farhana could have been with me that evening. But I had no clue how to get started with such a process or how lawsuits even worked in Japan. I also didn't know any Japanese lawyers or law firms. I figured that it was unlikely Toda San could help me in this regard, especially since she seemed so satisfied with the driver's apology. I figured I would go to Satoh San for his advice.

Instead of discussing this in the office, I decided to invite Satoh San to lunch. After chit-chatting for a few minutes, I brought up the possibility of suing the driver.

'Has the driver apologized, Asif San?' Satoh San asked.

I couldn't believe that I would have to have another long discussion about the whole apology thing with Satoh San. I quickly confirmed that indeed the driver had apologized, but again repeated my desire to sue the driver. Instead of giving me legal advice, Satoh San gave me a lecture on how trivial, meaningless and unnecessary such lawsuits are and how, unlike in America, they don't play a big part in Japanese society.

'You see, Asif San, Japanese people believe that when we all live in a society, people are bound to make mistakes. The main point is that the person acknowledges his mistake, takes responsibility and learns from it. The process starts with an apology. He must apologize for his mistake. If he apologizes, then the lawsuit becomes unnecessary, in my opinion.'

This was so different from our thought process that I wondered if Satoh San was really being serious or just blowing some Japanese smoke up my rear. But the more I thought about what he said, the more I started to see his logic and his point of view. Indeed, Japanese society is fundamentally not litigious. In case of mistakes, Japanese people generally tend to be more willing to take responsibility and face the consequences, apologize and try to meet their obligations. After giving it some thought, I decided that it was best to leave things as they were and not rock the boat, as I wasn't sure what such a lawsuit would actually solve anyway.

The next day, Toda San showed up in my office again and confirmed that all the paperwork had been settled and indeed the paper driver's insurance will soon reimburse all my related expenses. Indeed, the young driver not only fully compensated me for all my medical expenses, but even paid for my clothes and shoes, which had been damaged during the accident. I was glad that I had decided against litigation. Instead, Sharmeen and I went shopping at the Mitsukoshi Department store in the high-end shopping district of Ginza and bought a beautifully framed, gorgeous replica of Van Gogh's 'Wheat field with Cypresses' painting using the paper driver's vouchers. It is still proudly hanging in the dining room wall of our Boston home, reminding me of the accident.

* * *

Sharmeen was about to get ready for the second part of her medical licensing exam but had to delay her plans by about a month due to my accident. Farhana was well-adjusted and enjoying her time at the hoikuen, but we still felt that it would be nice to have some family around and decided that it was time for the grandparents to visit us again. It would be nice if Farhana could spend a couple of days a week at home, spending some quality time with them. This time, we decided that it was my parents' turn to come and visit us and help us out. After a few rounds of negotiations with them and my youngest sister, she agreed to make some special arrangements to have someone else take care of her twins while my parents spent about three months with us. My mom had always wanted to visit Japan. My dad would be returning here after a few decades. They had visited us in Korea and we had all had a wonderful time. I could sense that both of them were quite excited to come and visit us in Japan.

Their arrival day was about a month after my accident; I was still on crutches. The doctors had told me not to drive, but I found that driving was not so difficult, as my wounds had already started to heal nicely, and driving didn't require any movement of my left leg. I had not told my parents about the accident because I didn't want them to worry about it, especially since I knew that they would be in Japan soon. I figured that it was better to tell them face-to-face, and after I had got much better. Sharmeen and I drove to Narita to pick them up. When they came out of the immigration area and saw me on crutches, both of them were in total shock; my mom looked like she was about to have a heart attack. I told them the whole story about the accident as we drove home. They were a little upset at first that I hadn't mentioned anything about it to them, but they were relieved that I didn't get any serious injuries.

My parents ended up staying with us for about three months and helped us take care of Farhana. Since Sharmeen always commuted by train, she knew the Tokyo train system better than I did. She helped my dad by showing him how to get around by train from our local station to some of the main districts of Tokyo using train and subway maps. My dad had some idea about Tokyo from his trip, which also helped. She also bought Japan Railway (JR) and subway season passes for both of them. This way, they could just use the passes instead of having to buy tickets every time they took the trains or subways. Two to three days a week, my parents would drop Farhana off at the hoikuen and then use their JR passes to go all around Tokyo. I could tell that my dad was enjoying being back in the city that he had visited decades earlier. The rest of the days, Farhana stayed home with her Dada (grandfather) and Dadi (grandmother). After a few weeks, my mom felt that she had done enough exploring and decided to stay home with Farhana. My dad, on the other hand, continued to explore Tokyo. On weekends, I would take them to all the popular places in and around Tokyo. One weekend, I decided that I would take them to the city of Kamakura. This was my first visit to this ancient capital as well.

Kamakura is another ancient city, about an hour south of Tokyo by car. It had played an important role in Japanese history, serving as its capital from 1185 to 1333, during the Kamakura period. The period is significant and perhaps infamous in Japanese history, as it marked the beginning of the feudal system that lasted for the next 400 years. It was also when the samurai warrior class was first established. Today, Kamakura is renowned for one of the most famous icons of Japan—a forty-three-feet statue of the Buddha, known as the Kamakura Daibutsu or the 'Great Buddha of Kamakura'. This large outdoor bronze statue was built in the thirteenth century. Our main intention behind visiting Kamakura was to see this temple. My dad had visited it during his last visit to Japan, and I remembered it well from all the photographs which he had brought back.

We found the place after some effort, parked our car and walked a short distance to the entrance of the temple. We could see the large statue of the Buddha from the street, due to its sheer size. It was set against the backdrop of wooded hills; the day was a little cloudy, giving the area a mystical aura. My dad seemed very glad to be back at this famous spot and kept telling us how different and less developed it had been back then. Now, the outside of the temple area was surrounded by all kinds of souvenir shops. Farhana was quite taken with the large statue and especially enjoyed the fact that we could go inside it as it is hollow. I felt very happy not only to visit a place that I had seen so many photos of when I was growing up, but also because I was able to bring my parents here. After taking a ton of photos with the Daibutsu, we spent the rest of the afternoon exploring the ancient city full of quaint little Japanese stores, coffee shops and restaurants.

After many weekends of similarly exploring almost all the well-known places, we started to visit some of the parks in Tokyo. For a congested city full of concrete buildings, Tokyo has many large parks, each with beautifully manicured gardens and children's playgrounds. On a few Sundays, I would take them to visit Harajuku and Ginza. My mom fell in love with Ginza, which is the most exclusive and expensive shopping district in Tokyo. On Sundays, they close the main street to all traffic so that people can walk freely around the area. My dad preferred to spend time in the electronics district of Akihabara.

The three months flew by quickly, and soon, it was time for my parents to fly back to Dallas. We were not only grateful for their help with taking care of Farhana but also glad to be able to spend some quality time with our parents—first with Sharmeen's mom, a year earlier, and now with my parents. It wasn't always easy to be so far away from our families. I was particularly happy that Farhana got a chance to spend time with her grandparents. And besides, their company was definitely what we needed after such a harrowing accident.

Chapter 18

The Zen of Nara

Summer was almost over. I had completely recovered from my accident and was back on planes, trains and automobiles, along with my sarariman colleagues, pursuing various business opportunities. One morning, Shibata San came into my office with a big smile and said that the semiconductor division of Sharp wanted to see us. This was a breakthrough we had been waiting for. Shibata San and his sales team had been trying to get their business for some time, and till now, they had been avoiding our enquiries. He said that he would very much like for me to join him for this critical first meeting. The meeting was scheduled at their headquarters. I figured that, like most other large semiconductor companies, their headquarters was located either in Tokyo or some other big city. So I was quite surprised when Shibata San told me that they were headquartered in a very small town called Tenri, located south of Kyoto.

As usual, Shibata San and I took the Tohoku Shinkansen to Kyoto and then a series of local trains to the small station in Tenri. It was much smaller than Kyoto. We took a taxi to the Sharp office. Just like most of the Sony offices, they had a small Sharp museum in the lobby area, displaying many of their signature products that they had produced over the years.

'Do you know how Sharp started?' Shibata San asked me.

From my facial expression, Shibata San could tell that I didn't know this piece of trivia.

'The company started by making mechanical pencils. In fact, "sharp" in Japanese means mechanical pencils.'

That is quite a story, I thought. Indeed, Sharp did start out by making these mechanical pencils and grew into one of the giants of the Japanese electronics industry, a great example of the rise of postmodern Japan.

Soon, we were led to a meeting room on the sixth floor of the Sharp building. Four of Sharp's sarariman engineers showed up for our meeting, all key members of their engineering and procurement team, as we found out. We did our usual series of presentations, introducing our company and our capabilities. The meeting lasted a couple of hours, and they appeared pleased with what we had to offer. Shibata San and I also left the meeting pleased; both of us thought that it had indeed been a very successful first meeting. We were given some action items by the Sharp folks and invited back in a month to provide them with more information pertaining to their specific business opportunity.

It was 12.30 in the afternoon, and after taking a taxi back to the station, we decided to have a quick lunch before returning home to Tokyo. As we got off the taxi, Shibata San pointed to a small shop close to the station with a Japanese sign and said that it was a local ramen noodle shop.

'I love small local restaurants like this, and I am sure they have delicious ramen. Let's try it out.'

I looked around, and the place seemed unusually quiet for a station. I knew it was a weekday, but it still seemed a little unusual. But it was a welcome change as we were always battling our way through busy stations. I glanced at the shop that Shibata San had pointed at again. It looked kind of deserted.

'Are you sure that it is even open, Shibata San? The place looks like it is closed.'

Shibata San agreed, but we decided to check it out anyway. Turned out that the place was open. It was owned by an elderly couple who seemed genuinely delighted to see us. It was a very small place with mostly bar-style seating across from the small kitchen and a couple of tables. I wondered why the place was so empty if the food was as good as Shibata San had claimed. Putting aside my doubts, we ordered their special ramen. Shibata San was absolutely correct: indeed, it was absolutely delicious. While eating our noodles, I shared with Shibata San how I thought it was strange for Sharp to be headquartered in such a small town in the middle of nowhere. He didn't know why Sharp's head office was located in such a small town either, but said that it was not necessarily a bad location: it is a little over an hour from Kyoto and very close to Nara.

'You mean Nara is that close?'

'Yes, it is about thirty minutes by taxi', Shibata San said, slurping his ramen soup.

'Are you kidding me? We are that close to Nara?' I repeated again, hardly able to contain my excitement.

Sensing my excitement, he stopped eating and looked up at me.

'I am not kidding, Asif San. Tenri is *in* Nara prefecture and very close to Nara city. I thought you knew this', he answered while staring at me, clearly trying to figure out the reason for my sudden excitement.

'Have you been to Nara? It is also very historic, just like Kyoto', he said while still looking at me with his inquisitive eyes. 'If you want, we can go there after lunch', he offered.

I had learnt about Nara from my dad when I was in fourth grade. For some reason, his colourful description of this ancient city had struck a chord with me. I still remember how I was awed while listening to him talk about Nara, with its thousand-year-old traditional Japanese temples and pagodas, and the very famous Nara Park, where hundreds of people-friendly deer apparently roam around freely. He would show us the pictures he had taken, and I remember looking at them with interest over and over again. For some reason, I found the place intriguing and longed to visit it one day. In fact, it was on my bucket list for when I was in Japan. And completely unexpectedly, there I was, on a beautiful sunny day, having lunch only thirty minutes from the place, with my friend Shibata San, with the whole afternoon ahead of us. Of course I wanted to go!

'Nara is much smaller than Kyoto, and we will be able to walk to all the famous sightseeing places easily. You can see a lot in half a day, Asif San. I love Nara. Especially the park. It is gorgeous . . .' Shibata San was carrying on, also sounding a little excited by the sudden idea of visiting ancient Nara.

'Yes, of course I want to go. Please, Shibata San', I pleaded, cutting him off mid-sentence.

While we finished the rest of our ramen, I told Shibata San how I had always wanted to visit the place since my childhood. We thanked the couple for the bowls of delicious ramen. We got on a taxi from the station and just like Satoh San had said, arrived in Nara in about thirty minutes. The taxi driver dropped us off very close to Nara Park. I could easily recognize the place from all the photos I had seen hundreds of times. As I stood there surveying it, it looked even prettier in real life. A chill ran down my spine, still in disbelief at my sudden luck.

'Welcome to Nara, Asif San', Shibata San said with a pleasant smile. I looked at him, and it reminded me of the scene from the movie *Jurassic Park*, when Dr Grant (played by Sam Neill) was just mesmerized at seeing the live dinosaurs soon after arriving at the park, and Dr Hammond (played by Richard Attenborough) walks up to him and says, 'My dear Dr Grant, welcome to Jurassic Park.' Now I finally knew exactly how Dr Grant had felt.

Nestled amidst the rolling hills of Nara prefecture, this ancient city used to be the capital of Japan during the

Nara Period (710–784). It is considered one of the most glorious periods of Japanese history during which the economy, culture, religion, arts, and architecture flourished.[15] It was the first time the system of having a permanent capital was established in Japan,[16] even though the capital city would later move to Kyoto and finally to Tokyo. The period was heavily influenced by Chinese traditions and practices. It was modelled after the then Chinese capital of Ch'ang-an, or modern-day Xi'an. Chinese characters were adopted into the Japanese writing system for the first time, which in turn, led to the first-ever official written history of the country. Buddhism became widespread as the emperor embraced it as a key religion and philosophy. Japan's ancient glory from this period can be seen and felt in the sights of some of the most beautiful temples, shrines, pagodas and palaces that still stand today. Nara is home to eight ancient temples and shrines, all of which are UNESCO World Heritage sites, and located within a radius of eight kilometres, some of them located inside the Nara Park itself. It's where thousands of years of Japanese history, culture, and architecture are all harmoniously wrapped together in place by Mother Nature.

It seemed like a perfect day to visit the place. It wasn't very hot and humid as we were almost at the end of summer. This was an important factor for us as we were in ties and suits. We decided to take our ties off and put them in our respective office bags. Shibata San said that we should first visit the famous Todai-ji temple, which is one of the city's main attractions. After my

---

[15] Japanese history is divided into fifteen key periods. Nara (710–784), Kamakura (1192–1333), Edo (1603–1868) and Meiji (1868–1912) are considered key periods during which certain major events and changes took place. As of 1 May 2019, Japan is in the Reiwa Period.

[16] Prior to the Nara period, the practice was to move the capital with the commencement of the reign of a new emperor: the belief was that when an emperor passed away in the capital city, it became too polluted due to the emperor's death and hence could no longer serve as the capital.

experience of touring Kyoto with Shibata San, I knew that I was in good hands. I was sure he would take me to all the well-known places, time permitting. But frankly, I just wanted to walk around the Nara Park. So I had to ask him.

'Can we spend some time in the park first, Shibata San? It seems so nice and peaceful.'

'Of course. The temple is actually inside Nara Park. So, we will kill two birds with one stone', Shibata San replied with his usual boisterous laugh.

The 1,240-acre park in central Nara is one of the oldest and most beautiful places in Japan and a paradise for nature lovers. Established in 1880, it is one of the oldest parks in Japan. As we walked through the park to get to Todai-ji temple, I saw deer everywhere, indeed roaming fearlessly alongside the visitors. Since it was a weekday, it wasn't very crowded. I noticed that some of the visitors were feeding the deer. I was a little surprised as I just passed an English sign saying not to feed them. When I asked Shibata San, he said that people were allowed to feed them a special rice cracker known as *shika senbei* (deer rice crackers), which visitors could buy at some of the small stalls located at the entrance of the park. Most of the deer were perhaps spoiled, as they would approach almost every new visitor they saw, expecting to be fed.

After a nice leisurely stroll for about fifteen minutes, we arrived at the grand entrance of the famous Todai-ji temple. We worked our way through the gates and arrived at what looked like a huge courtyard. On the other side of the courtyard, I saw the main hall designed in a very traditional Japanese architectural style. Shibata San said that the large statue of the Buddha was inside the main hall. I thought it was just another famous temple and didn't know that it contained a large Buddha statue. I guess that explains such an overwhelmingly large structure. I couldn't wait to see the statue inside. As we got close to the many entrances of the main hall, the large statue came into view.

'There it is, Asif San. Look how big it is', Shibata San said, admiring the amazing piece of artwork.

As I entered the hall, I found the size of the statue even more overwhelming. There were a couple of placards with its history written both in Japanese and English. As I read it, I was surprised to learn that what I was looking at was built in the year 752. I found it hard to believe the Japanese had been able to build it over 1,200 years ago. As I kept on reading, my jaw dropped. Apparently, it is the largest bronze Buddha statue, almost fifty feet in height and weighing over 500 tons. How was it possible for the folks from so long ago, with minimal engineering skills and tools, to construct such a large and heavy statue? I just found it amazing. There were a group of tourists with a guide who was providing information in English. Curious, I slowly moved closer to them so that I could hear what the guide saying, while acting like I was just intently looking at this grand statue and had no interest in them. The guide was saying that the Todai-ji is considered to be one of the main Buddhist temples in all of Japan. I also learnt that the original structure had been rebuilt twice after being damaged by earthquakes and fire. The current structure was reconstructed about 300 years ago. Even at 30 per cent smaller than the original, the main hall of the Todai-ji temple is one of the largest wooden structures in the world. Rumour has it that the construction cost of the *Daibutsu* or the large Buddha statue nearly brought Japan to the brink of bankruptcy. Pleased to get this valuable historic information for free from the guide, I was still trying to process some of the amazing facts as we made our way out of the temple.

After taking in the grandeur of the Todai-ji temple, Shibata San suggested that we walk to the next attraction—the Kasuga-Taisha shrine. I was happy to hear that it was also located inside the park, which meant getting to spend more time walking through it. We were following a small map that Shibata San had picked up from the backseat of the taxi. Soon, we came up to an uphill pathway lined with stone lanterns on both sides. Apparently, there are 3,000 of them in total all around the temple compound. This Shinto shrine is also an ancient structure from the same period as the Todai-ji temple, around 768 AD. The main temple buildings are all designed in the old Japanese style of architecture and painted in bright orange colour. I found the colourful temple quite spectacular, especially against the backdrop of the lush greenery of Nara Park. There were bronze lanterns everywhere around the temple complex. I could only imagine how beautiful the place would look at night, when all the lanterns along the path and inside the shrine were lit. After walking around the temple for an hour or so, we emerged back in the main area of the park.

Shibata San and I decided to buy some rice crackers to feed the deer. Once they saw the food in our hand, a few deer rushed towards us. They seemed quite aggressive and not at all scared of the human species visiting them. But then we realized that perhaps feeding them wasn't such a great idea as some of the deer kept following us through the park, clearly expecting more food. Shibata San tried to communicate with them by throwing up his hands in the air to show them that it was empty, but his message was clearly getting lost in translation. After a long while, realizing that indeed we were of no further value to them, they went their merry way, most likely to harass some other visitors. By then, we had been walking for over three hours in our business suits and shoes and decided that it was time to take a short break. We bought some ice cream and coffee from one of the many shops lined along one side of the park. We walked a few minutes to find a small bench, sat down and started eating our ice creams, both of us quiet as we enjoyed and took in the peaceful surroundings of the lush Nara Park, but keeping our eyes peeled for the aggressive deer population. It seemed like a nice ending to a very nice and leisurely afternoon.

Shibata San suggested that we take our train from Nara Station instead of going back to Tenri, as it was much closer. We would

take the express train to Kyoto, then the Shinkansen to head back
to Tokyo. The weather was nice and the station was not far, so
we decided to walk. Apparently, there are a few other attractions
along the way. Shibata San mentioned that we would stop by one
of the most famous pagodas in Japan, which was just a short
distance away and on the way to the station. Even though I didn't
know the name, I knew exactly the one he was talking about, as
it is commonly featured as a major landmark of Japan in many
books and brochures, and of course, I had heard about it from
my dad. I was very satisfied with and thankful for our mini tour
of Nara so far. If Shibata San was going to take me to any more
historic or famous sites, it would be a bonus, I thought happily.

We had barely walked for five minutes from the park when the
impressive 122 feet, five-storey tall pagoda came into view. It is
part of the Horyu-ji temple complex. Shibata San told me that the
pagoda is the oldest wooden building in the world, even though
it was built over a thousand years ago, around 670 AD. Indeed, I
was right: it was the same pagoda I thought we were going to see,
easily recognizable as this ancient structure had been showcased
in many books, calendars and documentaries about Japan. I wish
we could go inside and go up the pagoda, but it was quite late and
the place was closed. Luckily, it was in an open area, so we walked
around the temple complex, admiring the pagoda. After taking a
bunch of pictures, we headed once again for Nara station.

As we arrived at the station, it brought us back to modern
times with all the glamour and glitz of the shopping stores and
restaurants both outside and inside the place, loud music coming
through the surrounding loudspeakers. After having a nice sushi
dinner, we boarded an express train bound for Kyoto.

On the Shinkansen back, I thanked Shibata San for making
my dream come true. He mentioned that he hadn't been to Nara
in a long while and also enjoyed visiting it after many years. He
also assured me that we had visited the most famous sites in the
city and that I could confidently check Nara off my bucket list, if

I wanted. While true, I knew that I had to be back with Sharmeen and Farhana and spend more quality time in this ancient place.

From then on, every time we had a meeting with the sarariman from Sharp at their Tenri headquarters, I would make it a point to try to stop by Nara. Sometimes, some of our sarariman would join me, while other times, I would just visit by myself. As many times I visited the place, it never seemed to get old. I always find that Nara Park emanates a Zen-like aura, at least for me, that just melts away my stress every time I visit the place. Taking a stroll in this beautiful ancient capital is like flipping through the pages of a beautiful picture book about Japan or Japanese calendars, which used to adorn many walls before the days of smartphones, tablets and laptops.

Chapter 19

The Fuji Expedition

By the time my second summer in Japan rolled in, our business had started to show significant signs of growth. We had been officially awarded the Sony business and we were expecting to gain a big chunk of revenue from it. Our efforts to win business from other customers had also started to pay dividends and the team was spending even more time on planes, trains and automobiles visiting customers. One early summer morning, Satoh San, Umehara San, Shibata San and I were travelling to Kyoto for a meeting with Panasonic. I had arrived early at the Tokyo Station, so I spent thirty minutes or so browsing the various kiosks at the station looking for my breakfast, even though I knew exactly what I wanted. I enjoyed doing this window-shopping at all the Japanese railway stations whenever I got a chance, looking at the variety of trinkets, souvenirs and especially the food, and in particular, the immaculate packaging it comes in, known as *bento* boxes. These rows of shops at any railway station or airport invariably reminded me of Christmas season, with their colourful small trinkets and hundreds of unique and vibrantly wrapped bento boxes stacked all around them.

Bento boxes are meant for takeaway food packaged in small square or rectangular paper or wooden boxes; each of them is beautifully wrapped as if they were birthday presents. Open the wrapper and one would find small portions of a variety of food items, meticulously arranged and colour-coordinated, looking more like a work of art than a lunchbox. A typical bento box will have multiple compartments separated by dividers, each filled with these small portions of assorted food items. Along with the main dish, for example, fried salmon or beef steak, it usually contains other stuff, such as a small portion of rice or noodles, some vegetables, a miniature omelette, along with some pickled radish. Some may also offer a couple of small mochi or Japanese sweet rice cakes for dessert. It is the most interesting form of takeaway food I have ever seen. Nowhere else in the world do they pay such attention to the packaging and presentation of a small box of breakfast, lunch or dinner. These bento boxes are available at almost all convenience stores throughout Japan. Interestingly, I have seen some of our sarariman bring these kinds of bento boxes for their lunch to the office. I always thought they had bought them from stores, but I later found out that they were all prepared at home by their wives. Japanese mothers and wives are well-known for their expertise in preparing elaborate bento lunchboxes for their children and husbands.

Anyhow, as it was getting close to our departure time, I quickly bought my usual breakfast: a single boiled egg inside a small clear plastic box, a single banana wrapped in clear plastic tied with a nice golden bow, a small piece of neatly packaged bread, a small packet of orange juice, and my favourite—a hot can of Café au Lait. Yes, one can buy hot and cold coffee in cans in Japan. They are even available in vending machines.

As I boarded the train and found my seat, I saw Shibata San, Umehara San and Satoh San already in their seats. I noticed that they had all bought bento boxes for their breakfast. As they were aware that I loved the view of Fuji San from the train, my sarariman colleagues always offered me the window seat on the right-hand side, which offered the best view of the majestic mountain. I was happy to see that Shibata San had kept the window seat for me. As our Shinkansen slowly pulled out of Tokyo Station exactly on time, we all settled down in our seats, three of them ready to enjoy their bento boxes, while I got ready to eat my assortment of Western-style breakfast.

The classic photo and video of the Shinkansen zooming along the beautiful Japanese countryside against the backdrop of snow-covered Mount Fuji have been used in numerous films, documentaries, calendars and books about Japan. That picture is a shot of the Tokaido Shinkansen either going towards or coming from Kyoto and Osaka. As it passes through the city of Mishima in Shizuoka prefecture, Fuji San comes into view. This was the same bullet train we were on that morning. Because of the high speed of these trains, the view of Fuji San lasts for only about five minutes. On top of that, the weather also has to cooperate. From my experience, the mountain is often covered by clouds, much to most of the passengers' dismay, especially during the summer season. The view of Fuji, while always majestic, is particularly enhanced during the winter season when almost half the mountain is covered in snow. There are more clear days during winter, which improves the chances of seeing the snowcapped Fuji from the Tokaido Shinkansen line.

Luckily, the weather was on our side that morning and soon, the grandeur of Fuji came into view. As it was early summer, most of the snow was gone, except for a little hint of it at the very top. As many times as I had seen it before, the view of Mount Fuji never seems to get old. Even today, when I am taking the Tokaido Shinkansen, I get so excited in anticipation as the train approaches near Fuji San, and I am equally disappointed if it can't be seen due to bad weather.

As my colleagues and I were enjoying the view, I mentioned our recent family excursions to the *go-gome* (fifth station) and the lakes around the mountain, especially Hakone. Satoh San adopted his senpai mode and gave me a detailed overview of the importance of Fuji San to the Japanese people. Mount Fuji is not only revered by the Japanese as the highest mountain and the coolest natural landmark, but since the seventh century, it has been a sacred site of the indigenous Japanese religion of Shinto. Shinto is a polytheistic Japanese religion believing in several *kami* or gods. The kami of Mount Fuji is known as Princess Konohanasakuya. Symbolized by sakura or cherry blossom, Konohanasakuya has an entire series of shrines dedicated to her, known as Segen Shrines. These shrines can be found at the base and on the top of Mount Fuji, and other places around the country. Satoh San mentioned that during summer, many people climb the mountain for the view of the sunrise from the peak of Mount Fuji, which is a sight to behold. He added that he and his wife had made the trek during their younger years.

This last bit of information particularly piqued my interest. *So, Satoh San had climbed Mount Fuji?* I had always wanted to climb Fuji but didn't think it was a good idea due to my fear of heights. So I quickly asked Satoh San how difficult the climb was. He said that there were a few trails going to the top of the mountain. Some are more difficult than others, but none of the trails really involve any 'climbing'. They are all more like a hike up a steep path. And one of the trails is less steep and easier to hike on, but it takes longer to reach the summit.

'I can take you up if you want to go', Satoh San offered. 'Many old people, even seventy-year-olds climb Fuji, Asif San. It's not too difficult.'

Really? Of course, I wanted to go! Even if I couldn't make it all the way up and could only make it halfway, it was worth the trip, I thought. Intrigued, I immediately decided to take him up on his offer in case he changed his mind later.

'I would love that, Satoh San. Let's do it.'

Umehara San, who had been listening to our conversation all this time, said that he would love to join us. Apparently, he also had been wanting to climb Fuji but had not had a chance to do so.

I looked at Shibata San with raised eyebrows. Before I even got the chance to ask, he said, 'Forget it, Asif San. I am not climbing Fuji. It's a stupid idea. Why not enjoy it from here? Look how nice it looks.' He pointed at it through our window, only to realize that the view of Fuji had long disappeared.

That's another thing I liked about Shibata San. In a country where few speak their mind, he was very direct. I often wondered if it was because of his long exposure to international business and especially his four-year assignment in Germany.

Our enthusiasm was not dampened by Shibata San's negative comments and we started to plan our climb. Satoh San mentioned that the climbing season opens from July to September. Since it was late May, we would have to wait a couple of months. He advised that it would be good if we used this time to prepare for our climb.

'Prepare for our climb?' I asked. 'I thought you had said it is more like hiking up a tall mountain. Surely, we don't need months of preparation for it.' I was worried that perhaps, indeed, it was more of a climb than a hike, which would make it difficult for me due to my phobia of heights.

'That's true, Asif San, but still, preparation is necessary', Satoh San said, sounding very serious.

Indeed, the hike up Fuji San can be quite strenuous, taking up to eight hours to the top at an altitude of 12,380 feet. At about 10,000 feet, the air becomes quite thin, and the hike becomes especially strenuous near the top. Satoh San also mentioned that it was important to have the right set of gear as it can help with the hike. The temperature steadily drops with higher altitude and is usually near zero degrees towards the summit, even during the summer months. Also, at a higher altitude, the weather can be quite unpredictable, changing drastically without any warning. One can get caught in heavy rain or be surrounded by thick fog, unable to see, at a moment's notice. Proper attire such as lightweight, warm and water-resistant jackets can make all the difference in the world. Satoh San advised that it was best to wear layers of clothes as opposed to wearing one thick jacket, so that we could easily add or take off the layers as needed to remain comfortable throughout the hike. We would also have to carry our own water and some food with us. He recommended that we buy a very lightweight backpack and ensure that we had the right hiking boots. If we wanted to see the sunrise from the top, we would have to hike mostly through the darkness of the night. A powerful flashlight is required, but Satoh San recommended that we buy a headlamp, so that our hands were free.

It was good to get all these information downloads from Satoh San. We had to agree with all his suggestions. Umehara San and I were a little worried about hiking for eight hours. Since my college days, I had always done some form of regular exercise, but since moving to Korea and then to Japan, I hadn't really been working out. Umehara San said that he was also out of shape. We also agreed that it was good to have a couple of months to try to get into better shape.

After returning to the office, Umehara San and I thought that we should try to recruit some more people for our climbing team. We figured that climbing Fuji San would be a very good team-building exercise. But unfortunately, very few people shared our enthusiasm, and in fact, some of them told me that it wasn't such a smart idea, sharing Shibata San's sentiment.

'*Muri, muri, muri desu yo*, Asif San', Junko San from customer service said, emphasizing that it was an impossible task for her. She asked me why anyone would go through such pain when one can simply enjoy the view from a safe distance, sounding exactly like Shibata San. Junko San also said that there is a well-known proverb in Japanese that says, 'A wise man will climb Fuji San once, only a fool climbs it twice.' Wouldn't this be Satoh San's second climb? I couldn't help but smile.

Junko San added that she had heard from her friends that the hike was quite boring, and the view up there was not as great. I could relate to this, having experienced the same feeling when we had driven halfway to the fifth station.

Despite the lack of interest shown by most of the office folks, Satoh San, Umehara San and I remained upbeat about our Fuji expedition. But after hearing so many negative comments from so many people in the office, I started to wonder if Satoh San had unintentionally made the hike sound easier than it really was. Regardless, I had no intention of giving up this golden opportunity. I had to give it a try.

In the end, there were only two other brave souls who agreed to accept our invitation and take up the challenge. They were Takamiyagi San, my admin, and a woman named Sasaki San from HR. There would be five of us going on our Fuji expedition.

Sharmeen wanted to join us as well, but I was a little worried that it might just be a little too strenuous for her. Then there was the issue of not having a babysitter for Farhana and none of us were comfortable leaving Farhana overnight with a nanny, especially since it was someone we didn't know well. I also didn't feel comfortable bringing her along, since it had morphed into a small company event with none of the others' spouses joining us. While Sharmeen was a little disappointed, she was kind enough to help me with shopping for the right gear. After several trips to the local North Face store, several hundred dollars poorer, and a few weeks of daily hour-long jogging on the treadmill, I was ready for our hike.

Of course, Satoh San, with his prior climbing experience had become our de facto leader. We all felt that we were in good

hands. He laid out a detailed plan for our hike. To see the sunrise
from the peak, we would be hiking overnight and arriving on top
just before sunrise. The good news was that we would not be
hiking from the very bottom, but driving to the go-gome and
commencing our hike from there. There are quite a few trails
going up the mountain, and the most popular and easiest one
was the Yoshida trail. The trail starts from the same go-gome
Sharmeen and I had visited, at an elevation of 7,500 feet (2,300
metres). The actual hike would require going up about 4,800 feet
(1,476 metres). This key information made me feel a lot better
and gave me some courage, although I still worried about my fear
of heights. Satoh San also informed us that there were quite a few
rest stops or stations along the Yoshida trail, each providing basic
amenities such as food, water and restroom facilities. Our plan
was to hike up to the seventh or eighth station, where we would
sleep for a couple of hours. Then we would walk the rest of the
way, arriving at the top just before sunrise, at around 4.30 in the
morning. Satoh San also advised that since the trails could get
quite crowded during the weekends, it was best to go on weekdays
when there was less foot traffic on the mountain. This was the
plan Satoh San outlined for us. He seemed very serious about
every aspect of our imminent expedition: anyone listening to him
and not knowing our actual plans could easily mistake that we
were climbing the Everest, not to the summit of Fuji.

It proved to be a little difficult for all of us to take a day off
at the same time in the middle of the week. So we decided that we
would leave the office early on a Friday afternoon instead. Since
I had driven to that particular go-gome before, I volunteered to
drive everyone in my little Toyota.

On a sunny Friday afternoon in mid-July, we left the office
at 3.30 p.m. and started our drive towards Fuji San. Since I had
learnt—from my many karaoke sessions—that the Beatles were
quite popular in Japan, I had brought a few of their CDs to

listen to in the car. Indeed, it turned out to be the right choice. Everyone seemed to know most of the songs in the album, and we all tried to sing along, despite not knowing most of the lyrics in any meaningful detail. I was using my Japanese-speaking navigation system in my Toyota, and while everyone was singing 'A Hard Day's Night', Satoh San kept giving me lessons on some of the key vocabularies used by the GPS. Soon, the majestic Fuji San came into view, looming large across the horizon in all its grandeur, covering the entire windshield of the car. All of us started to point it out to each other at almost the same time with some excitement.

The sight of Fuji always made me very happy, but this time, I found myself staring at it with mixed feelings. While I was also cheering with everyone, I could not help but question my decision to climb the highest peak in all of Japan. I felt like I was stuck on a rollercoaster, creeping slowly upward towards the top for the inevitable plunge into the abyss. But at this point, it was too late to get off this rollercoaster. However, it also occurred to me how far I had come since my arrival in Japan. Here we were, heading towards the summit of Fuji as a group, singing in a chorus, something that I would have found unthinkable a mere eight months ago.

We arrived at the Yoshida Trail's go-gome at 5.30 p.m. The sun was low on the horizon, and there was already a little chill in the air, considerably cooler compared to the heat and humidity of Tokyo. I looked up and stared at the trail: there were quite a few people on the trail, each slowly shrinking in size as they were hiking upwards, finally disappearing altogether into the crowd. Satoh San seemed happy and said that we were lucky and that the trail wasn't too crowded—the opposite of what I thought was the case. When I mentioned this to Satoh San, he burst out laughing.

'Oh, this is nothing, Asif San. Soon, it will start to get very crowded.'

'Well, in that case, we better get going', I responded, afraid of getting knocked off or knocking someone else off the trail while hiking up. The last thing I wanted was to bump into other climbers. I imagined the headlines on the next day's newspaper, 'Climbers perish as a stupid gaijin knocks them off the Fuji trail'. But I wasn't too worried as the trail started relatively wide and not super steep. If most of the hike was up such a slope, I was all set.

I couldn't help but ask Satoh San about it, and he confirmed that indeed most of the way up is very similar, except for a few spots, where it was a little steeper, but even those weren't too bad. My fear started to completely dissipate, giving way to a new sense of excitement as I stood there staring up the trail, ready to realize my dream of conquering Fuji San.

Satoh San said that we needed to get started as quickly as possible. So, all of us got ready, putting on our backpacks and with our climbing sticks in hand. As per Satoh San's recommendation, each of us was carrying one litre of water and some snacks. As we were ready to begin, I noticed that there were a few small temporary shops, selling all sorts of climbing paraphernalia. I saw some small oxygen bottles for sale and some of us bought them, just in case we needed them as we hiked through the thinner air near the summit. We also came across a small ramen shop and decided to have a quick dinner before we started our climb. Satoh San seemed a little displeased with our decision but reluctantly agreed. It was wonderful to eat the hot instant ramen sitting halfway up Fuji San, surrounded by the cold, fresh mountain air.

As soon as we were done eating, with Satoh San leading the way, we began our ascent. We were all quite excited for about the first thirty minutes, but soon realized how tough it was to continuously walk up a slope. Also, I remembered what Junko San had said back in the office: indeed, the grandeur of Fuji that we were used to seeing from far away disappeared pretty quickly. Instead, we found ourselves surrounded by a very barren landscape, full of rocks of all sizes and shapes. It almost felt like we were on some other planet. Soon, darkness started to set in, so we put our handy headlamps on our foreheads. Within another thirty minutes, it was pitch black and we all thanked Satoh San for his advice regarding this essential headgear. I was glad that I had listened to him and invested the 5,000 Yen (about $45) into this as it was very nice to have both my hands free. As I looked around, I realized that the mountain had completely disappeared in the darkness of the moonless night. The only thing visible was scores of moving headlamps and flashlights of the other climbers snaking up ahead of us, as well as down behind us. It was quite a sight to behold.

Soon it started to get cold as we gained altitude. I knew this would happen but was a little surprised as to how fast it started to get chilly. We started to add layers of clothing to keep warm. While the hike was tough and steep, we didn't face any of the rain or thunderstorms that the mountain is known for. Along with the tiredness and strain everyone had started to feel, the climb was relatively boring. The only entertainment was Satoh San's ongoing and continual annoyance at us. Because the climb felt increasingly strenuous, our frequency of breaks started to increase with altitude. Satoh San was clearly in a much better physical shape than the rest of us, and he didn't quite appreciate us stopping so often. On top of that, we were also chatting while we were hiking. This made Satoh San very annoyed. He kept telling us that our constant blabbering was what was making us so tired, which in turn, was making us take frequent breaks. He kept telling us to basically shut up to conserve our energy and concentrate on the climbing itself. Right after such mini-outbursts from him, we would stop talking, but only for about ten minutes or so, after which we would resume our chatting again. This made him even more mad at us. The rest of us found these outbursts quite hilarious, which we tried our best to hide quite unsuccessfully. That upset him even more.

We had been walking for a few hours and had started to feel a little exhausted. It was also freezing by the time we reached the seventh station. By this point, Umehara San and I had finished all the water we were carrying with us. Luckily, there was bottled water for sale at the seventh station. But we were both shocked at the prices. A regular 500 ml water bottle was selling for 1,000 Yen or about $10, almost ten times the normal price. It turns out that the price of water goes up exponentially as one gets to the higher stations. Despite my shock, it was an easy decision to fork out the 1,000 Yen: our body was in need of liquid. At that point, we would have paid $100 for a bottle of water.

We arrived at the eighth station around midnight, completely exhausted and tired, an hour later than we had originally planned, much to Satoh San's displeasure. Only Satoh San seemed to be in relatively good spirits with very little sign of any fatigue. I, on the other hand, was totally fatigued and wasn't sure if I could hike up any further. I had also started to develop a slight headache. It seemed like the thin air was affecting me more than the others. Luckily, the plan was to rest and nap for a couple of hours at the eighth station before continuing our ascent. Satoh San had said that there are lodges on both eighth and the ninth stations for tired hikers on a first-come-first-serve basis and rented by the hour. We found a lodge at the eighth station and proceeded to check-in, hoping that there was room for all of us. Luckily, there was. As we went inside, the place looked like a large room with rows of small individual sleeping spaces about four feet or so apart. The set of thick mattresses with even a thicker blanket on top in each of these individual spaces looked very inviting to me. We chose five of these spots in a row, and I couldn't wait to get rid of my backpack and get under the thick blanket. I noticed a small locker-type cubby hole next to my mattress. I quickly emptied my pocket and stored my personal stuff in the locker, put down my backpack on top of it, took off my shoes and quickly got underneath the warm blanket with all my clothes on. The temperature outside was below freezing at this altitude, but luckily, the room was heated. I stared out of my blanket to see what others were doing, and it seemed like Umehara San, Sasaki San and Takamiyagi San had decided to snack on the food they had brought along. Satoh San was already under the blanket. I fell asleep as soon as my head touched the pillow.

I had barely closed my eyes when I felt someone shaking me. I woke up, all startled and annoyed. I looked up, and it was Satoh San. What did he want now?

'It's time to wake up, Asif San. We need to start hiking. Otherwise, we will miss the sunrise', he said with a sense of urgency in his voice.

Still very tired, I glanced at my watch and was surprised to see that it was 2 a.m. I had been asleep for about two hours. But it felt like I hadn't had much rest. Everyone else was up and getting their gears ready. I forced myself to get up, afraid of missing the sunrise as Satoh San had just mentioned. With our backpacks on our backs and walking sticks in our hands again, we resumed our ascent. This time, we were all very quiet. I could tell that everyone was quite tired, despite the couple of hours of napping. Perhaps the thin air at that altitude was making us even more tired, I thought. After all, the eighth station is located at an altitude of 3,100 metres, or a little over 10,000 feet, and the air starts to get thin at this height. Soon, my headache returned and I started to feel lightheaded, affected by the lack of oxygen. I remembered that I had purchased the small bottle of portable oxygen. The bottle had a face mask, and all I was supposed to do was put the mask on my nose and breathe. I started to use it on and off as we climbed further, but it didn't seem to help much with my light-headedness. I decided not to mention anything about my headache to anyone, in case Satoh San got really annoyed.

It took us quite a bit of time to reach the ninth station at an altitude of 11,483 feet (3,400 metres). By this time, I was feeling nauseated and just didn't feel like I could climb any further. I decided that I must take another break, but at the same time, I didn't want to slow everyone down. I told the group that I was quite tired and needed a break, but I asked them to carry on without me. We could always catch up at the summit, I added. I could immediately sense that everyone was quite uneasy with this plan; they all chimed in saying that they didn't feel comfortable leaving me by myself, especially so close to the top. Takamiyagi San seemed especially worried that I was one of the few gaijins, and what if I got really sick? But I didn't want them to miss the sunrise on my account and insisted that they carried on, assuring them once again that I would be fine if I just had a chance to rest for thirty minutes or so.

While we were discussing all this, I noticed that Satoh San kept looking at his watch and seemed to be doing some quick calculations. Then suddenly, he said that I could easily sleep for about an hour and still be able to make it to the top to see the sunrise. He said he would have a quick discussion with the attendants at the lodge to ensure that I was awoken on time and to see that I was okay. The fact that I might still be able to make it to the top after taking an hour's nap sounded wonderful to me, even though all I wanted to do at that point was to get under a blanket. I rented a sleeping space at the ninth station, similar to the previous one, lay down, and after making sure to set my alarm, immediately fell asleep.

When I woke up after an hour, I felt surprisingly refreshed. The headache seemed to have got much better. I looked at my watch, and it was fifteen minutes to four in the morning. The hour of sleep had clearly helped my body get better acclimatized to the thin air at this high altitude. The sunrise was supposed to be around 4.30 a.m., which gave me ample time to walk the rest of the way to the summit. As I got out with my gears back on, it was pitch dark and freezing cold, and the wind had picked up a little, which made it feel even colder. It was quite crowded, so I didn't feel like I was at all left out, even though my teammates had moved on. Feeling rejuvenated, with my excitement back again, I started hiking upward with high hopes of catching a glimpse of the imminent sunrise from the top of Fuji San.

I was hiking in somewhat of a rush and wasn't paying attention to the time when suddenly, I heard what sounded like everyone around me whispering something in excitement. Almost instantly, the collective whisper from pretty much everyone on the slope sounded like a muted roar. As everyone up and down the trail suddenly seemed to have come to a stop, I almost bumped into the older lady in front of me. What was going on? Everyone seemed to be staring at the horizon. I quickly glanced at my watch and it was almost 4.30—almost time for the much-awaited sunrise. I felt an acute sense of disappointment as I realized that I was about to miss watching the coveted sunrise from the summit of Fuji San. I looked up and saw scores of headlamps snaking up the trail, but could not figure out how far below I was from the top. I stopped and peered out into the darkness, following everyone's gaze.

Within a minute or so, suddenly, across the horizon, a glimmer of red glow started to appear, and it seemed to grow brighter by the second. With the dance between the light and shadow of the early dawn, silhouettes of the people and the mountainous terrain began to appear before my eyes. As I gazed down across the horizon, for a minute, I thought we were surrounded by an ocean. Of course, I was aware that there is no ocean anywhere near the mountain. Were my eyes playing tricks on me? Then, just as the first bright ray of the sun appeared, I realized that we were above the clouds. What I thought was an ocean was actually a sea of clouds, well below us. And the sun started to come up from behind this sea. The next five minutes were one of the most amazing displays of God's work. As the sun continued to show its face a little bit at a time, the clouds below me turned from a dark shade of blue, to a faint shade of red, then into bright orange. Then suddenly, the sun popped out completely with a blinding brightness. And then there was light.

The whole process lasted for less than five minutes, but it felt mesmerizing. The hue of the clouds below had now returned to its usual white colour. Despite being disappointed at not making it to the top, I was very pleased to have witnessed this show of nature. As I looked around, I saw that everyone had a broad smile on their faces, shaking their heads in satisfaction, perhaps equally mesmerized by the brilliant sunrise, which we had all just witnessed. I realized that I was smiling as well. The couple in front of me looked at me and bowed slightly with their smile, which I reciprocated. I had a similar exchange with some of the people behind me. Nature clearly transcended nationality or language barriers. As I looked up again, I was even more pleased to see how close I was to the summit: it was barely a hundred feet above where I was standing. *Well, for all practical purpose, I essentially did end up witnessing the sunrise from the top*, I thought, doubting that the view from a mere hundred feet or so above would have been any different. I leisurely hiked up the rest of the way towards the summit, no more in a rush to reach the peak. Very close to the top, I passed a small iconic Shinto gate or *torii*. Soon—finally—I was on top of Mount Fuji. I couldn't believe that I was standing on the rooftop of Japan, something I had wanted to do since I was a child.

The summit seemed very crowded. I decided to take a break before exploring the top. I gulped down the freezing water from my water bottle and had a little snack, the food I had carried in my backpack. Rested but still feeling a little fatigued, I decided that it was time to explore the top of Mount Fuji. At first, I walked up a few feet to the highest point at the top, to ensure that I had indeed been at the very top (the terrain on the top is not absolutely flat). Then curious, I walked towards the centre to see what was down the middle of the crater. I was expecting to see some form of volcanic activity, even though I knew that the mountain had been dormant for hundreds of years: the last time it had erupted was in 1707. But like the rest of the mountain, it was just a barren crater. There is a small post office there in case someone wants to mail a letter from the top of Japan to their friends and families. I contemplated sending a postcard to Sharmeen and my mom, but then seeing the long line, decided not to do it.

In my excitement at successfully reaching the peak, I had completely forgotten about the rest of the crew. I got my mobile phone out, and but there was no signal. I started to wonder how to get a hold of everyone. I looked around but realized that it would be a miracle to be able to find them amidst the vast sea of people. I was debating if I should go around the summit and look for them, but decided against it. The diameter of the summit is quite large, and it takes about an hour to walk around the rim. After walking around for about thirty minutes or so and taking tons of pictures, I decided that it would be best to head back down in case I started to get sick again. I wasn't too worried about finding the others. I figured that they would all eventually make their way down and have to find me in the parking lot at go-gome if they wanted a ride back to Tokyo.

Going down, it was less crowded. Most of the hikers were likely still enjoying walking around the summit, as it was still quite early. The trail going down was different from the one we had taken up. This separation is by design, to ensure that hikers don't bump into each other. This descending trail seemed much steeper and rockier, but luckily was also a lot wider. I noticed some relatively scary signs all over the place warning the hikers against the danger of falling rocks.

Just as it had gotten rapidly cold on our way up, it started to get hot equally fast on my way down. As I started to shed layers, my body started to feel lighter and my backpack got heavier. Within a couple of hours, I was sweating and had removed everything, except for my T-shirt. The hike down was equally uneventful and boring in terms of the scenery, the same barren landscape I had seen during the initial part of our ascent. I took fewer breaks on my way down but made sure that I remained hydrated. After about four and a half hours, I was delighted to reach the fifth station and just ecstatic to see my Toyota. I bought a couple of more bottled waters, gulped down one and used the other one to wash my face and neck. I realized that my legs were shaking from exhaustion. I looked at the watch, and it was only 10.30 in the morning. I climbed into my Toyota, rolled the window down, laid the seat as far back as it would go. I tried to keep an eye out for the others, but my eyelids felt too heavy. I fell into a deep sleep in no time.

I dreamt that someone was calling my name and woke up, realizing that it was actually Umehara San knocking at my window and calling out to me to wake me up. It was 12.30 in the afternoon by then, and I had been asleep for two hours. Takamiyagi San was with him, and I was really glad to see them. As I got out of the car, they said that they were relieved to see me, adding that they felt really bad leaving me behind at the ninth station. But I briefly narrated my great experience, and they seemed happy to find out that it turned out okay for me. Then Umehara San asked me if I had seen Satoh San and Sasaki San. I was surprised as I thought they were all together. But apparently, after leaving me at the ninth station, the rest of the team couldn't keep pace with Satoh San; the group got separated during their climb towards the summit. We were sure that both of them would show up soon and started chatting, sharing our hiking experiences. Satoh San and Sasaki San did indeed show up within thirty minutes. They were also worried about me but were relieved and happy to learn that I had made it to the summit without any problems and seen the sunrise. We were all hungry and chowed down bowls of instant ramen noodle soup at the same shop, but this time, it tasted even better than the evening before.

As we were getting ready to leave, Umehara San suggested that we stop by an onsen on our way back. We all readily agreed. Soaking in a hot therapeutic bath sounded wonderful after such a strenuous hike. We found an onsen close to the base of Fuji San on our way back. It was indeed very relaxing to soak in the natural spring water: it seemed to wash away all the fatigue and exhaustion from our long hike. After spending a couple of hours at the onsen, which included a very nice Japanese sushi lunch, we drove back to Tokyo.

I was sure that I would be very sore all over for the next couple of days. But when I woke up the next morning, I was surprised to find that I had no soreness whatsoever in any part of my body. In fact, I felt great. Satoh San would later explain to me that this was because of soaking in the therapeutic spring water of the onsen. It seemed like a miracle, and my respect for the ritual of taking naked baths in public onsens went up a few notches.

I decided to remain wise and not go climbing Fuji San ever again. But I was happy to check it off my bucket list.

Chapter 20

The Panic Attack

After the Fuji expedition, my family and I decided to go visit Texas for our second home leave. On our way to Dallas, we decided to take a small detour to visit Amsterdam and Paris for a week. It was nice to get a break from my hectic schedule at work. And it was wonderful to be back home for a few weeks and spend some quality time with my parents, sisters, young nephew and nieces. Again, Tom asked me to stop by our head office before heading back to Japan. I spent a few days updating all the management and key stakeholders about our recent progress in Japan. The management couldn't be happier with our progress.

As the summer came to an end, Sharmeen and I had been itching to take another trip outside Tokyo. I had been meaning to take her and Farhana to Kyoto and Nara, especially after the whirlwind tour of both the ancient cities with Shibata San. Unfortunately, we didn't have a chance to visit these places as I had been busy with my work and she with her studies, and we spent a big part of the summer on our home leave. As fall rolled in, there was a long weekend ahead, and we decided to take a longer break by adding on a couple of days and visiting Kyoto and Nara. We figured that it would be nice to have our own transportation without having to rely on taxis and trains to get around while we were there. Despite the great public transit system everywhere in

Japan, it wasn't always easy to navigate with a three-year-old in tow, especially when one is carrying a diaper bag, a camera bag and a stroller. I figured that the drive would also allow us to see more of the Japanese countryside.

Kyoto is about 300 miles west of Tokyo on the Tomei expressway. Initially, I was a little worried as I had never driven this far and this long before on the wrong side of the road. But it turned out to be easy and quite a pleasant drive, without much traffic. I had always taken the train to Kyoto before this, and I found the driving to be comparatively more relaxing and enjoyable, allowing us to relish the scenery, which is not so easy to do in the fast-moving Shinkansen. Parts of the highway go through some very nice wooded and mountainous regions, especially close to the Fuji San area. Parts of it also go along the beautiful Pacific coastline. Since we weren't in any rush, we ended up stopping at most of the scenic spots along the way. It was also good to take these breaks with Farhana on board because within an hour or so of driving, she would itch to get out of her car seat, which would invariably start with a mild form of crying, soon to be followed by unbearable screaming. So these breaks served all sorts of purposes, making the drive quite enjoyable.

After about seven and a half hours of driving, we took our designated exit to enter Kyoto city. I gave the highway ticket to the toll booth attendant. He punched in something in his system, and the amount of our toll fee appeared on a small digital display outside the booth. I was shocked when I saw the amount and asked the attendant to verify that it was correct. He looked at me matter-of-factly and confirmed that the amount on the display was indeed correct. The total road toll was 14,900 Yen or about $130. Sticker-shocked, Sharmeen and I drove the rest of the way to our hotel relatively quietly, in somewhat of a dampened mood. Farhana remained cheerful, singing 'Bingo was his name-o' in the back, sitting in her car seat.

Highway and road tolls in Japan are horrendous and probably one of the highest in the world. To enter Shuto Expressway, the elevated expressway that loops around Tokyo, costs about $10. Whenever we drove to pick someone up at the Narita airport, a distance of about 55 miles, we paid 5,990 Yen or a little over $50 in road tolls. Having gone through the experience of paying these high road tolls, perhaps I should not have been so shocked. But still, to pay that much for a road toll was a little too much for me to swallow. The only satisfaction was that all the roads and highways in Japan were always in immaculate condition. I am yet to see a faded mark or sign on them.

Despite the initial shock, our trip to Kyoto and Nara turned out well. We visited more historic sites than the ones Shibata San and I had covered in one afternoon, a few months earlier, in both Kyoto and Nara. We also spent more time at each of the sites, taking out time to explore the associated Japanese history and culture. We felt bad that three-year-old Farhana wouldn't remember any of these wonderful places we were visiting. She seemed to be more interested in playing with the pebbles outside the Nijo Castle than visiting some of its historic and iconic halls. Sharmeen and Farhana fell in love with Nara for different reasons. Sharmeen, due to this old capital's ancient sites, and Farhana, at seeing all the free-roaming deer in the Nara Park. She probably thought of it as one large zoo.

From Kyoto, we drove to Nara and stayed there for a couple of nights. While the hotel where we stayed in Kyoto was a nice Western-style hotel, the small inn we stayed at in Nara was very different. Located inside Nara Park, it was a small privately owned place, with about twelve or so rooms. The place seemed like a hybrid between a Western hotel and a Japanese ryokan. With few guests, the staff were able to pay special attention to all our needs; we were treated like royalty.

It was early fall but some of the leaves of the trees had already started to change colour. It was truly magical to wake up in the morning, open the window and see the lush green and golden trees of Nara Park with deer roaming everywhere.

The rest of the trip was quite relaxing and uneventful, except for the last day, just before we left Kyoto. Farhana was a very picky eater. To get her to eat a decent lunch or dinner was a major event in our daily lives, which usually turned into a mini production when we were travelling. When we were on the road, most of the time, she would refuse anything other than just milk. But one thing she rarely refused was the chicken nuggets from 'McDoo', her term of endearment for McDonald's. I sometimes wondered if this was just an expression due to her baby talk or if she was truly in love with McDonald's. On the morning of our last day in Kyoto, before we started our drive back to Tokyo, we decided to get her some chicken nuggets in case she got hungry on the way. We had been visiting a McDonald's close to our hotel almost every day for Farhana. It was one of the larger ones, two storeys with plenty of seating and a small playground. We also decided to have a quick breakfast while there.

That morning, for some reason, the place was more crowded than usual and all tables were taken. It was filled with a lot of foreign tourists like us. Luckily, after waiting only for about five minutes or so, we found a small table on the first floor. Once we were all settled, I walked up to the counter to order the chicken nuggets. There was a long line, and it took more than ten minutes to get our food. As I was walking back to the table with the tray in my hand, I noticed that Sharmeen was sitting there all alone. I glanced around looking for Farhana but didn't see her anywhere, which I thought was kind of strange. Did Sharmeen let her go to the playground unattended? As I approached our little table, I asked Sharmeen where Farhana was.

'What do you mean where is Farhana? She is with you.'

'No, she is not. I went to order food leaving you two here, remember?' I replied, my concern quite clear in my voice.

'But I saw her following you to the counter', Sharmeen replied, sounding equally alarmed.

'But she is not with me', I yelled. 'I definitely left her with you.'

I felt all the surrounding eyes staring at us. Of course, at that point I didn't care. Sharmeen sprang up from her seat, and we started to look around frantically for Farhana. I quickly went outside to check the playground, but she wasn't there. A sense of sheer horror and paranoia started to come over me. It felt like the floor was giving way under my feet, and the room had started to spin. I felt paralysed, unable to move for a few seconds. I had started to sweat and could see a similar sense of fear on Sharmeen's face. Seeing her brought me back to my senses, and I realized that I needed to try to calm down to ensure that I didn't panic and end up losing our little daughter forever.

Sharmeen started to walk around the first floor, yelling her name, while everyone in the whole place just stared at us. I followed suit, shoving and pushing everyone around as we looked for our baby. Then it hit me that we were surrounded by foreigners. At that point, complete paranoia set in. *Is it possible that one of these foreigners is a child smuggler and has picked her up? What if they smuggle her out of Japan?* The feeling of paralysis returned, making me unable to move once again. But I knew that we had to keep looking. Mustering all my strength, I pushed aside my sense of paranoia and told Sharmeen to continue looking for her inside, while I dashed outside the McDonald's. I figured that as long as she didn't venture outside or no one had taken her out of the restaurant, it would be okay and we would surely find her somewhere inside.

As I came out through the door, there was no one in the parking lot: it was filled with parked cars. I went running around the whole place, looked in the nearby streets, but didn't notice anything suspicious. Was I too late? Has someone indeed taken her away? I felt completely exhausted as my legs gave way and I sat down on the kerb, almost weeping. Then suddenly, the thought that perhaps Sharmeen had located her inside allowed me to gather my strength and run back inside—only to find Sharmeen still looking for her. I could tell that she was also on the verge of crying, especially seeing me come from outside without Farhana. It seemed like our daughter had just vanished from the place. *Is it possible that we have lost our daughter?*

As Sharmeen started to cry and I was on the verge of having a nervous breakdown, I saw the set of stairs going to the second floor at the far end of the first floor. Again, with a little glimmer of hope of finding her upstairs, I ran towards and then up the stairs, looking for Farhana. As I started to run up the stairs, I managed to yell to Sharmeen to keep an eye on the exits. As I got close to the top, I saw Farhana standing alone, not too far from the edge of the staircase, weeping quietly. I raced up the rest of the way, picked her up and held her tightly. I could feel her trembling as tears rolled down my eyes. She held me even tighter and just started to bawl. As I walked down the stairs holding her, Sharmeen saw us and I could see the sense of relief on her face. The whole ordeal probably lasted a little over ten minutes, but it felt like an eternity. It is almost impossible to describe in words what it felt like during those moments: a sense of helplessness along with a feeling of utter despair, while being gripped by sheer paralysing fear, is probably a reasonable description. Relieved and delighted, the three of us quickly got out of the McDonald's, got into our car, and started on our drive back to Tokyo. It was as if we wanted to get as far away from that evil place as quickly as possible. Thirty minutes into our drive, Farhana said that she was hungry. That's when we realized that we had left the chicken nuggets back at the McDonald's.

Chapter 21

The Sarariman Pride—Drinking All The Way From *Tatemae* To *Honne*

After the strong dose of our panic attack, we decided to stay put in the safety of Tokyo for a while. Sharmeen was once again getting busy with her studies, and I was busy as ever at work. Our business was booming, and we were getting all kinds of new opportunities. During this time, I got a call from Tom one day, and he shared some very good news with me. He mentioned that Toshiba's semiconductor division had reached out to us to see if we might be interested in buying one of their manufacturing plants in Iwate prefecture, located in the northern part of Honshu, the main island. This was just music to my ears because buying their factory would mean that we would almost immediately experience a boost in our Japan revenue.

Perhaps sensing my excitement, Tom cautioned me that acquiring a factory from another company and successfully integrating it with our operations was not going to be easy, especially since it was a foreign entity. He added that we had a long way to go and a lot of work ahead of us to make it happen. I agreed with Tom but said that for a 100-year-old, top Japanese conglomerate to reach out to us for a potential merger and acquisition (M&A) was a big deal. He agreed with my sentiment. Tom told me that I may have to be part of the 'due diligence' process—an investigative process to understand whether Toshiba's factory would be a good fit for us to acquire. Indeed many M&As end up in failure due to a plethora of issues, starting from differences in company philosophy to product mismatch to differences in company culture to personal egos of the top management and so on. Before hanging up, he said that he would let me in on more details as needed and swore me to secrecy, asking me not to share this information with anyone.

Our inhouse expert for M&A was a gentleman named Jim Long. I knew of him and had met him a couple of times before but had never had a chance to work or interact with him in any meaningful way. He always came across as a serious person and a man of very few words, and I had hardly seen him chit-chat with anyone in the office. Tom called me back in a couple of weeks and told me that Jim would take the lead in the negotiations with Toshiba.

Sure enough, in a week, Jim showed up at our Tokyo office. I made sure that I said hello. We exchanged a few pleasantries, and I asked him about the M&A. He said that he was working on it and would let me know if he needed anything. That was pretty much the last time I heard from him. During the next few months, he visited Japan many times, but he would show up in the office only for a day or so and then disappear. I figured that he was in some meetings with the Toshiba folks. Whenever he was in the office, he pretty much kept to himself. He never said anything to any of us about what was going with the negotiation. In fact, we didn't even know if there was any negotiation going on. I never saw him involving anyone from our Japan office in whatever it was that he was doing in Japan.

My interest didn't lie so much in participating in the negotiations or the due diligence process, but more in ensuring that the deal was closed successfully as it meant significant revenue for us. Still, I was a little dismayed to be kept in the dark by Jim about such an important deal with a top Japanese semiconductor company. I called Tom a couple of times to follow up, and it seemed like even he wasn't fully aware how the M&A discussions with Toshiba were progressing. Finally, after about three months or so of being in the dark, I got a call from Tom. He informed me that there had been good progress made and that the deal was likely to close shortly. When I asked him why I had been kept in the dark, he confessed that even he had been kept in the dark. Apparently, the M&A with Toshiba was mostly a one-man show, with Jim doing all the work in secrecy.

Soon, the details of the M&A started to emerge. The agreement we had with Toshiba was that we would enter into a Joint Venture or JV arrangement, instead of buying their factory in Iwate outright. We would share ownership of the factory for three years, and during this period, Toshiba would pay us on a 'cost plus' basis. In other words, whatever our cost was to run the factory, they would pay a certain percentage on top of that. In return, we would utilize our expertise to reduce the operation cost every year. After the third year, we would fully own the factory. I had been waiting for months to see how much additional business this deal would bring for our sales, and it turned out that the deal meant a significant growth in our Japan revenue. I was delighted. Besides, a JV with one of the top Japanese conglomerates such as Toshiba would provide a sort of legitimacy to our Japan branch, which was not so easy for a relatively small and especially foreign company like ours. In fact, this had been one of our biggest impediments in growing our business, even though through sheer effort and hard work, our business had been growing. Using this JV as a springboard, we would have a much higher chance of winning even more business from other top semiconductor companies. I felt like the sky was the limit now.

Shibata San, Fujita San and I had been discussing this new JV and decided that sales may be called upon soon to take over the

Toshiba business. So, with the closing of the deal imminent, we started to make regular trips to the Toshiba factory in Iwate to get a better understanding of their facility, their process, their products and most importantly, their people. Along with the Toshiba plant, we would also acquire about a thousand of their employees. We figured that it would be good to establish a relationship with their sarariman as early as possible, to ensure a smooth transition once the deal was closed. The factory was located in a small town called Kitakami in Iwate prefecture, and was about a three-hour ride due north on the Tohoku Shinkansen line.

The head of Toshiba's Iwate manufacturing plant was a gentleman named Suzuki. He spoke English relatively well, having spent three years running a Toshiba factory in Malaysia. He was a key player of the JV, and during our multiple trips, we had quite a few meetings with Suzuki and his top people, always followed by dinners—the usual sarariman routine. Over the course of a few months, we had managed to build a good rapport with Suzuki San and some of his senior people, especially with three gentlemen named Takeru Honda, Kento Yamashita and Tomohiro Chida. I found Takeru San, who was from their engineering department, to be a little reserved. Yamashita San from the production department seemed very knowledgeable about the factory and came across as a rather open and amicable person. Chida San from their quality department was a very friendly and funny guy. They were all in key leadership positions at the factory, so their support would be crucial for the JV to succeed. But we had been hearing some rumours that some of the people from Toshiba were not very happy about the JV and preferred not to join our company. In fact, Tom called me one day regarding the same rumour and asked me to find out if indeed it was true. He said that our management was concerned that if many of the Toshiba employees were really unhappy about joining us, the chances of a successful integration could be hampered.

During our next trip, over dinner with my new sarariman friends from Toshiba Iwate, I decided to ask them about it directly. All of them seemed genuinely surprised to hear about such a rumour and assured me that it was not true.

'We are all happy to join an American company, Asif San', Chida San said. 'We feel like we have become international now', he added, smiling.

'But that's you guys, Chida San. How about all the other people, like factory operators and so on? Do you think they are happy to join us?' I enquired. 'I mean Toshiba is a very well-known company, and I wouldn't be surprised if some people weren't happy about this new business arrangement', I added.

Yamashita San said that it was certainly possible that some people weren't thrilled about working for a smaller American firm.

'Everyone was given a choice, and we all joined voluntarily, Asif San. So I am not worried about it', he said with confidence.

Yamashita San also elaborated that most of them had been working for Toshiba semiconductor manufacturing facilities within Japan, all their lives. Their internal customer was a Toshiba products division. Now they would have a chance to work with different overseas companies. And many of them were excited about this new prospect.

'Before this, almost no foreign guests visited our factory here in Iwate. But for the last six months, we have had so many foreign visitors. Good chance to practice our English', Takeru San added with a smile on his face.

I decided to not pursue this any further and just enjoy the nice sushi dinner with them instead. That evening, I called Tom and conveyed my conversation with the three sarariman from Toshiba. He seemed to be happy to hear what they had to say.

The final closure of the JV deal with Toshiba was cause for a big celebration. The factory held many events over a week-long period. Our top management from Arizona also came for the opening ceremony. Some of the folks from the Tokyo office were also invited. The following week, Suzuki San invited his direct reports and the management from our Japan office for a special dinner in Iwate. Fujita San, Shibata San and I joined, along with Takeru San, Yamashita San and Chida San from his team, among some other management folks from the factory. We had had a few meetings with some of the folks from the factory. In the afternoon, I ran into Suzuki San and he told me that he had arranged for a very special treat for all of us that night: one of the main delicacies from the Iwate area was on the menu. I asked him what it was but he wouldn't tell me.

'It will be a good surprise for you, Asif San. You will like it', he assured me.

With all the great meals I had had so far, I was sure that it was going to be good, especially since this was part of a major celebration. Still, I wished that Suzuki San would tell me what the special dish was. I couldn't help but worry. While my overall culinary experience in Japan had been great, there had been a few not-so-pleasant surprises.

Once, during a business trip to Nagano with Satoh San, the folks from Hitachi invited us to a 'special dinner', consisting of a local delicacy. I didn't bother to ask what was so 'special' about it, and was a little shocked when they served us raw horse meat sashimi as an appetizer, beautifully decorated on a pretty platter. I had heard that Nagano is well-known for horse meat. But still, to be actually served raw horse meat didn't feel very kosher to me, even though I did try it. There were other kinds of food, but I had lost my appetite by then, only to get hungry later in the evening when I was at the hotel. Luckily, I had found a Burger King close to where I was staying.

On another occasion, during a visit to Sony Oita, the head of all their manufacturing sites in Kyushu, Koga San, invited Shibata San and me to a 'special' restaurant serving a fish delicacy, for which Oita is famous. When we arrived, I was excited to see the well-lit, beautifully decorated restaurant designed in traditional architecture. I saw a large sign outside the restaurant with some elegant kanji (Chinese)[17] characters and a black-and-white artwork of a big round fish. It reminded me of the character Bloat, a blowfish from the Pixar animation movie *Finding Nemo*. When I asked Shibata San about the picture on the signboard, he said that it was a *fugu* restaurant.

Fugu is Japanese for blowfish or puffer fish. Turned out that the restaurant specialized in serving all kinds of blowfish dishes, including sushi and sashimi. But my excitement disappeared when Shibata San explained to me why fugu restaurants are so special. Apparently, blowfish are more poisonous than cyanide, unless handled properly. A simple mistake in preparing it can prove fatal. In Japan, the handling and preparation of fugu is strictly controlled by law. Only 'special chefs' are allowed to prepare fugu. These chefs must go through three or more years of training to meet the high standards required to properly handle the fugu fish. The restaurant only served fugu dishes, so I didn't have much of a choice but to eat some of them. The meal didn't taste so great after hearing Shibata San's comments about the danger it could pose. I looked for a Burger King or a McDonald's around my hotel afterwards, but unfortunately, I couldn't find one that evening.

* * *

Suzuki San had arranged for a minibus to take us to the restaurant. When we arrived at the place, it looked like a big traditional

---

[17] The Japanese alphabet consists of three different writing systems: hiragana, katakana and kanji. Kanji are Chinese characters or symbols, each character representing a word in itself. Hiragana and katakana are two different ways to write the same set of forty-six phonetic sounds. Hiragana is used to write Japanese words only, whereas katakana is used to write words borrowed from foreign languages.

Japanese home to me. I tried to see if there were any pictures on the large signboard which might provide some hint about the 'special delicacy', but there were no such signs. There were fifteen of us that evening, a fairly large group. Soon, we were ushered into a large dining area with floor seating. I love everything that is traditional Japanese and was glad to see that all the waitresses were wearing beautiful kimonos and the traditional decor inside. Yamashita San, who was sitting next to me, whispered that this was a very expensive place, and Suzuki San only invited people here on special occasions.

In sarariman tradition, the celebration started with a round of cold beer followed by various types of appetizers and Japanese sake. I was waiting for the menu, but none arrived. I asked Yamashita San about it, and he mentioned that the place had no menu. It was known for its special courses, and we would be served soon. Indeed, soon, a few large platters in the shape of wooden boats arrived filled with all kinds of sashimi. As always, the quality of the sashimi was great, and I felt a little relieved that there was no weird 'delicacy' like the ones I had experienced in Nagano and Oita. At least not yet. Just in case, I tried to eat as much of the sashimi as I could.

After the appetizers, a few waitresses paraded in with what looked to me like large soup bowls made of fine Japanese ceramic and covered with wooden lids. The outside of each of the bowls was decorated with artwork of various Japanese scenes, some with images of Fuji San, others with the famous temples of Kyoto, etc. They placed one in front of each of us. Yamashita San cautioned that it was very hot and not to touch the bowl. I wondered if this was the special delicacy that Suzuki San had told me about. When I asked Yamashita San, he just winked at me with a smile. The waitresses helped each of us take the lids off. Once mine was removed, I saw what looked like a dark-coloured soup with something round on the top. At first, I couldn't tell what it was, even though the 'round thing' looked faintly familiar to me. Then I realized what it was: there was a whole turtle floating in my soup. I just kept staring at it as everyone around me started to eat. My appetite completely disappeared.

Noticing that I wasn't eating and perhaps realizing that I might find their delicacy a little strange, Yamashita San assured me that it was tasty, and encouraged me to at least try it. He told me that it was called Suppon Nabe, or soup made out of soft-shell turtle, a well-known delicacy of the Iwate prefecture. I was worried that if I didn't at least pretend to eat, it would draw unnecessary attention towards me, and everyone would say how great it was and urge me to try it. So hesitantly and cautiously, I dipped my spoon into the soup, trying not to touch the turtle. I couldn't help but imagine the turtle crawling out of my bowl. I tried it a little, and it didn't taste as bad as it looked. I would have eaten the whole thing if not for the turtle floating on top. I pretended to eat it and luckily, everyone was too busy eating and chatting to notice me. I was glad that the bowl came with a lid. After a few minutes, I replaced the lid, pretending that I was done with my soup. I could tell that Yamashita San had noticed what I was trying to do, but the kind and gentle man that he was, he didn't make any fuss.

'Asif San, how did you like our special dish?' Suzuki San asked in his loud voice from the other end of the table.

'It tasted great, even though I must admit that the whole turtle in the soup seemed a little strange', I replied.

Everyone laughed.

'Never mind, I am glad you enjoyed it, Asif San', Suzuki San said, sounding pleased.

I became anxious for the waitresses to take away the soup bowls quickly in case someone found out that I actually ate very little. I hoped that there would be more food coming as I was still a little hungry. There was some rice at the end, but that pretty much concluded our dinner.

After dinner, the team invited us to a 'second place'. It was already past ten. Being in the very north of the main island of Honshu, Kitakami is much colder than Tokyo. It was early January, and there was snow everywhere. Apparently, the second place was a Japanese bar, about a fifteen-minute walk from the restaurant. Instead of taking taxis, everyone decided to walk, even though the temperature was a few degrees below zero with the wind howling, making it feel even colder. I wanted to go back to my hotel and try to take advantage of the McDonald's that I had seen before it closed. But the sarariman won't have any of it and insisted that I join them, reminding us that we were their special guests for the night. Shibata San and Fujita San also insisted that I join. Shibata San whispered that this was another good chance to build a relationship with these top management folks of the Toshiba facility. Reluctantly, I agreed to join them at the next place.

I was glad when we finally arrived at the karaoke bar. It was good to be inside a warm place. Soon, the drinks flowed and the singing began. I was too hungry to sing and asked Shibata San if we could order some food. He handed me a menu, and I was surprised to see that it was in English.

'Asif San, please order whatever you want', he said.

I was ecstatic to find that they had quite a few choices of Western food, such as chicken wings, cheese fries and pizza. We ordered all three of them, handing the menu back to Shibata San. Now, with some warm and normal food arriving imminently, I started to feel much better and joined in with the guys, singing some old Beatles songs.

After a couple of hours of chatting, singing, eating and drinking, everyone decided it was time to call it a night. Everyone got quiet all of a sudden. *Perhaps they are tired*, I thought. Then Takeru San, the quietest among the group, suddenly stood up and started to shout something in Japanese, while the others seemed be trying to calm him down. It was clear to me that Takeru San had had a little too much to drink that night. Then, he started to walk towards me while yelling something. The person who was sitting next to me had gone to the restroom and the chair was empty, so an inebriated Takeru San sat down next to me and said, 'Asif San, I hate Toshiba.'

I didn't know what to do with that information. Clearly, it was the alcohol talking. I felt like I had to say something.

'Why Takeru San, Toshiba is a great company.'

'No, it is a bad company. Very, very bad', he repeated a couple of times. 'Why did they sell the factory to you? I think Toshiba betray all of us', Takeru San continued with his finger pointing at me. Even though I was right next to him, he was shouting in my ears. I was at a loss for words. Obviously, Toshiba didn't sell their factory to me but to the company that I worked for. I guess, at that moment, I was representing our company to Takeru San.

'My family is not happy at all. My wife's family is now ashamed of me. No one knows your company here. Everyone knows Toshiba. I hate Toshiba. No one is happy to join your company.'

Up until now, I was writing off this incident just as some silly remarks of a drunk man talking gibberish. But what he had said captured my attention. Wasn't this the same rumour that we had heard before—that some of the Toshiba employees were not so happy with this JV arrangement?

'What do you mean your wife's family is now ashamed of you, Takeru San? What does that mean?' I asked him, wanting to know more.

He was about to answer but a few people, including Yamashita San and Chida San, came over and escorted Takeru San out of the bar. They returned in a while and Yamashita San sat down next to me and apologized.

'I am very sorry about that, Asif San. Please don't mind Takeru. He always acts strange when he drinks.'

'No problem. I hope he is okay. He seemed really upset.'

'He will be fine. We put him in a cab. He has been working very hard.'

Everyone went very quiet after the incident. The party ended, and we all went our own ways.

The next morning, Fujita San, Shibata San and I caught the Tohoku Shinkansen back to Tokyo. I was still bothered by what Takeru San had said the night before. Shibata San was sitting next to me, and I decided to discuss the matter with him.

'Kitakami is a very small town, Asif San. Toshiba is the largest company there. Everyone is very proud of it, and especially the local sarariman are very proud to work for Toshiba. Now, they have to work for our company, and no one has heard of us. Not everyone is happy about the whole thing.'

'Really?' I was surprised since I had asked the three gentlemen from Toshiba about this, including Takeru San. They had all denied it.

'Of course they will say that to you, Asif San. But don't worry. It will be fine once they start working for the JV. It is not so easy to accept change for many people. And this is a very big change for them.'

I always liked Shibata San's pragmatism and was glad to hear him say that things would be okay.

What about the assurance from Yamashita San and Chida San a few days ago, when they were very happy to join an American company? Why couldn't they admit that everyone wasn't excited about the JV? Most of them had worked for the plant all their lives. Toshiba is indeed a household name, not only in Japan, but around the world. On the other hand, very few people outside our industry were familiar with our company. I would be very worried if I were them. There was nothing wrong with admitting some apprehension; this was indeed a major change for all of them.

It hit me at that point how unusual it had been not to hear any kind of complaints or *concerns* during the last few months from any Toshiba employees. Everyone appeared to be excited about joining an American company. Could it be that their *tatemae* was on display instead of their *honne?* I had read about these two Japanese traits in a magazine recently.

Japanese society puts a high value on conformity and social harmony, wa, where the needs of the many always outweigh the needs of the few. People are expected to prioritize what is best for the country, the community, the company and the group over their self-interests. To maintain harmony, public discord and disagreements are avoided whenever possible. As a result, it is common for most Japanese people to avoid voicing how they actually feel or what they really think in public settings, especially if it goes against popular beliefs, opinions and decisions. This is also one of the main reasons why they rarely say 'no' to even the toughest of requests, causing confusion and misunderstanding among foreign businesspeople and visitors.

One's true feelings and thoughts, which are rarely displayed in public, are known as honne. A person's honne is only shared with the closest of family members and friends. What is displayed to the outside world instead is called tatemae. The word 'honne' literally means 'true sound' and 'tatemae' literally means 'the front of a building'. Honne and tatemae play large roles in all walks of Japanese life, in business settings, among broader family members and even among close friends. Tatemae is invariably what foreigners see for the most part when they visit Japan. In my opinion, that is why Japanese people *always* seem to come across as super polite, kind and helpful. While indeed, the Japanese in general tend to be very polite, there is a certain degree of superficiality in such behaviour.

When everyone at the Toshiba plant was telling me how happy they were with the JV for the past few months, some of it was their tatemae on display. In his drunken state, that night, Takeru San expressed how he actually felt about it, accidentally exposing his honne, sharing his genuine concern and dislike for the imminent JV.

But I was still wondering about his comment about his wife's family now being ashamed of him. I asked Shibata San, and he told me to forget about it.

'It is probably his English. He wasn't saying it properly, I think.'

'C'mon, Takeru San's English is not that bad. I think he meant what he said, that his wife's family is not so happy about the change. But I don't understand why they were ashamed. It's not like Takeru San did anything wrong', I carried on.

As we discussed it further, Shibata San's explanation started to make sense. Indeed, there was some issue with the language Takeru San had used, but it could also be true, Shibata San explained. In a small town such as Kitakami, working for a large Japanese conglomerate such as Toshiba was a matter of pride for all the sarariman and other employees. Takeru San's in-laws were probably very proud of the fact that their daughter was married to a Toshiba sarariman. So they were probably unhappy with this change. Perhaps, Takeru San had used the word 'ashamed' to emphasize how strongly they felt about it. Whatever it was, clearly he seemed to be under some sort of family pressure for having to leave Toshiba. Of course, Takeru San's tatemae would not allow him to express such concern to his office workers or to us—certainly not to a gaijin sarariman like me, who was sent by the head office.

Now that I got a firsthand example of the tatemae and honne, I figured if I wanted to find out what my fellow sarariman were really thinking and feeling about something, it would most likely be pointless to ask them directly as all I would get would be their tatemae. To get access to their feeling or honne, I would just have to get them drunk.

Chapter 22

Change of Guards

The Toshiba JV was a very big deal for our company, not only in terms of additional revenue stream but also in terms of being able to close such a high-profile M&A deal with a top Japanese conglomerate. Japan was now prominently on the radar of all the key folks at our head office. The top management couldn't be happier with our accomplishments. The Japan office had now moved from their peripheral vision, squarely on to their main screens.

Within a couple of months after the successful JV, Suzuki San began to appear regularly in our Tokyo office, even though his primary job was to run the factory in Kitakami. Many of us didn't understand at first what the purpose of his regular visits to our Tokyo sales office was. But pretty soon, Suzuki San started to inject himself into various meetings and decision-making processes related to the sales activities. It became clear to most of us that Suzuki San saw himself as the head of all of our Japan business, both operations and sales, despite the fact that his job was to run the factory, and Fujita San was already present as our head of sales. The two of them started to clash often on various issues. Initially, it came across as a subtle tension between the two of them. Then they began to disagree on almost every issue openly, in front of all of us: clearly, their tatemae was thrown out the window due to their egos as two leaders of our Japan region. Soon, it became clear that there was only room for one. For me, going to some of these meetings was like watching two samurais battling it out for the top position.

Originally from Okinawa, Suzuki San was a big man with a boisterous voice. He was direct and often abrupt, nothing like a typical Japanese sarariman. His demeanour reminded me of a sumo wrestler, ready to push his opponent out of the ring at any moment. In comparison, Fujita San was mild-mannered, a perfect gentleman. Suzuki San always seemed nice to me. I wasn't sure if it was because he liked me or because he knew that I had ties with the upper management in Arizona. Regardless, personally I didn't have any problem with him. I rather enjoyed his direct mannerism. It was a breath of fresh air in a place where most of the people were only showing their tatemae. But their constant rivalry was damaging the morale of our office, something we had worked very hard to build in the past few years. At times, I felt like dismissing both of them and taking on the leading role myself, but I felt like I was too junior, only a director, whereas these guys were both senior vice presidents.

While our Japan office was struggling with this in-fighting, I had to go to Arizona for a week for some important meetings related to one of our customer programmes. While there, I happened to bump into our CEO, Steve Sullivan, and he asked me how things were going. *Business has been good but we have an issue with Suzuki San and Fujita San, which is getting quite serious.* I really felt like sharing this with him but didn't quite know how to start. Steve must have sensed my hesitation. He invited me to his office, closed the door and asked me to speak freely about any issues. Being totally frustrated with the situation back in Tokyo and with no solution in sight, I decided to tell Steve what was going on between Suzuki San and Fujita San and how it was affecting our office folks negatively.

Steve seemed a little surprised. Clearly, he wasn't aware of the situation. I wasn't surprised as I hadn't shared this information with Tom yet. He asked me a few questions and then promised to look into it. I told him that if the issue was not resolved soon, we might lose some of the progress we had made in the last few years. He again promised to take care of it one way or the other, and asked me to give him a little time. Hearing this straight from our CEO, I returned to Tokyo with a sense of relief, even though I was wondering how exactly Steve was going to sort this out. Either FujitaSan or Suzuki San had to go, in my opinion. Who was Steve going to let go? We needed Fujita San for our sales, but Suzuki San was one of the key guys for our JV to be successful, especially with his influence in the new JV factory. It wasn't going to be an easy decision. But I knew that it needed to be resolved quickly. Before I left, I also brought it up with Tom and informed him of my discussion with Steve. He seemed a little surprised and annoyed that I hadn't shared all these details with him, but I explained to him that this was a relatively recent phenomenon that I was indeed planning to discuss with him. But Steve beat him to it, unfortunately. He seemed to be fine with my explanation.

When I returned to the office, I started to notice that Fujita San wasn't quite himself. His attitude had changed significantly in the two weeks that I was gone. Whereas before he was standing his ground as the head of sales in his confrontation with Suzuki San, now he almost didn't seem to care any more. Moreover, I was surprised to see that he was allowing Suzuki San to run the show, to a certain extent. In the battles of the two samurais, Suzuki San seemed to clearly be winning. I felt concerned as I wasn't sure that this was the best outcome for our sales office. While Suzuki San had good leadership skills, his background was running operations and factories for almost forty years for Toshiba. He had no experience running a large sales organization.

Also, having worked for Toshiba for forty years, I felt like Suzuki San sometimes still acted like a Toshiba sarariman. I sometimes wondered if he still thought that he was working for Toshiba, instead of us. Having witnessed Suzuki San's very strong and aggressive personality, I wasn't surprised that he was winning the battle with Fujita San, but I wasn't happy with this outcome.

I was expecting some change imminently, such as a call from Tom any day with a resolution to this office fiasco. But two months passed by, and there was no action or mandate from the head office to address the issue. Suzuki San was more in control of our office now. Every day, more and more, Fujita San was keeping to himself. Many of us would still go to him for his inputs regarding sales matters and he always provided them. But I could tell that his heart and mind weren't in the game as they used to be.

Then one day, I got a call from Mike Anderson. Mike was the head of one of our business units, and he was one of the few people who had believed in my initiatives in Japan from very early on. His support, along with Tom's, was crucial to getting support from most of our product folks. Mike had visited Japan a few times during the last three years. Whenever he was here, I would accompany him to all the customer visits and we would go out for dinner and drinks. I really enjoyed his great sense of humour and we got along very well. I also admired him for his leadership skills and very strong family values.

'How are you doing, buddy?' Mike asked in his usual happy mood.

'Truth be told, Mike, things are not the best around here these days.'

'I heard. Guess what? I will be helping you out, my friend.'

'That's great, Mike, but the issue at hand is not due to the lack of support from the US side but our two samurais here who just can't seem to get along. Their infighting is bringing everyone's morale down.'

Mike laughed, hearing me refer to Suzuki San and Fujita San as two samurais.

'That's why I am calling you, my friend. General MacArthur will be coming to your rescue soon', referring to the famous American general who led Japan's rebuilding efforts after the devastation of the Second World War.

'Steve Sullivan had told me something like this might happen, but it has been two months already. Besides, who is going to be our General Macarthur?'

'Me', Mike replied.

'What do you mean, Mike? Are you planning to move here?'

'That's the plan and that's why I am calling you.'

This was very good news indeed, I thought. But I still couldn't believe it. While Mike was very supportive of our Japan business, I had a hard time picturing him living in Japan.

'I can' believe it. That is awesome, Mike. Is Leah okay with this?' I asked, referring to his wife.

'Well, not quite yet. But I am working on it.'

'I see. But what is the plan? Will you be running the sales group and rescuing us from Suzuki San? In any case, just a warning. He is a force to reckon with.'

'Forget about Suzuki. Tell me about life in Tokyo. I still have to convince Leah about the move. I may need your help. But for now keep this news under wraps till everything is finalized.'

I wondered how Suzuki San and Fujita San would react to this news when they found out.

A week later, Mike arrived in Tokyo with Leah, for a house-hunting trip. But I was also sure that the main purpose was to 'sell' Tokyo to her. Leah had heard horror stories about how most Japanese homes tend to be very small. I could relate as they would be moving from their mini ranch in Arizona. With the help of our HR, I had already arranged to show them a few nice houses in some of the nicer neighbourhoods. Just like us, both Mike and Leah were somewhat sticker shocked when they heard the exuberant Tokyo rents. But both Mike and I kept reminding her that the company was going to cover for it along with many other things, including the very high tuition at the international schools for their kids. But it was interesting to see their face with the look of the same shock that we experienced when we had first arrived. Sharmeen and I took them around the city, focusing on all the positive things, of course. I wanted Leah to like Tokyo so that Mike could move here and help us out of our predicament.

I guess the trip was a success as Mike called me two days after they left to confirm his move. Even though I was supposed to keep this a secret, I had shared the news with Shibata San, as we would often lament over the bad situation in the office. Within a week after Mike's trip, Fujita San was informed by our head office of Mike's assignment and he told everyone in the Japan office. With his exact role not so clear, my sarariman friends and colleagues were abuzz with rumours and asked me about it. I told them that I also wasn't sure what was the truth. I felt that they didn't quite believe me, though, as they knew that Mike and I were close.

Mike returned in about two weeks to officially meet and greet everyone in the office. I introduced him to Suzuki San and could immediately sense the subtle tension between them. But unlike Fujita San, Suzuki San seemed more tense this time, whereas Mike looked comparatively more relaxed. Suzuki San said that he would schedule an office meeting later that morning to introduce Mike to the whole team. I took Mike to see Fujita San as well, but the meeting with him was quite brief.

Suzuki San scheduled the meeting for 11 a.m. and we all gathered in our largest conference room in the office. After welcoming everyone, Suzuki San proceeded to introduce Mike in English. While he didn't quite say it outright, it came across as if Mike was there to run sales for him.

'Sorry, Suzuki San, but that's not really right', Mike interrupted him with almost no emotion in his voice.

Here we go, World War II all over again, I thought. However, I was quite happy that Mike at least addressed Suzuki with the honorific 'San'. Mike wasn't known to be the most culturally sensitive person in the world.

'What do you mean, Mike San?' Suzuki San said in his boisterous manner and loud voice.

'I am not here to run sales for you. I was told that I am here to run all of Japan—be the country head.'

That was the first time I saw Suzuki San at a loss for words. He seemed to be getting a taste of his own medicine. There was pin-drop silence in the room, a sense of disbelief as these exchanges were taking place between the two.

'Ah ah, that is not what I was told', Suzuki San replied, managing to get his composure back quickly and letting out a fake laugh. I wondered if anyone had ever openly challenged him like this before.

'That's what the CEO told me', Mike said.

'I think difficult, Mike San. You are not Japanese.'

Suzuki San's comment reminded me of my first encounter with Satoh San.

'Well then, looks like we have a problem', Mike countered.

Once again, Suzuki San seemed to be at a loss for words. 'Well, I am the head of Japan', he managed to say, but this time in a much softer tone.

'Great, then you can run Japan. I will call our CEO and let him know that he was wrong and that you are running Japan. Guess I will not be moving here after all.'

With that, Mike walked out of the meeting room.

Everyone else had been listening intently in disbelief and seemed to be completely taken aback at Mike's sudden exit from the meeting room. No one knew exactly how to react or what to do. Suzuki San said something in Japanese and adjourned the meeting, much to everyone's relief.

When I returned to my office, I found Mike sitting there, waiting for me.

'Lunch?' Mike asked.

'Lunch? What just happened there, Mike?' I asked, even though I was impressed at how Mike had managed to rattle Suzuki San at their first encounter. But still, I figured it might have been best to have rocked the boat so violently on his first day.

'Don't worry about it. Let's go to lunch.'

Just as we were about to leave, Suzuki San showed up in my office.

'Mike San, gomennasai. Looks like some misunderstanding, perhaps. Let's go to lunch and have a good discussion', Suzuki San said.

'Oh, thanks. I can't go to lunch today. I have a very important lunch appointment.'

'Oh, I see. We can talk later then.' With that, Suzuki San left my room.

'Why did you ask me to go to lunch if you have an important lunch appointment?' I asked Mike, all confused.

'I do have an important lunch appointment. With you, buddy. Let's get out of here.'

Did he just blow off the head of Japan to have lunch with me? I knew then that Mike was certainly going to come out ahead in this second round of the battle for our leadership position.

Within two weeks, there was an official announcement from our CEO. It said that Mike was moving to Tokyo to lead the sales team reporting to him. Suzuki San was going to return to Iwate to run the factory and report to the Chief Operating Officer. It also said that I was going to report directly to Mike and Fujita San had decided to leave the company. With that one message, the whole thing was finally settled.

Mike moved to Tokyo with his family after a few weeks and Suzuki San returned to Kitakami to run operations as he was originally supposed to do. Fujita San stayed with us for two more months to help with the transition and then left our company. I was glad to see that things were finally getting back to normal. Unfortunately, these changes were a little too much for Satoh San and he decided to quit as well. I was sad to see him go as we had worked very closely together and gone through some tough times to turn the place around. Also, I had formed a friendship with him in the process. But I could see that he felt very out of place with all these changes in the office. So while I was sad, I realized that this was for the best for him as well as the company. I took both Fujita San and Satoh San out separately for farewell lunches.

By the time Mike had relocated to Japan, we had already established a solid team in the office, quite capable of handling the new business growth. His primary function was to take on a leadership role and provide guidance to the team. With him at the helm, our overall support within various functions of the company improved even further.

A man of staunch evangelical faith, Mike is originally from New Jersey, but lived in Arizona most of his life. Back home, he drove a bright yellow, jacked-up Ford F-350 pickup truck. With a crew cut and lean build, he looked more like a marine than an executive. He was also one of the most culturally insensitive persons I had ever met. He made no effort whatsoever to understand and abide by the Japanese culture. It took some time for the local sarariman and employees to get used to his ways. He often made insensitive jokes and not everyone saw the humour in them. While this didn't bother me, I worried about how the sarariman and others would react. But his unwavering support for the local team, his pragmatic management style, and his ability to find humour even in the bleakest of times, made up for what he lacked on the cultural sensitivity side—at least for most of the sarariman. Once the core team realized how important he was for the business to grow, they ignored or tolerated his insensitivities. I would often try to help bridge any cultural gap whenever I felt that it was necessary.

During the first month, we got quite busy taking Mike to meet all of our customers and introducing him as the new head of sales. Subsequently, Mike, Shibata San and I, along with some of our sales folks, would travel regularly for various customer visits. It was always fun to travel with Mike because of his humorous nature.

During one of such business trips, just outside Tokyo, Mike, Shibata San, Umehara San, Y.C. Park and I were on a local train. Usually, Mike would be talking to us about a plethora of subjects but today, he seemed very quiet for some reason. To me, he also appeared to be in some sort of discomfort. I asked him if he was all right. Mike leaned towards us and said that he needed to use the bathroom. Most local trains in Japan do not have bathroom facilities. We were still a good thirty minutes from our destination, and unfortunately, we were on an express train. This meant that the train was not going to make frequent stops. Mike said that there was no way he could wait thirty minutes. YC offered to go and look, in case the train had a restroom. He disappeared into the crowded train, then returned in a few minutes and announced that there indeed was a toilet at the very front of the train. Immediately, Mike dashed towards the front section, navigating through the crowd. It felt like he was gone for an unusually long time and we started to get a little worried. I wondered if he might have got sick. After about fifteen minutes or so, just as I was about to look for him, we saw Mike, walking towards us with a smile on his face. As he approached us, he kept pointing at his toes. It was hard to see what exactly he was pointing at, due to the crowd. When he got nearer, he burst out laughing.

'What's so funny?' I asked while laughing with him for no reason.

He pointed towards his toes, this time lifting his pants up a little. I noticed that his socks were missing.

'What happened to your socks?' I asked, totally confused.

'Well, they didn't have any toilet paper.'

This time, we all burst out laughing. We all thought that he was a genius for coming up with such a practical solution. Also, most people would not share such a story, but Mike wasn't like most people. It became big news in the office the next day and everyone thought it was funny and totally weird behaviour by another gaijin.

There were many funny incidents like this with Mike involved, both inside and outside the office. Our sarariman found him to be hilariously strange. Shibata San bestowed him with the title henna gaijin or a 'strange foreigner'.

It was very nice to have Mike around in Japan for all sorts of help and support. Additionally and soon, my friend Ron Ellenberger would also move to Japan to help integrate the Toshiba plant with our company. With Mike and Ron in the office, I found the whole environment very different compared to when I had first started. It was good to have them around as I could have conversations in the office without having to worry about the cultural nuances or language issues, whenever I felt like it. I couldn't be happier.

Chapter 23

A New Home

The wind of change was not only blowing in the office but on the home front as well. Our little Farhana was ready to graduate from her hoikuen and start kindergarten that fall. We wanted to enrol her at the Tokyo American School, but it was more than an hour-long bus ride away from our house and we didn't feel comfortable with the idea of such a long commute for a four-year-old. For a while, I contemplated moving close to the American School, but that would mean almost an hour and a half of commuting for me every morning. As we started to look around for other international schools, we discovered one in the Setagaya Ward, quite close to us. It was an all-girls, Catholic school called Seisen International School. Unlike the international hoikuen, Seisen was truly an international school, with the majority of its teachers hailing from Canada, Ireland and the US, and with English as their language of instruction. We arranged to take a tour of the school and met with a few of their kindergarten teachers. Satisfied, we enrolled Farhana in Seisen for the fall session.

But we soon ran into a problem, which we had completely forgotten to take into account. Despite being quite close to us, the school wasn't within walking distance. The train wasn't convenient either as the school was a twenty-minute walk from the nearest station. We had only one car which I was using;

besides, Sharmeen still wasn't very comfortable driving in Tokyo. How were we going to drop off and pick Farhana from school? I was still busy travelling during the weekdays, so I could not do it on a regular basis. It wasn't convenient to rely on taxis every day.

We spoke to a couple of friends of ours whose kids were going to Seisen, but their kids were in high school and could commute by themselves. They all recommended that we move closer to the school. They mentioned that the school was right in the middle of a residential neighbourhood, and there were many nice homes around the school. I did some initial research and found out that, indeed, the neighbourhood consisted of quite a few two and three-storey houses. Sharmeen and I drove around the school area and saw some really nice homes, and a few of them had the 'To-Let' sign out front. But just by looking at them, I could tell that the rents for these places were going to be much higher than what we were paying for our maanshon. Still, I decided to explore the possibilities, and once again, enlisted the help of our old friend Miku San from IBM HR.

Always diligent, Miku San found a few nice places within a week and arranged for us to do a tour. The very first house we saw was a nice three-storey house, literally within five minutes' walking distance from the school. It was a really lovely house sitting at a corner of a quiet neighbourhood intersection. As we walked in, we liked the dark wooden floors all over the first floor. There was a large living room and a dining room adjacent to it. There was a door from the dining area that led to the kitchen. Sharmeen and I really liked the kitchen area. It was small but it felt very cozy, with a small counter-top area where we could sit and have breakfast. There were three large bedrooms upstairs, including the master bedroom. The third floor was a single room that we could use as an office or a large storage space. We felt that it was just perfect for us. We also liked that the neighbourhood streets were lined with rows of sakura trees. I could only imagine how nice it would look during the cherry blossom season. Just as it happened with our current maanshon, Sharmeen and I immediately fell in love with the place.

I cautiously asked Miku San about the rent, half scared of what she might say. Indeed, it was higher at about $8,500 per month, a significant hike from the $5,000 per month we were paying for our current maanshon. This meant it was time for me to do another round of negotiation with our head office. But with our business booming, I felt more confident, this time around.

With the change of guards, we now had Mike and Ron living in Japan. Our office was no longer a stranger to the higher expenses of the expatriates. Instead of contacting our HR in our head office, I decided to seek Mike's approval first. After all, he was the boss. I explained to him what was going on with Farhana's school and the issue with the transportation. I also told him about the house Sharmeen and I really liked and how it was walking distance from the school. As I was going on trying to justify the higher rent, Mike stopped me mid-sentence.

'Asif, go for it. I have no issue. If you are seeking my approval, I approve.'

'Wow, that was easier than I thought it would be', I replied honestly.

'Look, you have done a great job in Japan. I know it and our management knows it. Your work and effort have been crucial to getting us to over $300 million in annual revenue for Japan. I don't see this as an issue at all. In fact, let me know if you get any pushback from the HR.'

I was really at a loss for words, which rarely happened to me, hearing my boss praise my efforts for the last three plus years in this way. It felt very good and satisfying and gave me even more incentive to work harder. Grateful for his kind words and quick approval for the higher rent, I thanked Mike for his kindness.

'Yeah, yeah, yeah . . . don't say that I never gave you nothin',
Mike said jokingly—just Mike being Mike. With that settled, we
moved into our new home in Setagaya Ward during the summer,
a couple of months before school started.

Since we wouldn't be able to travel as freely once Farhana
started her kindergarten, we contemplated taking a trip during the
long Obon holiday that was coming up in August. The Obon Week
is a major week-long holiday season in Japan. Obon is a Buddhist
holiday when family members get together to commemorate
their ancestors. Having no family in Japan, we decided to travel
to Nagasaki and Kumamoto in southern Kyushu during the
Obon week.

I had been to Nagasaki a few times to visit Sony, and now was
fulfilling my self-promise to bring Sharmeen and Farhana to this
beautiful city by the bay. Nagasaki always reminded me of San
Francisco, with its hilly roads and the blue water of the harbour
visible from various parts of the city. Nagasaki was a major port
used by the Portuguese and Dutch merchants during the sixteenth
through the nineteenth centuries. Unlike the Dutch traders, the
Portuguese merchants also had a mission to introduce Catholicism
to the island. The ruling Shogun looked at this as a threat and
expelled and prohibited the Portuguese from engaging in any
trade activities with Japan. They preferred the Dutch merchants
instead, whose only objective was trade. During the 264 years of
self-isolation (1603–1868) mandated by the Tokugawa Shogunate,
Nagasaki was the only port open, and it was open only to Dutch
merchants. The city houses the oldest church in Japan, the Oura
Church, built in 1853. There is still a strong Dutch influence in
Nagasaki, which can be seen in the city's old architecture to its
famous Castella Cake.

We rented a car and visited all the touristy places of the city.
Sharmeen and I found visiting the Peace Memorial Hall to be
the highlight of our trip. This is where the second atomic bomb

was dropped during the Second World War. It was a sobering experience amidst an otherwise colourful time in the city. From Nagasaki, we drove to Kumamoto to see one of the famous castles of Japan. It was about a four-hour enjoyable drive through scenic mountain regions with very few other cars on the highway. After about a week of exploring southern Kyushu, we returned to Tokyo. By the time Farhana started her school in September, we had settled into our new home.

* * *

By this time, Sharmeen had completed most of her US medical licensing exams. When our parents had visited us during the past couple of years, it was mostly to take care of Farhana, so that Sharmeen could concentrate on her studies and I could focus on my work. Now, we decided that it was time to invite them back without the 'obligation' of having to watch over their granddaughter. Of course, they'd say that it was their pleasure to watch over Farhana because it gave them an opportunity to bond with their cute little granddaughter. But still, it would be nice to take them around Japan, something we weren't able to do when they were here before. We invited my parents first and they arrived in mid-March, right on time for Hanami with sakura in full bloom. Our plan was also to take them to Kyoto and Nara this time, so that they could experience and appreciate more of Japan.

We didn't even have to go to a park to enjoy the cherry blossoms. Our new neighbourhood street became almost unrecognizable as the lines of sakura trees on both sides of the streets were in full bloom. My parents were very impressed at getting to experience the very brief but very famous Japanese sakura season.

Since I was busy at work, and it was difficult for me to take too many vacation days, I booked a tour of Kyoto and Nara just for my parents. Our plan was that once they were done with those two cities, we would join them and continue on to visit Hiroshima and Island of Shikoku, which we hadn't had a chance to visit yet. Hiroshima is another two and half hours west of Kyoto. So I figured that there was no point for my parents to come back to Tokyo. Instead, I decided that we would join them in Kyoto to go on to Hiroshima. We would be taking the Shinkansen from Tokyo towards Hiroshima. I booked my parents' tickets on the same train and in the same compartment, except that they would get on at Kyoto Station. It required some meticulous planning on my part, but with the help of my admin, Takamiyagi San, it was all arranged.

As our Shinkansen approached the Kyoto station, I started to get worried. *What if my parents were on the wrong platform?* The train would stop for less than a minute. *If they miss the train, how would we find them? I should have given them a local mobile phone.* As the train rolled into Kyoto Station, Sharmeen and I anxiously looked out the window to see if they had made it. Even Farhana joined us in our search for her Dada and Dadi. All of a sudden, Farhana started to yell, 'Look, Dada and Dadi!' Her eyes seemed to be sharper than ours. Following Farhana's gaze, we were relieved to see them standing on the right platform with their carry-ons. They were very excited to see us as well and told us all about their adventures in Kyoto and Nara.

We arrived at Hiroshima Station and checked in a hotel close by the station. We quickly grabbed some lunch at one of the Western restaurants at the hotel and headed out to visit the Peace Museum. It was the first time for all of us, except for my dad, who had visited the place during his trip to Japan, many years ago. As in Nagasaki, visiting the Peace Museum in Hiroshima was another sobering experience. We had read all about the devastation of the first atomic bomb, but to see some of the preserved artefacts portraying the power of the bomb and pictures showing the level of destruction it had caused was horrifying. Ironically, three months earlier, we had visited Pearl Harbour when we had stopped by Hawaii on our way back to Tokyo from our home-leave. Visiting both memorials within a span of four months and seeing such devastation and the sheer number of lives lost on both sides was a sombre reminder that no one really wins in a war.

I had rented a car in Hiroshima so that we had access to our own transportation and would not have to rely on public transportation. The next morning, we checked out and started driving to our next destination, Matsuyama City on Shikoku Island. Matsuyama is most famous for the oldest onsen in Japan, known as Dogo Onsen. Our main purpose for coming to Shikoku was to visit this iconic onsen. It was almost a four-hour drive from Hiroshima to Matsuyama, including a ferry ride for about an hour. We arrived in Matsuyama in the late afternoon, checked in at our hotel, and after relaxing for a couple of hours, went to dinner at a nice Japanese restaurant.

During the ferry, I told everyone about the beauty of the Japanese onsen and its amazing therapeutic qualities. I also told them about Dogo Onsen, how it was the oldest onsen in Japan and a national treasure. My parents were not too keen on it once they heard the details of the etiquette, especially the requirement to be naked despite the baths being segregated by gender. Sharmeen had not had a chance to visit an onsen yet, and this was going to be her first time. She was also not very keen, but was curious as I had shared my onsen stories with her many times before. But still, I thought that I had successfully convinced everyone to take part in the onsen experience. After dinner, as we walked back to the hotel, I told everyone to get ready for our nighttime adventure to Dogo Onsen. Sharmeen was still hesitant, but I managed to convince her to join us. We put on the customary yukatas provided by the hotel and went to my parents' room. My mom opened the door, and I was disappointed to see that she wasn't ready and neither was my dad. They declared that it had been a long day and they really didn't feel like going to the onsen. Instead, they said they would prefer to stay at the hotel and get some rest. A little disappointed, Sharmeen, Farhana and I left by ourselves. But I understood how they felt, remembering my own inhibition during my first onsen experience in Oita, a few years ago.

We decided to walk to Dogo Onsen as it was only a ten-minute walk from our hotel. We noticed quite a few numbers of tourists walking on the sidewalk along with us, also wearing the yukata, surely heading in the same direction as us. Soon, we arrived in front of the majestic three-storey wooden structure of the Dogo Onsen. I was quite stunned to see such stunning architecture in the middle of nowhere. It looked more like a small Japanese castle to me than a bath house. Established over 300 years ago, Dogo Onsen is truly a testament to the richness of Japanese history. While it may not be well-known overseas, it is quite famous in Japan. The onsen was used as the main backdrop for Hayao Miyazaki's 2001 Oscar-winning anime masterpiece, *Spirited Away*.

Just as I had expected, no one spoke any English, but I had done some research beforehand. I knew that Dogo Onsen had two public baths. The larger baths were on the first floor and were called *Kami no Yu* (bath of the gods) and the second set of baths, located on the second floor, are smaller and known as *Tama no Yu* (bath of the spirits). Apparently, locals consider bathing with the spirits or Tama no Yu to be more prestigious, so it costs more. In the lobby area, I paid for all of us, and we parted ways at the entrance. Sharmeen and Farhana went through the red set of curtains, while I through the blue into the Kami no Yu bath area.

This time, I entered confidently, fully versed in the ways of the onsen etiquette. I kind of felt proud and even looked around to see if there were any gaijin needing my expert guidance. But that evening, it seemed like we were the only gaijin inside the onsen, at least in the men's area. After enjoying Japan's oldest baths for an hour, I came out into the main entrance area, fully relaxed, and found Sharmeen and Farhana already waiting there for me. I could tell from their faces that they had had a good time as well. As soon as she saw me, Sharmeen excitedly started to share her experience. Just like my first time, she felt a little shy at first, but once she entered the bath, she found it very relaxing, with all her inhibition quickly melting away along with all her stress. She told me that Farhana was the only baby in the bath that evening and all the Japanese women were quite taken with the cute gaijin toddler. Some of the older women were very nice and had helped Sharmeen with the onsen etiquettes, making things easy for her. They were probably intrigued to see gaijin in such a remote location.

Next morning, after breakfast, we checked out of the hotel, ready to explore the last destination on our itinerary before we headed back to Hiroshima to catch the Shinkansen back to Tokyo—the Matsuyama-Jo (Matsuyama Castle). After spending six days on the road, my dad seemed to be in no mood to visit another historical site and was ready to head back home. He was very annoyed to learn that we were planning to visit another castle. A homebody, he would rather spend time watching the sports channel sitting in our Tokyo home than roaming around in old castles, temples and museums. After six days, it was clear that he had had enough of Japanese history. Since he was a retired civil engineer, I found it odd that he didn't enjoy traditional architecture, design and learning about the construction of these old structures as much. My mom, on the other hand, is the opposite. A retired professor of literature, she loves history and enjoys visiting ancient and historical sites. She pays close attention to everything, carefully reads all the placards and signs, and inspects all the artefacts in detail and even jots some of them down in her notebook, which she carries with her all the time (she published a book about her trip to Japan).

'How many castles does one have to see? Besides, it's a very hot day. Let's skip the castle and just go home', my dad said in a very annoyed voice.

'Dad, how can you come all the way here and not pay a visit to one of the famous castles on the island? This was built by one of the lords in the sixteenth century who was a close ally of the Tokugawa Shogunate. He was an important figure in the famous Japanese battle of Sekigahara . . .'

'You see one, you have seen them all. They all look the same to me. Besides, how can an important castle be on this small island?' my dad said, cutting me off mid-stream, having no interest in my Japanese history lesson.

'It will not be wise to leave without seeing the Matsuyama Castle', my mom chimed in, worried that we might skip visiting this historical site.

'Of course, you must visit the place since I don't want to go', my dad said.

Worried that they may start to fight, Sharmeen offered a reasonable option. 'How about we go to the castle and take a quick look, instead of spending a lot of time there?'

My dad didn't seem too pleased with this suggestion but agreed to it as a reasonable compromise. It was indeed a very hot and humid day. In fact, after walking around the grounds of the Matsuyama Castle for fifteen minutes, all of us were ready to return to the air-conditioned rental car. My parents were glad to be back home in Tokyo after a six-day whirlwind tour of some of the major cities of Japan. It was wonderful for us to spend such quality time together as a family in faraway Japan. Even in my wildest imagination, I could never have thought that I would be so lucky. My parents spent a restful week with us before returning to their home in Arlington, Texas, right outside of Dallas.

Chapter 24

Clubbing Sarariman Style—*Okaa San Nihon Jin Desu*

As the summer was coming to an end, we got the good news that Sony had awarded us another piece of big business. This time around, I hadn't been as involved, but I was happy to see that our sales team had done a good job in getting this new project closed. They invited us to Oita for a celebration. Shibata San, Umehara San and I showed up at the Sony Oita plant for a meeting, followed by an enjoyable dinner. All the key Sony members were there, including Yamazaki San, the gentleman I had met during my first sarariman adventure, Sakamoto San, Mitsumata San, and Koga San. All these sarariman were no longer strangers to me after having worked with them for the past three years.

After dinner, the Sony team took us to the 'second place' at a hostess bar. As we all got settled in a large room, the waitstaff brought in our drinks, nuts, chips and dried squid, a common item served in Japanese bars, and set them down on the large coffee table in front of us. I looked around and there was a small stage at the front of the room with full karaoke systems. As the waiters left, an elegant older woman in a beautiful pink dress entered our private room. From the way all the sarariman from Sony greeted her, it was clear to me that they had met her before and frequented the place often. After greeting everyone else, she turned towards me and said 'hello' in English. She continued with something else in Japanese. I knew enough Japanese by now to understand that she was inquiring about the gaijin sarariman in the room. Shibata San took the lead and introduced me to her. I asked who she was, and Shibata San said that she was the 'Mama San' of the bar.

Mama San gave me her meishi and introduced herself also as 'Mama San'. Along with the elegant look, she had a very cheerful personality. She seemed to be quite popular with the Sony folks. The few minutes she was with us, Mama San made all the sarariman laugh aloud a few times. Before she left, she said something to Shibata San and then bowed, deeply apologizing to me. As she was leaving, Shibata San explained that all the girls at the bar were Japanese, and no one spoke any English. The Sony folks started to apologize to me. Frankly, I wasn't surprised. In fact, most of the hostess bars that I had visited in the last few years had all had the same issue. It was a phenomenon I was used to and told them not to worry.

Soon, Mama San returned with a line of young Japanese ladies parading behind her. All were dressed nicely and wearing heavy makeup; in unison, they bowed and welcomed us. Then each one of them squeezed between each of the sarariman. Now each of us was partnered with a woman from the bar. The lady who sat next to me smiled, bowed slightly and introduced herself as Chikako. She appeared to be in her late twenties, older than the rest of the ladies. I introduced myself using the little Japanese that I knew.

That was the extent of our direct conversation, as we didn't speak each other's language. Everyone else, on the other hand, seemed to be enjoying talking to their respective dates for the night. While Chikako San focused on pouring my drink, ensuring that my glass was never empty, I decided to focus on singing and picked up the thick book that listed all the songs available in their karaoke system. There was a good selection of English songs. I found one of my favourite songs by The Doors, 'Light My Fire'. As I looked up to figure out how to work the system, I saw Chikako San holding a large remote-control unit, ready to add the song for me. I pointed at it on the book, and she expertly punched in the corresponding number on the large screen of the remote controller.

Everyone, half-drunk, stopped chatting, clapped and cheered as the music started to play. I sang the song to my heart's content. It turned out that Mitsumata San knew the song and joined me using a second microphone. We all sang several songs during the course of the night, mostly by the Beatles, of course. After an hour and a half, Mama San returned, joining in on the conversation, making sure that everyone was having a good time. Before she left, she whispered something to Shibata San. I looked at Shibata San, asking him with my look what was going on. Shibata San said that our time was up and we should leave soon. Most of the hostess bars charge by the hour and by the number of people attending. Drinks and food are not included in the hourly rates. It was late, so we ended the party. Shibata San paid the bill and we bid our farewell to all the ladies first, and then to the sarariman from Sony, thanking them once again for the continued business.

Hostess bars are very popular among the Japanese sarariman. They are usually quite expensive. For example, Shibata San had paid over $1,000 for ninety minutes at the hostess bar that night. The price was on the low side because we were in a small town in Oita. But an evening at such a bar in a high-end location like Roppongi in Tokyo, can cost over $3,000 for a party of six or seven sarariman. These are not bars that most of the sarariman frequent regularly, but usually for special occasions. These hostess bars provide a young, Japanese lady as a 'date' for the sarariman for the evening. Their primary job is to keep the sarariman entertained through small talk, ensure that their glasses are never empty, and that each of them participates in the evening's entertainment. The more the sarariman drinks, the higher the bill at the end of the night. Essentially, these women are like modern-day geishas, who have discarded the traditional kimono and face-painting for fashionable Western dresses and modern makeup. Just like the geishas used to entertain the lords and the daimyos in the past, these women keep the modern sarariman entertained.

* * *

A couple of weeks later, we were celebrating another big business award, this time from Toshiba. The plan was to celebrate with some of the sarariman from Toshiba, just as we had done with the Sony folks. We had a nice dinner, and then one of the sarariman proposed that we go to his favourite hostess bar in downtown Oita City. Everyone cheered in agreement at first, but then the mood turned serious, followed by an intense discussion between one of the sarariman from Toshiba and Umehara San and Shibata San.

After a while, curious, I asked Umehara San what was going on. He told me that the Toshiba folks wanted to go to a local popular hostess bar, but they weren't sure if foreigners were allowed there; it was apparently for Japanese people only. They wanted me join them and were scheming how to get me inside the bar. By now, I was no stranger to these pockets of 'discriminatory' behaviour in Japan. In fact, I felt glad as this would be a great opportunity to excuse myself and go back to the hotel to get a good night's sleep instead of yet another night of singing with a bunch of drunk sarariman. But none of them would hear any of it. I had now become their gaijin sarariman friend. I wasn't sure if I should be happy to be part of the sarariman family, or sad as

I was tired and wanted to go back to the hotel. They decided to try their luck, and we all got into a few taxis and headed for this popular hostess club.

Their concern turned out to be warranted. As we gathered around the entrance of the bar, a relatively big guy wearing a dark suit stopped us. The guy was giving me a look-over and then, in extreme politeness and deference, said that gaijin are not allowed in this particular establishment. Umehara San and Shibata San and some of the sarariman from Toshiba huddled around him, and tried to convince him to let me in.

After fifteen minutes of intense negotiation with doorman, Umehara San came over to me smiling and said that everything was fine, I could join them at the bar.

'How did you manage that? The man at the door seemed quite stubborn about not letting any gaijin in.'

'Well, sumimasen (sorry), Asif San, but we lied. We told him that your mother is Japanese', he said, looking a little apologetic but with a mischievous smile.

'By the way, we also told him that you didn't grow up in Japan, so you can't speak Japanese well, but you can speak and understand a little bit. He may ask you a few questions in Japanese, Asif San. *Gambatte kudasai ne* (please do your best), I told him to ask you questions in easy Japanese.'

With that, he led me to the entrance, and I was now face-to-face with the man in the dark suit. He seemed to be looking at my face intensely, clearly trying to find some trace of Japanese heritage in my appearance. I am sure he found my Asian look a little confusing. After a few minutes, he either bought into it or gave up finding my Japanese features and decided to test my language skills instead.

'*Sumimasen, Nihongo wa shabere masu ka* (Excuse me, but can you speak Japanese?)', he asked.

'*Hai, chotto dake deki masu yo* (yes, I can speak a little)', I replied, glad that I had been practising my Japanese skills regularly.

'*Ahh, ii desu ne. Nihongo wa jouzu desu ne* (Ahh, that's great. Your Japanese is very good)', the man in the suit complimented me politely, looking satisfied.

'*Sumimasen, mo hitotsu dake arimasu. Anata no Okaa San wa Nihonjin desu ka?* (Sorry, just one more question. Is your mother Japanese)?'

'*Hai, Okaa San Nihonjin desu*', I lied, following Umehara San's instruction.

This time, the big guy seemed completely satisfied. I had passed his test. And with that, we were led into the hostess bar for another night of sarariman karaoke party.

As I was going through this experience, my mind raced back a couple of years, when I was told by IBM's HR Miku San that some of the houses close to our station were available for rent to Japanese only. As in that case, none of these guys were worried or troubled about sharing with me the fact that the bar was for Japanese only. To them, it wasn't discriminatory, as it hadn't been to Miku San. Besides, I was also sure the big guy at the door that night was quite aware that I wasn't really Japanese. Yet, everyone somehow figured out a way to allow me to go into this 'Japanese only' bar, avoiding any conflict. It left me more convinced that this 'Japanese only' practice was less discriminatory and more to avoid an awkward situation where their guests could be uncomfortable because of the differences in language and culture.

Again, we all sang our favourite songs to our hearts' content at the Japanese-only hostess bar till two in the morning. Tired, we said our goodbyes to the Toshiba folks and returned to our hotel for a short nap before catching our flight back to Tokyo, early the next morning.

Chapter 25

Madogiwa

We had been working with Renesas, another top semiconductor company, starting almost at the same time we had started to work with Sony. One of the senior executives of their microcontroller division was a gentleman named Masaki Sanada. Through many meetings over the last three years, some of us had got to know him well. In his late fifties, Sanada San was one of the most pleasant people to work with and projected a relaxed and easy-going style. Despite the many challenges we faced to bring their business to fruition, he had always been one of our cheerleaders inside Renesas, and always seemed to have a positive attitude, encouraging the teams to work closely together and never give up. His leadership skills were invaluable in our endeavours to work through some of the challenging and complex product designs we had done. Along with Sanada San, we had also established good relationships with some of the sarariman from the outsourcing and engineering team at Renesas.

Sanada San didn't always join all our meetings with Renesas—and we had had many of them over the past three plus years—but always made it a point to show up, even if only for a few minutes, to greet us and hear about how things were progressing. But he loved to join us for lunch or dinner. Whenever we invited him to our official dinners, he would often be accompanied by a young woman, a different one every time. But he was also one of the few sarariman I found who would fondly talk about his family quite often during these dinners. Every now and then, he would even lecture us on the importance of one's family and how one should always keep one's wife happy, while accompanied by a young woman who was clearly not his wife. I found this dichotomy in his behaviour both interesting and amusing, but I wasn't quite sure how to interpret it. There were many times I meant to ask him about it, but always ended up deciding against it. I simply wrote it off perhaps as the typical behaviour of an older, happily married sarariman enjoying the company of a young and attractive woman.

In my experience, many Japanese sarariman seemed to have a special fondness for young women, especially those of small stature. In most cases, I believe that it is innocent in nature, as they seem more to be idolizing them. After all, the biggest fan group of Japanese teenage female pop bands, known as J-Pop, are middle-aged, older or retired sarariman. As long as Sanada San was happy and happily married, as he always claimed to be, who was I to judge?

During our fourth year of engagement with Renesas, suddenly, Sanada San stopped showing up to our meetings. We invited him for dinner a few times, but were told that he was very busy with other projects, which we found quite unusual. Shibata San would try to unsuccessfully get a hold of him over the phone, which we also found to be odd. After a couple of months, I started to wonder what Sanada San was up to. Had he got in some kind of trouble due to his regular association with all those young ladies? Or had he moved to some other division within Renesas? That would not be good for us as his support was crucial for us to expand our business with them. Shibata San had known him for years, since they both used to work for Hitachi Semiconductor. So I asked Shibata San to try to find out what had happened to Sanada San through some of their mutual contacts.

'Sure, Asif San. But I think he has probably become *madogiwa*', Shibata San replied to my request.

Madogiwa? What on earth was that? It sounded like a bad disease to me.

'Sometimes companies want sarariman to leave or retire early, Asif San. But in Japan, it is almost impossible to fire or let go of employees. So the companies will take all the responsibilities away from the sarariman. Basically, he has nothing to do. We call these sarariman madogiwa.'

'But he still gets paid?' I asked.

'Yes. He still gets his salary. Sometimes, the company may reduce the salary, especially for the older sarariman, who are close to the retirement age of sixty. The company hopes that these madogiwa sarariman will find some other consulting job somewhere else and leave the company on their own, thus saving the pain of forced separation. Alternatively, they will just stay as madogiwa till their retirement age of sixty.'

I knew that Sanada San was in his mid-fifties. 'So, are you saying that if indeed he had become madogiwa, Sanada San will collect his salary for the next four or five years while doing nothing?' I asked incredulously.

'Yes, that might be the case with him', Shibata San replied.

I was very curious and Shibata San explained this concept to me in detail. '*Mado*' in Japanese means window and '*giwa*' means towards. The term literally means 'facing the window'. What it implies is that madogiwa sarariman have nothing to do other than to gaze out the window the whole day. The practice of turning sarariman into madogiwa is a common practice in Japanese companies, especially in large conglomerates. Japanese labour laws tend to be more employee-friendly and favour employees over the employers. Laying people off just to save costs, while a common practice in America and many other parts of the world, is legally not allowed in Japan.

I had witnessed this firsthand during my second year at our office. We had an employee named Watanabe, who was responsible for managing our Japanese suppliers. He had nothing to do with our Japan sales and reported directly to the head of our supply chain group in Arizona. There was a company-wide employee entrenchment, and Watanabe San was supposed to be let go as part of this process. For some reason, no one in our head office had thought of consulting with the local HR people about this. Instead, the head of the procurement team in Arizona had handled it the American way. They just called Watanabe San on his mobile on a Friday morning and told him that his services were no longer required as of that afternoon. Stunned by this sudden news, Watanabe San walked to our HR office and told them what had just happened. Our Japan HR folks were shocked and had to go into damage control mode.

Toda San had to call the HR office in Arizona and explain that this kind of entrenchment is not allowed under the Japanese labour laws. She also made it clear that if we were to go through with it, Watanabe San would probably file a lawsuit against us, and he would most likely win. In which case, the company could be liable for significant monetary compensation. After a few chaotic days of trying to manage the situation, the company ended up reaching a special agreement to let Watanabe San stay with us until he found another job. He ended up staying with us for eight months, basically doing nothing while collecting his full salary. He would show up every morning at 9 a.m. and leave office at 5 p.m. but he just wasn't doing any work, at least for the company. Eventually, he did find another job and left. I heard later that we had to give him a very generous retrenchment package which included a year's salary.

In Japan, it is not only that layoffs are not allowed, but it is also difficult to fire people, even in the case of nonperformance. I had personally gone through a painful experience because of such strict labour laws. During our first year, I had hired a young engineer named Mori in my technical team. He seemed very knowledgeable during the interview process and came across as a hardworking person with a good command of English skills. But within a few months, it became clear that he wasn't up to the challenge. He started to slack off, and soon, even some of our customers started to complain about his lack of technical capability and his inability to follow through on commitments. After having some discussion with our HR, we sent him to some training classes, but it was of no use. Then things turned for the worse. He started to avoid us in the office, often calling in sick. It was clear to us that Mori San was a liability who needed to be dealt with quickly.

Having witnessed what had happened with Watanabe San, I approached Toda San first. I figured that this was a more straightforward case due to his poor performance, and thus it would be relatively easy to fire the guy. But she informed me otherwise—apparently, it was not going to be as easy as I had thought. To comply properly with the labour law, all the issues with Mori San's performance would have to be clearly documented, and we would also have to prove that we used all means necessary to try to make it work. The whole process could take anywhere between six months to a year, Toda San added. I was a little taken aback to hear of such long and lengthy firing processes.

Mori San had already started to negatively impact our business. If it was in Arizona, we would have let him go with less than a couple of hours of notice. Toda San mentioned that the first step would be to have an unofficial chat with Mori San, where we will 'encourage' him to leave on his own, perhaps even offering some sort of a package. This way we would not have to worry about any legal issues. Toda San explained that it would help Mori San 'save face'. *Why would we care about his face-saving when this guy not only isn't capable but also has an attitude problem?* When I mentioned this to Toda San, she told me that allowing people to 'save face' is very much a part of the Japanese work culture. She said that the process was quite simple, and there was a high chance that Mori San would leave on his own if we did it right. The plan was that we would have a discussion with Mori San about how things were just not just working out between him and the company, and how it would be best if he could perhaps find another opportunity, thus 'encouraging' him to leave. I had no choice but to agree with following the right process, hoping that Mori San would get the message and leave on his own quickly.

'But what if he refused to leave on his own?' I asked.

'I think he will leave, Asif San. In fact, he will be happy that you gave him a way out and a chance to "save face". If he doesn't leave, then we would have to go through the other option, which is documenting everything, sending him to more training and so on. It will take a longer time. *Shoga nai*, Asif San. This is the Japanese way', Toda San said. She offered to set up and help with the meeting with Mori San.

The meeting with Mori San was interesting, to say the least. Toda San did most of the talking, mostly in English, for my sake. She was extremely polite to him the whole time, explaining how we would love for him to keep on working, but how things weren't working out. Mori San acknowledged this and went on to say how tough things were for him. I couldn't believe what he was saying and got quite annoyed, but I decided to keep quiet and let Toda San carry on. She never once mentioned anything about him leaving, but asked him what we should do instead. Mori San said that he would think about it and get back to us.

'Toda San, you never really "encouraged" him to leave the company', I said, sounding annoyed as soon as the meeting was over.

'Don't worry, Asif San. I think he got the message', Toda San replied.

After another two months, during which time Mori San became madogiwa, he gave us his one-month notice and finally left the company.

* * *

A few months later, Shibata San confirmed that, indeed, Sanada San had become a madogiwa sarariman.

Towards the end of my fourth year in Japan, things in the office had become very smooth for me. I had established a strong team, and they had all become quite self-sufficient, needing my assistance less and less. With Mike Anderson at the helm, I didn't have to worry about interfacing with our management as much either. As a result, I wasn't as busy as I had been during my first three years, and I was enjoying the relatively relaxed work environment. But I also started to wonder if I would soon join the madogiwa club. Perhaps, it was time to start thinking about returning home. The last thing I wanted was to become a madogiwa gaijin sarariman.

Chapter 26

The Gaijin Sarariman Goes Home

Expatriate assignments have interesting lifecycles of their own. During the first year, the expatriates and their families typically experience a mixture of emotions—euphoria from being put on the new foreign assignment, concern at being in a new place with so many unknowns, increased stress levels due to having to learn many basic things anew, wide-eyed excitement at discovering so many new things, confusion at some of the local cultures, rules and regulations, which many times may not make sense; all while invariably missing their family and friends back home. We had also gone through these cycles during our four years in Japan. Our initial excitement at moving to Japan gave way to anxiety at both work and home—from the cold shoulder I had received during my initial months, to trying to find a suitable home, to the very difficult task of ordering a pizza properly.

The second year brings a sense of comfort as the new location becomes one's new home, as surroundings start to look more and more familiar and faces of strangers start to look friendly. The second year is also the year where an expatriate starts to become productive at work, having figured out how the local entity operates, its needs and how to get things done—basically, the trick of the trade. I remember my wife mentioning that it was good to be back home when we landed back in Tokyo

after our second month-long home-leave in Texas. I found
the comment interesting because this city had indeed become
our new home.

During the third year, life in the temporarily adopted country,
which was so foreign not too long ago, starts to feel very normal
and natural. But typically, towards the end of the third year, families
tend to start missing home, especially their friends and families,
whom they have left behind. Being so far away and not being able
to see and interact with them regularly tends to weigh heavy on
one's mind. If the assignment continues, during the fourth and
fifth years, the families and even the expatriates find themselves
looking for excuses to spend more and more time at home and in
their home office. The rule of thumb is that the first five years of
an expatriate assignment are crucial. If the expatriate, along with
the family, successfully makes it through the first five years, then
most of them can endure to stay longer, and in fact, many end up
staying in the country for long periods of time.

By the time our fourth year rolled in, we found that the
novelty of Japan had started to wear off, and we felt like we were
ready to return home. Sharmeen and I were itching badly to go
back. Our Japan revenue was on track to grow over tenfold by
the end of that year, compared to when I had first started—a
tremendous achievement. Additionally, in the last three and a
half years, our Japan organization had grown, and now we had
a very competent and large team in our office. Most of my team
members were now well-versed in the ways of our company
and well-aware of how to get things done. We had come a long
way from my early days, when everyone was coming to me for
solutions. They were rarely coming to me seeking help any more:
I felt that it was a sign that I had done my job well. After all, by
definition, an expatriate's primary objective is to make his role
obsolete as quickly as possible, finding and training local talent.
I felt that I had accomplished what the company had sent me

to do. So I started to think about how I could repatriate back to our head office in Arizona.

If expatriate positions are coveted and hard to come by, repatriating to one's home office can be even harder and more challenging. During the period of an expatriate's assignment in a faraway land, things in the head office invariably change; some people and colleagues get promoted, some people leave, while new folks join the company. Typically, the expatriate will find that the head office has moved on while he or she has been away. In many instances, the expatriates tend to slowly fade away from the management's radar, missing out on new opportunities and promotions. It is common for many expats to leave their company within a year after their repatriation, not being able to find their 'right place' or 'fit in' at the evolved organization. In fact, most of my expat friends at the company had suffered the same fate— they had left the company within six months after their return.

So I was very cognizant of the importance and the difficulty of finding the 'right role' in our head office for my repatriation. Luckily, just like the Japan assignment, a new role back home almost just as easily fell into my lap. Once again, I found myself to be at the right place at the right time. All I had to do was recognize that and seize the opportunity.

Towards the middle of my fourth year, in early summer, the head of our product group, Robert Darveaux, happened to be visiting our Tokyo office. I knew Robert well; he was one of our smartest technologists and I had a lot of respect for him. Mike and I decided to take Robert to visit our customers, and we had a great week together, travelling all over Japan. During one such customer visit just outside Tokyo, we were sitting at a Starbucks having cappuccinos, since we had arrived early. We were chatting away as always about various things, from business, family, kids, to sports and religion. Robert started to talk about some of the challenges he was facing at home. He seemed particularly worried about the future of one of the emerging product lines. His Image Sensor Product Group was in need of new leadership. Image sensors are critical components of most modern digital cameras, including the cameras that are on our mobile phones. Our company was embarking to serve this market segment, apparently without much success.

'The person who is running the group is really struggling', Robert continued, 'I need to replace her quickly if we want to grow in this area.'

As soon as I heard this, I knew that I had to take a shot at it, even though I had no experience in image sensor technology. This could be my chance to get back home.

'I would love to help you out if you are okay with it', I blurted out.

Both Mike and Robert stopped talking and looked at me surprised.

'Well, if you are really serious, Asif, the position is yours. But I thought you are busy here in Japan', Robert said.

'You are not going to leave me in Japan by myself, are you, Asif?' Mike added on, sounding a little disappointed. Mike was aware that we were getting homesick and were ready to return home. In fact, I had had a detailed discussion with him a couple of months earlier, where we had agreed that I would stay in Tokyo for one more year, helping him out. But opportunities don't come often, and I had to seize what seemed like a great chance for repatriation.

As Mike and I were talking about this, especially how he needed me for a little longer in Japan, Robert seemed to be listening with interest. Always the pragmatic one, he jumped in with a solution.

'I see no reason Asif can't start the job from Tokyo and eventually move back to Arizona within a year.'

Mike and I looked at each other. I could do that. Of course, it meant that I would have to do two jobs during that period, continue my business development role in Japan while managing the image sensor product group in the US. I looked at Mike.

'What do you think, Mike? This could work out, right?' I asked.

'Well, as long as you are here, at least for the year to help me out, I am okay with it', Mike said in agreement.

With all of us in agreement, I shook hands both with Robert and Mike. I couldn't believe my luck. I knew of a few cases where it took some of our expatriates more than a year to find a suitable role to return home. The dual responsibility didn't bother me so much as I knew that the local team was now quite capable and strong. Besides, by that point, I was quite willing to put up with the additional tasks and responsibilities if it meant that I was on a path back home.

In the end, I renegotiated with Mike to stay on for six more months, instead of a full year. I did end up getting very busy during that time. I had to travel extensively to the US to start to take on the new role and, at the same time, still had to interact with our Japanese customers for various business opportunities. I also had to start travelling to our factories in Korea more often and visit some of our customers in Europe, as part of my new role. My wife claims that I had spent only a handful of nights at home during that six-month period when I had started to do both the jobs, just like a true sarariman and almost like a tanshin-funin.

In October, my repatriation plan was officially announced to everyone at the Japan office. Everyone seemed to be in a bit of a shock at the suddenness of it and almost everyone started to stop by my office to say how sorry they were to see me leave, with some even pleading with me to stay on, seeming genuinely disappointed. Shibata San and Umehara San didn't seem happy at all with my repatriation idea. I was taken aback at this outpouring of emotion from everyone.

As news of my repatriation reached our customers, with whom I had worked closely for the last four years and grown our business, they all wanted to see me and have a farewell dinner. So in my last month there, I got busy crisscrossing all over Japan, bidding my farewell to all the sarariman with whom I had become close. People in the office started to take me to lunch to bid me their own personal farewells. Finally, the office threw me a great big *sobetsu-kai* or farewell party in December before I left. In true sarariman tradition, the spouses were not invited, of course. But I had a wonderful time with the whole team eating, drinking, chatting and listening to the farewell speeches. Of course, such a party can't finish early. Some of us went on to a second place for drinking and finally to a third place for karaoke, where we all sang to our hearts' content, way into the night. We called it a night around two in the morning, bidding our farewells to each other for about ten minutes.

Finally, it was the day for us to leave. We had moved into the Shinjuku Hyatt for a week, as all our personal belongings had been packed and shipped out, and we had to vacate our home. It was the same Hyatt where we had first stayed when we moved to Tokyo. On a clear and crisp winter morning, very similar to the day when I had first arrived at our Ebisu office, we boarded the Narita Express bus to leave for the airport. I was pleased to see that a few people had come down to the bus stop to bid us their final farewell, despite the fact that it was in the middle of a working day.

With mixed feelings, I boarded the Japan Airlines Boeing 747 at Narita Airport that would take us to Hawaii for a well-deserved seven-day vacation before heading back home. I felt a mixture of joy and sadness as we settled down into our seats at the very front of the big jumbo jet—sad to leave Japan and my fellow sarariman and other colleagues, but at the same time, feeling happy at the prospect of returning home.

I couldn't help but feel a real sense of achievement and satisfaction as some of the people who expressed their sadness at my leaving were the same people who weren't very excited about my Japan assignment during my initial months there. I felt like I had come full circle. As the plane took off from Narita and crossed over to the Pacific Ocean, somewhere over Chiba, well north of Tokyo, a sense of sadness started to linger over me. I looked back at our four years, and I began to realize how rich the whole experience had been for all of us. The plane had not yet left the Japan airspace, and strangely, I had already started to miss Japan. I closed my eyes and started to reminisce about my many memories, trying to identify the most rewarding moments. That's when I realized the entire four-year journey in Japan had been a reward.

The End

Acknowledgements

First and foremost, I would like to thank my Mom and Dad without whom I wouldn't be who I am today. I am eternally grateful for the countless hours my Mom spent with me (and my sisters) to ensure that we were getting a great education, among many other things. I am equally grateful to my Dad for all the little but important things he helped me with and for getting me acquainted and fascinated with Japan.

Thanks to my wife, Sharmeen, for never objecting to our multiple moves all over the US and Asia, and putting up with my extensive global business travels over the years. While the process of moving and getting settled in these new locations and countries wasn't easy and was often challenging, in the long run, they all turned out to be excellent experiences for the whole family, which both of us enjoyed thoroughly.

My daughter Farhana and my son Rayan, both of whom I am very proud of, are constant inspirations to me just by being themselves.

Even though I have been thinking about this book for some years, I didn't realize that I needed a nudge and some inspiration to finally start the writing process. My friend Robert Darveaux provided this much-needed 'nudge' through his typical inquisitive questions during a dinner in Singapore.

I am eternally grateful to all my friends in Japan for everything they have taught me as well as for their help, guidance and an overall wonderful experience during my four years there. While there are too many to name, I would be amiss if I don't particularly thank three people—my friends Ken Shibata, Norito Umehara and Tadashi Sano. I have many wonderful memories with all of them, especially with Shibata San and Umehara San.

My thanks also go to John Boruch and Scott Voss, my big bosses at the company in question, who made my assignment in Japan possible.

Finally, I am most grateful to my editors, Nora Nazerene and Udyotna Kumar, and publisher Penguin Random House Southeast Asia for being so patient with me and playing a major part in shaping the book into its final format.